Palgrave Studies in Global Human Capital Management

Series Editors

Sumit Kundu
Florida International University
Miami, FL, United States

Ashish Malik
The University of Newcastle
Callaghan, New South Wales, Australia

Surender Munjal
University of Leeds
Leeds, United Kingdom

Vijay Pereira
University of Wollongong in Dubai
United Arab Emirates and University of Portsmouth
Portsmouth, United Kingdom

Globalization has led to spatial division and disaggregation of work across the globe, leading to the evolution of novel forms of work organization and contextually-embedded approaches such as co-working and co-creation in an interconnected and interdependent ecosystem. Whilst there are many advantages of scale and scope associated with these work design forms there are also many problems and challenges. Palgrave Studies in Global Human Capital Management presents new research that examines the intersection of globalization, technology, innovation, HRM practices and work organization. With an emphasis on human capital management in international business, the series stresses the importance of culture and contextually-situated knowledge a dynamic work environment, especially in the context of big emerging markets to enhancing productivity and competitiveness with a skilled work force.

More information about this series at
http://www.springer.com/series/14623

Sumit Kundu • Surender Munjal
Editors

Human Capital and Innovation

Examining the Role of Globalization

Editors
Sumit Kundu
Florida International University
College of Business
Miami, Florida, USA

Surender Munjal
Leeds University Business School
University of Leeds
Leeds, UK

Palgrave Studies in Global Human Capital Management
ISBN 978-1-137-56560-0   ISBN 978-1-137-56561-7   (eBook)
DOI 10.1057/978-1-137-56561-7

Library of Congress Control Number: 2016954253

Printed on acid-free paper

This Palgrave Macmillan imprint is published by Springer Nature
The registered company is Macmillan Publishers Ltd.
The registered company address is: The Campus, 4 Crinan Street, London, N1 9XW, United Kingdom

Foreword

In my 1984 book (Tung, 1984), I attributed the post-World War II "economic miracle" in Japan to its human power. Even though the Japanese economy has entered into the doldrums since the 1990s, the fact remains that human capital is pivotal to a country's competitive advantage as a nation's ability to innovate is very much a function of its success in nurturing, attracting, and retaining human talent. Kundu and Munjal's edited book of readings highlights this important theme, namely, the critical relationship between human capital and innovation.

In the pre-globalization era, human capital was assumed to be more or less static, that is, a country either possesses it in abundance or not. With globalization, there is greater mobility of human talent across countries despite the emergence of de-globalizing trends as evidenced in Britain's referendum vote to leave the European Union. Freer human flows across countries have contributed to the worldwide war for talent. This latter phenomenon has been brought on largely by, one, the ascendancy of emerging markets, particularly that of China's and India's; two, the aging of the workforce in many countries; and, three, the shortage of people with a global mindset (Tung, 2016). This competition among nations to recruit the best and the brightest, regardless of their country of origin and nationality, has paved the way for "brain circulation" (Saxenian, 2005) and the growing use of global virtual teams. Brain circulation is particularly prevalent in societies with sizable diasporas, such as that of China's and India's. As far as global virtual teams are concerned, the magnitude of diversity of such teams is indeed substantial since human talent can hail from any country and/or region of the world.

The chapters contained in this book address many of these themes and thus help shed important and useful insights into how countries and companies alike can leverage these resources to their best advantage.

Rosalie L. Tung
The Ming & Stella Wong Professor of International Business
Simon Fraser University

References

- Saxenian, A. (2002). Brain circulation: How high-skill immigration makes everyone better off. *The Brookings Review, 20*(1), 28–31.
- Tung, R. L. (1984). *Key to Japan's economic strength: Human power.* Lexington, MA: Lexington Books, D. C. Heath.
- Tung, R. L. (2016). New perspectives on human resource management in a global context. *Journal of World Business, 51*(1), 142–152.

Contents

Notes on Contributors

Peter Enderwick is Professor of International Business at Auckland University of Technology, Auckland, New Zealand and in recent years a Visiting Professor at the Centre for International Business, University of Leeds, UK. His interests are in the areas of international strategy, international HRM, services, and emerging markets. He is the author of eight books as well as a number of book chapters and articles in professional journals.

Kowoon Kim is currently a PhD student in Management and International Business at Florida International University. She attended the Dongguk University, in the Republic of Korea, where she received her BA in International Trade in 2011. She earned her Master's in International Management Studies from the University of Texas at Dallas in 2014. Her research interests include cross-cultural management, international human resource management, and multicultural management.

Sumit Kundu is James K. Batten Eminent Scholar Chair in International Business in the College of Business Administration at Florida International University, USA. He is the Vice President of the Academy of International Business and sits on the editorial board of several premier journals. Kundu has published several articles in prestigious journals and has been a consultant to several multinational corporations including Novartis, MasterCard International, Ingersoll Rand-Hussmann International, Boeing, and CPI-Sears Portrait Studio.

Yasmina Lazrak has held executive marketing positions within Fortune 500 companies such as Unilever, Danone, Colgate-Palmolive, and The Coca-Cola

Company. She holds a bachelor's degree in business administration and marketing from Institut supérieur de commerce et d'administration des entreprises (ISCAE) in Casablanca, Morocco, and a master's degree in international business from Florida International University in Miami, Florida. She currently serves as Vice President for Strategy and Development at Skiversity, Inc., a Florida corporation specializing in international business strategy. She is Adjunct Professor of International Management at Florida International University.

Paula Makkonen is a Finnish scholar with a PhD in Management from University of Vaasa, Finland. She has a long and intensive international business career. Her primary research interests are: cross-cultural careers, talent and change management, and different modes of global talent flow.

Ashish Malik is a senior lecturer at the University of Newcastle, Australia. He earned his PhD from Victoria University of Wellington, New Zealand and has published and/or presented over 90 papers in reputed international journals including *Industrial Marketing Management, International Journal of HRM, Health Care Management Review* and *Knowledge Management Research & Practice*. He has guest edited four special issues in reputed international journals. He has also authored/edited four books and serves on the editorial board of numerous international journals and is a co-editor of Palgrave Studies in Global Human Capital Management.

Mohammad Haris Minai is a doctoral student at the Indian Institute of Management Lucknow. He has about 13 years of industry work experience in leading multinationals, including leading semiconductor design teams. His areas of interest are leadership, innovation, and creativity.

Surender Munjal is the Director of James E. Lynch India and South Asia Business Centre and Lecturer of International Business and Strategy at the Leeds University Business School, United Kingdom. He earned his PhD from the University of Leeds, United Kingdom. He has earned many accolades for his teaching and research, including the Best Paper award at the Academy of International Business and Dean's award for excellence in teaching. He has published in mainstream international business journals, *Journal of World Business, International Business Review* and *Management and Organization Review.*

Vijay Pereira is Associate Professor of International and Strategic HRM at the Australian University of Wollongong Dubai campus. He earned PhD from the University of Portsmouth, United Kingdom and has published and presented over 75 papers worldwide in reputed international journals including *Human Resource Management* and *Journal of World Business*. He has guest edited four special issues in reputed international journals. He has also authored/edited three books. He was the Area/Associate Editor (OB/HRM) of the Journal of Asia Business Studies and is currently on the international advisory board for the journal *South Asian History and Culture* and on the board of the *Financial Times*-listed journal *POMS*.

Srinivas Rao Pingali is a founding member of Quatrro Global Services and has 25 years of varied experience in product development, sales, and marketing, market research and business operations in global organizations such as NFO, Tata Group, and Accenture. Pingali is a Chemical Engineer and holds an MBA in Marketing from the University of Illinois at Urbana-Champaign.

Janet Rovenpor is Professor of Management at Manhattan College. Her research combines her training in organizational behavior with her concern for successful strategic management outcomes for corporations. Her articles focus on the impact that personality traits have on employee productivity and organizational performance. She also writes about business ethics, managerial values, and organizational crises.

Juan I. Sanchez is Professor of Management and International Business and Knight-Ridder Byron Harless Eminent Chair of Management at Florida International University. He has served as an elected member of the Academy of Management's Human Resource Division Executive Committee. Sanchez has published approximately 20 book chapters and 100 articles in refereed journals including the *Academy of Management Journal, Journal of Applied Psychology, Personnel Psychology, Journal and Organizational Behavior,* and *Journal of International Business Studies,* among others.

Grishma Shah is Associate Professor of Management at Manhattan College. Her research interests include economic globalization and cultural change, specifically in emerging economies. She received her PhD from Rutgers University in 2008.

Shailendra Singh holds a PhD from Indian Institute of Technology, Kanpur. Singh is Senior Professor at Indian Institute of Management Lucknow and the Past President of the National Academy of Psychology. He has more than 28 years of post-PhD academic experience and more than 80 peer-reviewed publications. His research interests are in leadership, high performance organizations, stress, and citizenship.

Arup Varma holds a PhD from Rutgers University. Varma is Professor of Management at Loyola University Chicago. His research interests include performance appraisal, expatriate issues, and HRM in India. He has published over 75 papers in leading academic and practitioner journals, and has presented over 90 papers at national and international conferences.

Mary Ann Von Glinow is the Knight Ridder Eminent Scholar Chair in International Management at Florida International University. She was the 2010–2012 President of the Academy of International Business. She has a PhD from the Ohio State University. Von Glinow was the 1994–1995 President of the Academy of Management, and is a Fellow of the Academy of Management, Academy of International Business and the Pan Pacific Business Association. She sits on 15 editorial review boards and numerous international panels. Von Glinow has authored over 100 journal articles and 14 books.

Norhayati Zakaria is an associate professor at the Australian University of Wollongong Dubai campus and the School of International Studies, Universiti Utara Malaysia. She is a principal investigator and global research collaborator for several international grant bodies such as Asian Office of Aerospace Research Development, Japanese Society for the Promotion of Sciences, Nippon Foundation, and National Science Foundation.

List of Figures

List of Tables

1

Exploring the Connection Between Human Capital and Innovation in the Globalising World

Surender Munjal and Sumit Kundu

The volume of investment in the development of human capital by multinational enterprises (MNEs) as they innovate and compete for markets around the world has seen a sharp increase since the advent of the twenty-first century. At the same time, MNEs rummage around for novel means of governance that facilitate innovation and an efficient utilisation of human capital. MNEs are pursuing integrated business models, namely globally linked and locally leveraged (Bartlett & Beamish, 2015), reinventing the organisation in the form of a global factory (Buckley, 2011a, 2011b; Buckley & Prashantham, 2016) and, as key strategies in this regard, orchestrating head office efforts with that of subsidiaries (Mudambi, 2011). Consequently, the business world witness architectural, radical as well as disruptive innovations (Pisano, 2015) in the

S. Munjal (✉)
University of Leeds, Leeds, UK

S. Kundu
Florida International University, Miami, FL, USA

© The Author(s) 2017   1
S. Kundu, S. Munjal (eds.), *Human Capital and Innovation*,
DOI 10.1057/978-1-137-56561-7_1

market place that profoundly affects many industries. Consider, for example, the cases of Apple in the communications (cell phone) industry, Uber in transportation, and Amazon in retail. The business world is also witnessing competition from new players in emerging markets, like China and India, where enterprises focus on indigenous innovation (Chittoor, Aulakh, & Ray, 2015; Lema, Quadros, & Schmitz, 2015; Li, Strange, Ning, & Sutherland, 2016; Rui, Zhang, & Shipman, 2016). MNEs focus on developing innovative capabilities in developing countries in the way of reverse innovation (Govindarajan & Ramamurti, 2011; Govindarajan & Trimble, 2013; Ramamurti, 2016). It shows that intellectual human capital is prevalent around the world, not concentrated in developed countries. Thus, the onus of progressive companies is to foster a global mind set of brain circulation, which commonly refers to mobility in the workforce of highly talented individuals. Centres of excellence are sprawling from Silicon Valley and Boston Route 128 to Beijing in China, Bangalore in India and Sao Paulo in Brazil. The innovation landscape has been redefined and conventional wisdom challenged. This is the dawn of a new era where the connection between human capital and innovation is to be affected by forces of globalisation as well as localisation. Enterprises of all sizes, industries and countries of origin have to embrace these new realities as they face competition from others in developed and developing countries.

Clearly, to understand the complexities in the role of human capital in fostering innovation, one has to understand that the ecosystem of innovation has to encompass different levels of human capital analysis. The aim of this book is to explore the connection between human capital and innovation. Our conceptualisation in Fig. 1.1 shows the relationship between human capital and innovation at various stages of human capital aggregation. It suggests that even though human capital is fundamentally generated at the individual level, its importance as a critical resource comes from the collective accumulation of individual human capital at manager (Lepak & Snell, 2002; Zhu, Chew, & Spangler, 2005), entrepreneur (Davidsson & Honig, 2003; Marvel & Lumpkin, 2007), firm (Chen & Huang, 2009; Hitt, Biermant, Shimizu, & Kochhar, 2001), industry (Ranft & Lord, 2000; Shan, Walker, &

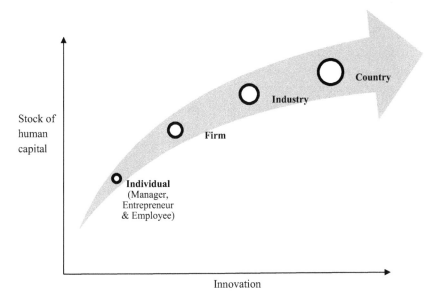

Fig. 1.1 Stages in the aggregation of human capital and innovation. *Source*: Compiled by authors

Kogut, 1994) and country (Benhabib & Spiegel, 1994; Dakhli & De Clercq, 2004) levels.

The book comprises nine chapters, including this introduction as Chap. 1, identifying the relationship between human capital and innovation at manager, firm, industry and country levels. The second chapter by Enderwick sets the foundation for subsequent chapters by providing an overarching framework that unlocks the connections between human capital and innovation both within and outside of the firm. Taking cognisance of rising uncertainties in the global marketplace, he stresses the need for managers to create an ecosystem of innovation that allows the firm to be innovative and maintain flexibility for the effective elimination of market uncertainties.

Enderwick uses the global factory framework (Buckley, 2009, 2011a, 2011b, 2016) to illustrate how firms are reinventing themselves (e.g. by creating a balance between internalisation and externalisation of activities) in order to stay competitive in the wake of the competitive global environment. The global factory thinking suggests core functions that capture a higher proportion of the overall value added by the firm should be internalised, while non-core functions, such as production activities, should be outsourced to external parties that can best perform them taking advantage of their embedded locations.

Core functions comprise high value adding activities such as product conceptualisation, design and implementation, technology development, product branding, marketing and customer service. Essentially, these core activities are reflected in the competitive advantages for the firm while human capital remains the backbone in their development. Enderwick suggests that innovation in each of these areas is critical. MNEs should invest in the development of human capital employed in the core functions. While the human resource practices of recruitment, selection, training and retention remain important in this process, Enderwick stresses the autonomy and flexibility at the workplace to boost creativity in the human capital.

The third chapter by Minai, Singh and Varma extends this argument by emphasising the role of leadership. The authors argue that challenges of 'leading for innovation' need to be understood at an individual and enterprise level to properly understand the process of building creativity in human capital employed by the firm. The authors suggest that to accomplish this, it is necessary for the firm to allow each leader to adjust his or her approach when the individual factors or the situational demands vary from location to location (an argument further examined in Chap. 4). The authors attempt to combine two streams of research in leadership: one that places emphasis on the motivational component of leadership and another that emphasises the role of leaders in influencing behaviour. They build different propositions for the leadership approach to foster innovation when core teams comprise diverse individuals in various situations.

Chapter 4 by Sanchez examines the balance between *centripetal* and *centrifugal* forces in managing human capital for innovation. The author argues that the literature on managing human capital is possibly skewed in favour of localisation, thereby ignoring that a global strategic imperative often houses the key drivers of innovation in global firms. The literature suggests that localisation of human capital management practices is vital given that individuals are psychologically tuned to local institutional environments and in order to exploit local talent the firm needs to adapt accordingly (Björkman & Budhwar, 2007). This eventually leads to a higher degree of interdependence among head offices and their subsidiaries, which may result in improved performance (Mudambi, 2011; Mudambi & Navarra, 2004; Pereira, Munjal, & Nandakumar, 2016).

In contrast, the author proposes several arguments for a global imperative arguing that too much focus on localisation efforts may endanger a firm's innovative spirit. Sanchez proposes a bi-dimensional model of the global mindset, where localisation and globalisation represent two distinct sets of paradoxical forces that need to be managed by the firm in order to facilitate its innovative performance. This is a logical conclusion for the global factory set-up that acknowledges the twin informational aspects of innovation reinforcing the importance of explorative knowledge production, alongside the exploitation of existing stocks of skills and talent.

Human capital is considered a socially complex, intangible resource (Black & Boal, 1994). The management of global–local integration of diversity in workforces further contributes towards the complexity of human capital. On the one hand, diversity can be recognised as a valuable component of human capital that breeds new ideas and different perspectives for problem solving; on the other hand, it can contribute to the challenges of managing human capital.

Chapters 5 and 6 analyse the role of diversity in human capital for innovation. The authors argue that in a competitive global environment, the diversity and complexity associated with management of human capital are increasing. Firms increasingly recruit employees who are not only spatially away but also have different racial, sexual and cultural orientations, indicating that firms put more importance on international and non-traditional human capital. The management of diversity in human capital involving factors such as race, sex and culture, as studied in these chapters, is an under-researched topic and studies in this area with a focus on innovation have the potential to be quite rewarding.

Chapter 5 by Kim and Von Glinow examines the ways in which non-traditional human capital may supplement talent and innovation gaps. Chapter 6 authored by Zakaria, on the other hand, argues in favour of diversity on account of race and culture. Both studies present diversity as an innovative work structure with implications for how a firm's agenda can improve innovation performance. The authors illustrate how this type of ecosystem promotes innovation and describe what challenges it presents for managing culturally and geographically distant employees.

Kim and Von Glinkow specifically analyse the role of lesbian, gay, bisexual and transgender (LGBT) expatriates in promoting innovation and the challenges associated therewith. The authors argue that even though talent pools across the globe are widening, firms are finding it difficult to find qualified traditional human capital locally. Firms thus often rely on teams of non-traditional expatriates. The authors raise two important issues that have implications for the firm. First, the MNE develops an internal labour market in the form of teams of expatriate managers where the human capital is trained (and retained) to take up challenges arising in foreign markets; second, the gap in creativity required for innovation in performing core functions of the MNE can be filled by the use of non-traditional human capital. The authors conclude that diversity and inclusive workplaces are more innovative and productive than those that are homogeneous.

Zakaria's Chap. 6 examines global virtual teams as an innovative work structure. The author argues that global virtual teams allow the firm to stay competitive and agile. Focusing on innovation in the process of teamwork, the author proposes what she calls the CAB (cognitive, affective and behaviour) framework for understanding cross-cultural competency in global virtual teams that can aid in understanding aspects of cultural competency such as awareness, sensitivity and adroitness. The author presents certain propositions for successful teamwork in a virtual multicultural workplace. Her work also has important implications for the management of human capital in the global factory, that is, managers should inculcate open mindset and appropriate attitudes towards the cultural diversity of global virtual teams as an innovative work structure.

A similar approach is required for managing human capital outside a firm's boundaries as firms are increasingly outsourcing knowledge-intensive activities to leverage skills and talent possessed by third parties. The move to access specialised knowledge externally is catching scholarly attention (Mudambi & Venzin, 2010; Yang, Mudambi, & Meyer,

2008). Chapter 7 by Pingali, Rovenpor and Shah explore this phenomenon by examining the trend and drivers of the shift in outsourcing and offshoring from traditional economic consideration to knowledge-seeking motives. The authors give a historical review of outsourcing with some useful contemporary statistics. They suggest that with advances in communication technology the outsourcing phenomenon is not only growing but also changing its nature. Online platforms act as marketplaces allowing efficient matching of skills and talent between buyers and sellers. The authors thus refer to the global search for talent and innovation in the current electronic age of a knowledge-driven economy as 'Best Sourcing'. The authors argue that the growing trend in the outsourcing of high-end, value-creating knowledge-based activities has significant benefits in innovation.

The evolving stream of research (e.g. Govindarajan & Ramamurti, 2011; Govindarajan & Trimble, 2013; Ramamurti, 2016) in this area further suggests that skills and talent in emerging economies are increasing. The availability of promising human capital raises the innovation profile in emerging economies and attracts multinational enterprises from advanced economies looking for specific skills and talent.

Chapter 8 by Mckkonen examines the role of local talent in different phases of China's innovation performance. The author's thesis revolves around the mobility of people across geographic and cultural boundaries and argues that mobility has fundamental implications for innovation because talent flows with the movement of people and helps in the transfer of technologies and knowledge across borders. Mckkonen associates the mobility of professionals in the global labour market with the development of countries' innovation performance. Taking the case of China, Makkonen identifies three innovation performance phases, the eras of copy and imitation, evolution and revolution. The author argues that China's ability to move from evolution to revolution is influenced by global talent flow, cultural factors and regulative institutions at home. The study thus highlights the role of macroinstitutional environment on a country's innovative capabilities.

The final chapter by Malik and Pereira extends the analysis to the case of India. The authors argue that globalisation imposes an increased need for investment in human capital. However, there is little theoretical basis for understanding how skill formation affects innovation. The authors propose a theoretical model for understanding the interactions and relationships between various units in the formation of human capital with innovation. With respect to the formation of human capital, they specifically place importance on the need for and nature of training and development, customised according to the existing state of affairs of the workforce.

Overall, this book integrates different levels in the study of human capital and its connection with innovation. It tackles this timely topic within the context of globalisation. Given the complexity of relationships, organisations must take an integrative perspective to leverage the usage of human capital in fostering innovation in a globalised world. The success of firms is determined by the optimal allocation of resources, the most precious of these being human capital. It begins with recruitment and retention of talented individuals who are available globally and discusses how firms sustain innovation capabilities within as well as outside their organisational boundaries. We are familiar with the role of offshoring and outsourcing of different activities in the value chain as firms have come to realise that not everything can be done within the internal boundaries of the organisation. The continued success of an enterprise in a fast-changing world witnessed by disruptive, radical and architectural innovation has to be understood and examined from the creation of knowledge and the transfer of best practices across the organisation.

We hope readers will find this compilation of articles useful. Given the nature of the subject, it remains a comprehensive, yet focused, exploration of the connections between human capital and innovation in the globalised world. We trust the book will not only serve as reference material for academia but also provide useful guidance to managers and policy makers. The chapters present many examples in support of our assertion, highlighting managerial action to achieve an ecosystem for innovation and human capital development, for instance, managing diversity, customising training and improving leadership to enhance creativity among the workforce employed in the core functions of the MNE. The important managerial action of balancing tensions between *centripetal* and *centrifugal* forces is identified. In addition, the book draws attention towards the development of human capital in emerging economies, which reflects policy implications. While, the global mobility of talent has vastly contributed to the economy of the United States and, in recent years, to the Indian and Chinese economies, the European Union is still debating the pros and cons of it. This suggests that global mobility may have positive effects on the innovativeness and competitiveness of the host economy; however, a well-thought-out policy is needed to harvest its economic benefits.

References

Bartlett, C., & Beamish, P. (2015). *Transnational management: Text, cases & readings in cross-border management*. New York: McGraw-Hills.

Benhabib, J., & Spiegel, M. M. (1994). The role of human capital in economic development evidence from aggregate cross-country data. *Journal of Monetary economics, 34*(2), 143–173.

Björkman, I., & Budhwar, P. (2007). When in Rome…? Human resource management and the performance of foreign firms operating in India. *Employee Relations, 29*(6), 595–610.

Black, J. A., & Boal, K. B. (1994). Strategic resources: Traits, configurations and paths to sustainable competitive advantage. *Strategic Management Journal, 15*(S2), 131–148.

Buckley, P. J. (2009). Internalisation thinking: From the multinational enterprise to the global factory. *International Business Review, 18*(3), 224–235.

Buckley, P. J. (2011a). *Globalization and the global factory*. Cheltenham: Edward Elgar.

Buckley, P. J. (2011b). International integration and coordination in the global factory. *Management International Review, 51*(2), 269–283.

Buckley, P. J. (2016). The contribution of internalisation theory to international business: New realities and unanswered questions. *Journal of World Business, 51*(1), 74–82.

Buckley, P. J., & Prashantham, S. (2016). Global interfirm networks: The division of entrepreneurial labour between MNEs and SMEs. *The Academy of Management Perspectives, 30*(1), 40–58.

Chen, C.-J., & Huang, J.-W. (2009). Strategic human resource practices and innovation performance—The mediating role of knowledge management capacity. *Journal of Business Research, 62*(1), 104–114.

Chittoor, R., Aulakh, P. S., & Ray, S. (2015). Accumulative and assimilative learning, institutional infrastructure, and innovation orientation of developing economy firms. *Global Strategy Journal, 5*(2), 133–153.

Dakhli, M., & De Clercq, D. (2004). Human capital, social capital, and innovation: A multi-country study. *Entrepreneurship & Regional Development, 16*(2), 107–128.

Davidsson, P., & Honig, B. (2003). The role of social and human capital among nascent entrepreneurs. *Journal of Business Venturing, 18*(3), 301–331.

Govindarajan, V., & Ramamurti, R. (2011). Reverse innovation, emerging markets, and global strategy. *Global Strategy Journal, 1*(3-4), 191–205.

Govindarajan, V., & Trimble, C. (2013). *Reverse innovation: Create far from home, win everywhere*. Boston, MA: Harvard Business Press.

Hitt, M. A., Biermant, L., Shimizu, K., & Kochhar, R. (2001). Direct and moderating effects of human capital on strategy and performance in professional service firms: A resource-based perspective. *Academy of Management Journal, 44*(1), 13–28.

Lema, R., Quadros, R., & Schmitz, H. (2015). Reorganising global value chains and building innovation capabilities in Brazil and India. *Research Policy, 44*(7), 1376–1386.

Lepak, D. P., & Snell, S. A. (2002). Examining the human resource architecture: The relationships among human capital, employment, and human resource configurations. *Journal of Management, 28*(4), 517–543.

Li, J., Strange, R., Ning, L., & Sutherland, D. (2016). Outward foreign direct investment and domestic innovation performance: Evidence from China. *International Business Review, 25*(5), 1010–1019.

Marvel, M. R., & Lumpkin, G. T. (2007). Technology entrepreneurs' human capital and its effects on innovation radicalness. *Entrepreneurship Theory and Practice, 31*(6), 807–828.

Mudambi, R. (2011). Hierarchy, coordination, and innovation in the multinational enterprise. *Global Strategy Journal, 1*(3-4), 317–323.

Mudambi, R., & Navarra, P. (2004). Is knowledge power? Knowledge flows, subsidiary power and rent-seeking within MNCs. *Journal of International Business Studies, 35*(5), 385–406.

Mudambi, R., & Venzin, M. (2010). The strategic nexus of offshoring and outsourcing decisions. *Journal of Management Studies, 47*(8), 1510–1533.

Pereira, V., Munjal, S., & Nandakumar, M. K. (2016). Reverse dependency: A longitudinal case study investigation into Headquarter-Subsidiary relationship in the context of an emerging country. *International Studies of Management & Organization, 46*(1), 50–62.

Pisano, G. P. (2015). You need an innovation strategy. *Harvard Business Review, 93*(6), 44–54.

Ramamurti, R. (2016). Internationalisation and innovation in emerging markets. *Strategic Management Journal,* forthcoming, DOI: 10.1002/smj.2553.

Ranft, A. L., & Lord, M. D. (2000). Acquiring new knowledge: The role of retaining human capital in acquisitions of high-tech firms. *The Journal of High Technology Management Research, 11*(2), 295–319.

Rui, H., Zhang, M., & Shipman, A. (2016). Relevant knowledge and recipient ownership: Chinese MNCs' knowledge transfer in Africa. *Journal of World Business, 51*(5), 713–728.

Shan, W., Walker, G., & Kogut, B. (1994). Interfirm cooperation and startup innovation in the biotechnology industry. *Strategic Management Journal, 15*(5), 387–394.

Yang, Q., Mudambi, R., & Meyer, K. E. (2008). Conventional and reverse knowledge flows in multinational corporations. *Journal of Management, 34*(5), 882–902.

Zhu, W., Chew, I. K., & Spangler, W. D. (2005). CEO transformational leadership and organizational outcomes: The mediating role of human–capital-enhancing human resource management. *The Leadership Quarterly, 16*(1), 39–52.

2

Flexibility, Labour Utilisation, and the Global Factory

Peter Enderwick

Introduction

A growing number of global industries are experiencing significant changes in organisational and ownership structures as environmental change increases both volatility and governance options. In essence, the traditional internally owned and managed structures characteristic of international business in the 1960s and early 1970s are being eclipsed by a growing reliance on partnership or network-type structures. These organisational forms have been termed the global factory (Buckley, 2014) refining a concept first coined three decades ago (Grunwald & Flamm, 1985). The global factory describes a network of organisations providing input services for a set of products or services. These services are typically collated across national borders from organisations under different ownership, coordinated by a lead firm through the global factory network.

P. Enderwick (✉)
Faculty of Business, AUT University, Auckland, New Zealand

© The Author(s) 2017   **13**
S. Kundu, S. Munjal (eds.), *Human Capital and Innovation*,
DOI 10.1057/978-1-137-56561-7_2

While progress has been made in understanding the core principles of the global factory (Buckley, 2014) and how such systems differ from more traditional multinational enterprises (Enderwick & Buckley, 2015), there remain important elements that are poorly understood. The global factory has evolved to deal with increasing uncertainty within the global marketplace. A growing pace of innovation, new sources of competition, rising consumer expectations, and technological convergence all encourage the adoption of flexible organisational forms and strategies. When we examine the competitive advantages of the global factory, we see it is well placed to compete in a demanding global environment. Its core advantage is its cross-border coordination or 'interface competence': the ability to manage a geographically dispersed value chain. This is coupled with superior skills in governance: to know what activities should be undertaken internally and what should be outsourced. At the same time, the focal firm or lead multinational enterprise in the global factory system, has to invest in and maintain its critical firm-specific advantages in technology, branding, and supply chain management. The consumer provides focus for the global factory, with all activities directed to satisfying customer needs. It is also apparent that an implicit strength of the global factory is flexibility: the ability to survive volatility and respond rapidly to changing circumstances. Despite its obvious importance, there has been very little analysis of flexibility within the global factory model.

In response to this gap, this chapter examines the importance, role, and sources of flexibility within global factory systems. It contributes to our understanding in a number of ways. First, it examines the importance of flexibility within global factory systems, highlighting the impact of a key driver in location and governance decisions. Second, our discussion is firmly embedded in the context of the global factory, an international cross-border network of service providers differentiated by location, ownership, and purpose. We consider flexibility in broader terms than simply resource or system flexibility. We suggest that the very structure of the global factory bestows the organisation with significant advantages when pursuing a strategy of enhanced flexibility. Third, we extend existing concepts of flexibility beyond that of primarily labour market flexibility and from the level of the establishment to networks, and in particular, directed networks. Fourth, we develop a simple schematic conception of flexibility within global factory systems that highlights the diverse forms of flexibility that are available to such organisations. Finally, the discussion highlights some of the costs of pursuing enhanced flexibility and how many of these can be mitigated through a global factory network.

The discussion is organised around five substantive sections. Following this introduction, we consider the importance of flexibility to the global factory, highlighting its centrality in managing volatility. Section three discusses the sources and forms of flexibility and the considerable literature that has developed in this area. Building on this literature, and firmly embedding our discussion within the context of the directed network, we offer a simple conception of flexibility within global factory systems. In section four, we consider some of the traditional costs associated with increased flexibility, in particular, transaction costs, conflict, commitment, learning, innovation, and the links between flexibility and firm performance. We show how the global factory is able to alleviate many of these costs. The final section offers concluding comments.

The Importance of Flexibility Within the Global Factory

Global factory structures offer a number of benefits to participant firms, particularly to the lead or focal firm. They enable the firm to specialise to undertake itself those tasks where it has clear advantage and to outsource more peripheral activities. Such specialisation should result in a more efficient utilisation of resources and enhanced opportunities to capture scale and experience advantages. In part, such specialisation should contribute towards a second benefit, lower costs of production and distribution. However, cost savings may also occur through the allocation of activities to optimal locations with access to lower-cost inputs. The global factory may also enjoy flexibility benefits over more conventionally organised rivals. We define flexibility within a global factory system to mean the ability to effectively reallocate resources and restructure processes in response to uncertainty. This raises the interesting question of why flexibility is of importance to the global factory system.

The answer lies in the reality of contemporary globalisation. The growth in globalisation has undoubtedly increased business opportunities in opening up new markets and production locations. But it has also increased interdependency and competition. This, in turn, has increased volatility. Volatility has increased within the three major market groups—financial, product, and labour. Financial and product markets have experienced growing interdependency and, financial markets at least, are highly global with shocks rapidly spreading through contagion effects. Product markets are also characterised by mounting levels of global independency bringing increased competition, new sources of competition, shorter product life cycles, and immense pressure to reduce costs. While labour markets are characterised by lower levels of global interdependency, their volatility levels have also increased. This has occurred through cross-border flows of labour (legal migration in the case of integrated regions such as the European Union [EU]), illegal migration (resulting from significant unrest in areas such as the Middle East) and the transfer of work overseas through offshore sourcing.

Higher levels of volatility are now characteristic of a wide range of tradable products and services and are apparent on both the demand and supply sides of international business activities (Buckley & Casson, 1998). On the demand side, product standardisation enhances consumer choice reducing buyer loyalty. Sellers seek to reduce such volatility through continuing innovation, branding, and the extension of brands to signal life style, as well as various lock in mechanisms such as loyalty schemes. Supply side volatility results from rapid innovation, shorter product life cycles and the need to achieve economies of scale and cost minimisation. Producers have access to a far wider range of potential suppliers as the worldwide market for market transactions (Liesch, Buckley, Simonin, & Knight, 2012) has both widened and deepened. Accessing factors in overseas locations has been facilitated by the adoption of more open market regimes as trade and investment restrictions have been relaxed (Sauvant, 2016). At the same time, technological innovations in transport and communications have facilitated the management of externally sourced transactions (Hummels, 2007; World Bank, 2009).

There have been a number of changes in the international business environment that have contributed to growing volatility. One has been the rise of significant new competitor nations, most notably, some of the major emerging economies that have added to global competition and locational choice, marking an end to the 'Golden Age of Western Capitalism' when global production was dominated by a smaller number of enduring nations (Marglin & Schor, 1992). Some of the growth of emerging economies has been at the expense of traditional industrial powers including the USA and parts of Europe (Baldwin, 2013). Second, a number of governments seeking to improve national competitiveness have initiated policies, including liberalisation, deregulation, privatisation, and enhanced labour flexibility, that have added to global volatility through growing market interdependency. Changes in political and social attitudes towards economic power and domination have been reflected in increased internal competition within large international businesses, which have added to operational uncertainty and volatility. In the face of significant volatility, international businesses seek flexibility which contributes to resilience, the ability to absorb and adapt to shock events.

Volatility also affects structural decisions of the firm. If markets are growing strongly, sunk investments in supply or distribution facilities can be offset against rising sales volumes. Similarly, investments are unlikely to be reversed. For these reasons, the firm may be happy to internalise such activities, undertaking them under shared ownership. However, market volatility emphasises the need to seek lowest costs and increases the likelihood that some markets may need to be abandoned. In such a scenario, externalisation, pushing some of the risk onto partner organisations, both upstream (supplying inputs and products) and downstream (distribution and sales), may be the preferred option. For these reasons, volatility, the pursuit of flexibility, and growing externalisation, are all interrelated.

Sources and Forms of Flexibility

When we examine the concept of flexibility within the global factory, context is imperative. This is because the global factory is characterised by its adoption of network relationships: it is not an autonomous entity undertaking all elements of the value chain itself. It is linked into, and reliant upon, other organisations. In addition, it has international scope and is involved in a number of national markets. These two characteristics, partial externalisation and locational diversification, may themselves contribute to flexibility. For these reasons, existing classifications of the sources of flexibility may be of limited value when applied to the global factory.

There have been a number of important efforts to identify and classify sources of organisational flexibility. Atkinson (1984) focusing on labour flexibility, highlighted the following four key forms of flexibility: functional; numerical; financial, and temporal. Functional flexibility addresses the utilisation of skills with greater flexibility resulting from cross- or multiskilling of employees. Numerical flexibility results from changes in the level of labour input, utilising part-time workers for example. Financial flexibility may be achieved by aligning payment and reward systems to achieve flexibility objectives. Temporal flexibility refers to hours worked. While useful, this taxonomy suffers from its restrictive applicability (primarily to internal employees) and its view of the organisation as a predominantly closed system. Other scholars have attempted to broaden the concept of flexibility to look at systems, particularly manufacturing and supply chain systems (Upton, 1994). This work highlights similar ideas— functional, strategic, time horizon, and hierarchical concepts—underpinning system flexibility (D'Souza & Williams, 2000; Duclos, Vokurka, & Lummus, 2003; Lummus, Duclos, & Vokurka, 2003). While these studies do extend thinking to consider system flexibility (Olhager & West, 2002), they are still of limited value when analysing the global factory. In part, this is the result of conventional classifications, for example Zhang, Vonderembse, and Lim (2003) divide flexibility along two dimensions— flexible competences—those attainable within the internal producing organisation, and flexible capabilities—those perceived by the buying organisation. While it is recognised that external flexibility is likely to have a more significant impact than internal flexibility initiatives (Jordan & Graves, 1995), such taxonomies pay scant regard to the organisational and governance complexity of the global factory.

A central theme of the firm flexibility literature is the internal separation of employees along the lines of a core and a periphery (Kalleberg, 2001). The pursuit of functional flexibility with cross-skilling and enhanced responsibilities creates a privileged group of core employees enjoying high levels of job security and favourable employment conditions. Numerical flexibility, in contrast, produces a group of employees on less favourable employment and payment conditions whose numbers can be readily adjusted because they are part-time, temporary, or contracted through outside agencies. Core employees contribute to firm flexibility because they possess multiple skills and can be readily redeployed. Their commitment is assured because of their favourable treatment, links between pay and firm performance, as well as their increased employability that results from access to greater responsibly and development opportunities. Peripheral employees contribute to flexibility, primarily to operational flexibility, because of the ease of adjusting numbers and hours worked as well as through their engagement on less costly terms. Peripheral workers are seen as assuming some of the 'risk' of volatile markets (Jacoby, 1999).

A dilemma for the firm is the successful combination of these two forms of flexibility. Workforce segmentation with groups on contrasting employment conditions is likely to create resentment and conflict (Geary, 1992). While the concept of dualism, with a core-periphery workplace divide, is well established (Doeringer & Piore, 1971), studies of their compatibility report mixed results, ranging from a negative relationship (Cully, Woodland, O'Reilly, & Dix, 1999; Osterman, 1999) to a positive one (Morishima, 1995). One of the ways to overcome internal workforce conflict based on segmentation is the use of network relations, to externalise one group, typically peripheral employees. This is achieved through the use of subcontracting, widespread in manufacturing, and back office service activities, in a growing number of industries. Networks replace duality *within* organisations with distinction *between* organisations.

For our purposes, existing work on flexibility suffers a number of key weaknesses. First, much of it focuses on technical systems and how to optimise such systems. In a global factory where superior cross-border coordination or interface competence may be the key source of advantage, technical effectiveness is likely to be a small part of overall system optimisation.

Second, the focus of much of the flexible firm work is internal. It is based on a view that traditional hierarchical organisations, adopting Fordist production principles, forego flexibility in the pursuit of scale and cost mini-misation. Such principles of production require stable, predictable, and ideally, growing markets. Where these conditions cannot be assumed and markets are volatile, greater flexibility is desirable. From this perspective, flexibility can be achieved by internal restructuring through initiatives such as multi-skilling, job rotation, and the increased use of contract or part-time workers. In essence, flexibility can be pursued through changes in the employment terms and conditions of current resources.

Third, as discussed above, this literature pays insufficient attention to interdependencies between the various sources of flexibility. While it is recognised that enhancement in one flexibility dimension does not nec-essarily result in an improvement in overall system flexibility (Gupta & Somers, 1996), the diversity of potential sources of flexibility and the relationships between these, have not been fully researched. For example, attempts to inculcate both functional and numerical flexibility within the same organisation (effectively a dual labour market), is likely to lead to conflict. Spatially separating or distancing these activities, and their asso-ciated workforces, is a capability that exists within global factory systems.

Fourth, the flexible firm literature pays scant regard to the issue of how a network of collaborative firms is managed. Implicitly, the network is seen to offer mutual benefits and is coordinated through market forces. In practice, such networks are more likely to be consciously directed and this is certainly true for the global firm. The focal firm builds, directs, and manages a complex network in its own interests, part of which is the pursuit of enhanced flexibility.

Finally, any conceptualisation of flexibility within a social system as complex as the global factory needs to acknowledge the likelihood of trade-offs. Achieving greater flexibility is clearly not costless: doing so may be at the expense of other organisational dimensions, for example commitment, coordination, uncertainty, information capture, or innova-tion. These are relevant considerations that need to be incorporated into any meaningful analysis.

In the light of these weaknesses, we offer a conceptualisation of flex-ibility within the global factory system, summarised schematically in Fig. 2.1.

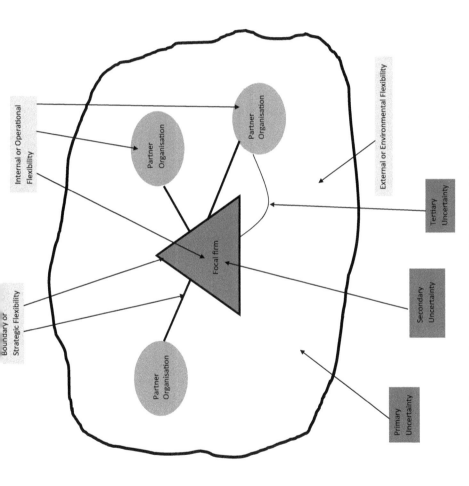

Fig. 2.1 Conceptualisation of uncertainty and sources of flexibility in the global factory

In this simplified conception, the centre of the global factory is the lead or focal firm internalising key activities such as innovation, branding, and critical management tasks. The focal firm is likely to be hierarchical to some degree in its organisation. For the sake of exposition, the focal firm is shown to be involved with just three external partner organisations. These may be upstream (suppliers for example), or downstream (distributors, retailers, after sales service providers). Both the focal firm and its partners exist within a wider international business environment, shown by the orange boundary line in Fig. 2.1. This implies that transactions between the focal firm and its external partners cross national borders.

Figure 2.1 suggests that the firm faces three types of uncertainty, termed primary, secondary, and tertiary uncertainty (Buckley & Carter, 2002). Primary uncertainty arises in the business environment and may be the result of social, economic, technological and political changes, or competitor actions. Primary uncertainty encourages broad environmental scanning as such changes create both opportunities and challenges for business. Scanning results in the collection of significant volumes of information, much of it pertaining to exogenous changes. It is the collation, integration, and synthesis of such information that gives rise to secondary uncertainty. Secondary uncertainty is an internal management issue that occurs because of incomplete or unproductive synthesis of knowledge. It results from the ineffective combination of knowledge where, for example, managers are not aware of intentions or actions of other members of the management team. In Fig. 2.1, secondary uncertainty is depicted as an internal management problem but is likely to involve a wide range of knowledge inputs drawn from a variety of international sources. Secondary knowledge problems may be addressed through changes in organisational structures and incentive and reward systems. A third type of uncertainty, tertiary uncertainty, arises from interactions with external parties and can create opportunism (Williamson, 1996), where those holding valuable knowledge fail to reveal or share it, misrepresent it, or use it for their own benefit. These sources of uncertainty create a series of organisational problems involving the effective acquisition of information (primary uncertainty), its synthesis and integration within the management task (secondary uncertainty), and ensuring its effective deployment (tertiary uncertainty) (Buckley & Carter, 1996).

For the global factory, flexible structures and systems contribute to resilience and a reduction in the costs of these forms of uncertainty. Systems are resilient if they can absorb shocks. Flexibility is developed in three key areas.

The first, termed external or environmental flexibility, is concerned with the acquisition of knowledge about environmental conditions and how these can be used to the advantage of the firm. The global factory is likely to invest heavily in environmental scanning, in part because of the significant options it enjoys in location choice. It is able to access optimum locations, selected in terms of cost, resource availability, and quality. We would expect flexibility considerations to be factored into location decisions, for both the firm's own operations and in the selection of partner organisations. If the pace of environmental uncertainty increases, location switching might be expected to rise. The more diverse are the operations of the global factory—both geographically and number of partner organisations—the more environmental information the focal firm can secure, contributing to more efficient location decisions. Access to overseas locations can bring significant flexibility gains as the example of Apple illustrates. For iPhone manufacture in 2013, Apple used suppliers in more than 25 countries, who, collectively undertook more than 767 fabrications. Of these, 637 fabrications (83 per cent) were undertaken in Asia. China was the most significant source country responsible for 330 fabrications (FinancesOnline, 2013). Part of China's attraction to Apple was the flexibility it offers, with one estimate suggesting that ramping up production where 8700 engineers are needed to manage 200,000 factory employees, would have taken 9 months in the USA, but just 15 days in China (FinancesOnline, 2013).

The second form of flexibility shown in Fig. 2.1 is termed operational or internal flexibility and refers to the deployment of labour within establishments, by both the focal firm and its suppliers. We have discussed the most likely scenario under which this might occur, labour market dualism based on a core-periphery division. There is evidence that such dualism occurs both within focal firms and between the focal firm and suppliers. Amazon provides an example of a company that apparently uses labour intensification in some of its secondary activities that it directly controls such as warehousing (Soper, 2011). However, recent reports suggest that the company encourages a highly competitive, even ruthless, work culture throughout all its operations, negating the argument of a core-periphery division (Kantor & Streitfeld, 2015). Reports of dualism between plants in global factory networks encompass a range of industries including clothing, footwear, electronics, cut flowers, and even false eyelashes (Balch, 2015; Chamberlain, 2013). Industrial accidents, such as the Rana Plaza fire in Bangladesh in 2013, illustrate the dangerous working conditions that some suppliers offer (Burke, 2013). As mentioned in the previous section, it is more likely that the global factory will use its locational differentiation to utilise core-periphery divisions between plants (both owned and contracted) enabling it to avoid the challenges of duality within a single establishment.

The third type of flexibility identified in Fig. 2.1 is strategic or boundary flexibility that arises from the ability of the global factory to exploit global locational and governance differences. In this case, the focal firm gains flexibility advantages through placing activities in less regulated locations, or managing operations in ways that provide enhanced flexibility.

Locational differentiation contributes to flexibility in several ways. One is simply the pricing advantage that access to lower-cost sites provides. In the event of a decline in product demand or an increase in competition, the firm could exploit the gap between (lower) costs and retail prices since it has access to lower costs of production. In addition, offshore locations may offer more favourable production and regulatory conditions where, for example, there is a plentiful supply of skilled labour, a competent supply base, or fewer restrictions on labour utilisation. It is perhaps not surprising that global factory systems are heavily focused on China and South-East Asian economies where there are fewer operating restrictions than in areas such as Europe. State-led capitalism, characteristic of many of the most popular Asian locations, helps underpin competitive operating conditions (Amsden, 1992; Leftwitch, 1995).

A second flexibility benefit of locational differentiation results from a more effective application of segmentation. The global factory conceives of segmentation in terms of activity fragmentation or 'fine slicing' rather than simply labour deployment. This type of segmentation allows the firm to avoid many of the difficulties that arise when dualism is introduced in a single location. For example, the focal firm is able to implement distinct knowledge strategies with exploration occurring in higher value-based locations and exploitation within assembly or distribution plants where flexibility is provided by efficient routines (March, 1991). Appropriate and differentiated leadership styles and corporate cultures can be operated across plants, particularly where ownership is not shared. Trying to operate dual cultures or leadership styles within the same establishment is likely to be extremely challenging. In addition, locational differentiation enables a network to work in a matching fashion, where core and peripheral workers complement one another and the latter is not simply a buffer protecting the former, as conceived in core-periphery labour models. Such differentiation can also be taken further where the focal firm opens its internal markets to competition, perhaps requiring internal units to service both inside and outside customers. This can bring benefits of both scale and market discipline. A third benefit of locational differentiation is in increasing information sources and facilitating adjustment to change. A network offers multiple sources of information, increasing awareness of volatility. It also provides specialist suppliers who, because of their high-quality knowledge, may be better able to anticipate change. This attenuates adjustment costs and increases flexibility in a cost-effective way.

Strategic flexibility can also result from governance advantages enjoyed by the global factory. Establishment differentiation based on ownership helps to overcome some of the challenges of implementing flexibility strategies. These include the difficulties of overcoming inertia or administrative heritage, violation of employee perceptions of psychological contracts, and internal conflict (see below). In addition, governance differentiation brings risk advantages. Externally sourced suppliers and partners provide more strategic options than growth based on vertical integration and allows for real option strategies, joint ventures or contractual supply relations. While the core-periphery labour market literature suggests that employers are seeking to pass risk onto employees, we would argue that more accurately this risk is being assumed by supplier and partner organisations within a global factory network. Ownership or governance separation also reduces reputational costs in the face of adverse events. Heavy investments in technology and brand building may be better protected where membership of a global value chain is less than transparent.

Our discussion highlights a number of features of flexibility strategies within the global factory. First, we suggest that flexibility is a complex and diverse concept, stemming from several sources. The global factory enjoys a number of distinct sources of such advantage, some of which are not available to the domestic or more traditionally organised international business. Second, the structure of the global factory enables it to better exploit the various forms of flexibility and to minimise conflict that usually arises when increased flexibility is sought. The analysis also highlights the advantages that the global factory enjoys in managing continuous disequilibrium. The challenges of balancing stability and change are considerable, particularly when the two are pursued simultaneously within a single organisation. Our model highlights the possibly of relative stability within the focal firm coexisting with continual disequilibrium within other parts of the factory network. The challenge for the focal firm directing the network is in balancing differential rates of change within elements of the system. This is a quite distinct management task.

The Costs of Flexibility

Flexibility is not costless: as well as the direct costs of building and maintaining flexible strategies and structures, there may also be indirect costs if the pursuit of flexibility involves trade-offs with other desirable goals. In this section, we consider some of the key costs.

Coordination and Transaction Costs

If flexibility is achieved through externalisation to partner organisations, then coordination or transaction costs will arise. These costs can be compared to those necessary for the management of an internal hierarchy, but which may imply a lower level of flexibility. In situations such as employment, hierarchies may be a lower-cost option than contracting through the market (Williamson, 1975) but do carry coordination costs. The relevant comparison is thus between the costs of hierarchy and the (likely higher) costs of externalisation where the difference is a premium for enhanced flexibility. However, the pursuit of flexibility is likely to impact not just the volume, but also the nature, of coordination costs. If, for example, greater flexibility necessitates multiple sourcing, or the regular switching of suppliers to ensure lowest cost, then average supplier tenure is likely to fall. Cooperation based on loyalty is liable to decrease, and incidences of cheating may rise since perceptions of a continuing and significant business relationship are reduced. In such a situation management priorities may change. Managers would need to place greater weight on identification, effective screening, and comprehensive due diligence when selecting partner organisations. The creation of a transparent corporate culture emphasising loyalty could assist in reducing incidences of cheating or opportunism. Inculcating such values and behavioural changes is likely to add to coordination costs.

There are reasons to believe that the costs of contracting may have fallen in comparison with management by fiat. This has occurred as technological developments in communication and control have facilitated integration, particularly cross-border activities, a world market for specialist skills has emerged (Liesch et al., 2012), and global factory firms have invested heavily in developing their coordination skills. Indeed, we would argue that such skills are now the primary source of competitive advantage of the global factory (Enderwick & Buckley, 2015).

Flexibility and Conflict

As discussed earlier, the coexistence within the same organisation of employee groups engaged under different terms and conditions, and possibly involved in the same or interrelated tasks, may be a source of resentment and conflict, hampering organisational performance. Conflict is particularly likely if peripheral employees are used to cushion core employees, with the former effectively assuming a disproportionate share of employment risk. The response of the global factory to this paradox may be to ensure that dualism occurs between organisations rather than within a single establishment (Harrison, 1994). Such segmentation not only helps avoid direct conflict but allows greater differentiation if it occurs between operations subject to varying cost and regulatory regimes.

Flexibility and Commitment

High-performance workplaces are likely to be characterised by high levels of employee commitment. Traditionally, commitment has been secured through the provision of job security and favourable pay and working conditions. However, the growth of less secure employment and performance-based evaluation have eroded this fundamental bargain, with, at best, opportunities for training and development to enhance 'marketability' replacing security of tenure. Opportunities to increase capabilities, while valued by many employees, do little to encourage commitment to a single employer. Ensuring employee commitment is likely to be problematic, particularly where employment conditions of a group of employees are changed unfavourably. Since such changes often coincide with lower levels of institutional and regulatory workplace support such as trade union coverage or social security benefits, they can trigger unconstructive responses. In essence, some employees may believe that their 'psychological contract', the terms of the exchange relationship between employee and employer, has been breached (Hiltrop, 1996). Maintaining psychological contracts within a flexible organisation pursuing some form of dualism necessitates significant investments in training and development opportunities. If the organisation is reluctant to make these investments, perhaps because it is primarily seeking to cut costs, commitment levels may be expected to plummet. For the global factory, the simplest solution to this problem is to differentiate activities and to ensure that tasks which are likely to be restructured are outsourced. This no longer means externalising a complete function such as production, but through 'fine slicing' targets specific tasks and employee groups. For the global factory, dualism (or more broadly, significant differentiation) may exist between network members, but does not have to occur within a single establishment.

Flexibility and Organisational Learning

The purpose of flexibility is to enable the firm to better respond to changing opportunities and volatility. This highlights the importance of learning within an organisation since the degree of organisational knowledge and capability determine the extent and direction of flexibility (Volberda, 1998). The strategic management literature increasingly stresses the dynamic nature of firm capabilities and how these enable the firm to respond to rapidly changing conditions (Kandemir & Hult, 2005; Teece, Pisano, & Shuen, 1997). Dynamic capabilities require continuous renewal and this occurs through organisational learning (Beer, Voelpel, Leibold, & Tekie, 2005). Organisational learning contributes to firm flexibility in a number of ways. Continual learning improves information processing capabilities, enabling the firm to identify and respond to new opportunities before competitors (Dickson, Farris, & Verbeke, 2001). Recurrent learning also facilitates 'unlearning' when obsolete mental models and approaches must be abandoned (De Holan, Phillips, & Lawrence, 2004). Learning adds to the firm's stock of accumulated experience and this is likely to be positively correlated with the ability to adjust to a rapidly evolving environment (Kenny, 2006). The limited evidence suggests that organisational learning contributes to firm flexibility and the ability to deploy resources in anticipation of change (Santos-Vijande, Lopez-Sanchez, & Trespalacios, 2012).

Flexibility and Innovation

Since innovation in products, processes, and coordination provides a primary source of competitive advantage for the global factory, understanding the links between flexibility and innovation is important. Unfortunately, this is not a simple matter. One reason is likely causal ambiguity between innovation and flexibility. Does successful innovation require a flexible organisation or does the implementation of innovation create flexibility? The reality is that multiple causation is likely to exist. A further complication is the complex nature of innovation. The term has been applied to a wide range of activities, rarely clearly defined. If we take the position that most innovation results from new combinations of existing processes, products, and ideas (Freeman & Soete, 1997), then functional flexibility might be expected to be positively related to innovation. Employees who are multiskilled, enjoy autonomy in their work and have expectations that their input will be valued, are likely to be more creative. There may also be an information technology effect if such workers are more socially connected, since innovativeness and social networking are correlated (Metcalfe, 2004).

Empirical evidence supports the view that functional flexibility and innovation are positively related (Hammond, Neff, Farr, Schwall, & Zhao, 2011; Shalley, Zhou, & Oldham, 2004; Spiegelaere, Gyes, & Hootegem, 2013; Zhou, Dekker, & Kleinknecht, 2011). However, the opposite seems to hold for other forms of flexibility, particularly numerical flexibility (Michie & Sheehan, 2003; Pieroni & Pompei, 2007; Probst, Stewart, Gruys, & Tierney, 2007; Spiegelaere et al., 2013). Explanations for this focus on the likelihood that employment insecurity reduces commitment and undermines training investments made by the firm (Sverke, Hellgren, & Näswall, 2002; Zhou et al., 2011). The counter to this view is that flexible contracts add to the resources of the firm with high rates of turnover injecting new knowledge and perspectives. Storey, Quintas, Taylor, and Fowle (2001) offer a more nuanced explanation suggesting that contract employees may complement an organisation's (other) innovative employees, implying a positive, but indirect, relationship. Research focusing on organisational characteristics suggest that flexible employment policies are rarely used as part of an innovation enhancing strategy and that more innovative organisations avoid such contractual arrangements (Lorenz & Valeyre, 2005; Michie & Sheehan, 2003; Storey et al., 2001). The use of temporary employees may also affect the type of innovation that a firm produces, with one study suggesting that their presence is associated with imitative, rather than original, innovation (Zhou et al., 2011). In summary, the research suggests that while functional flexibility may be positively related to innovativeness of individuals and organisations, numerical, or contractual flexibility appears to have a negative influence.

For the global factory, the logical conclusion may be to acknowledge the twin informational aspects of innovation, utilising the distinction between explorative and exploitative knowledge production (March, 1991). Knowledge exploration involves the creation and acquisition of new knowledge, emphasising the stages of search, discovery and experimentation. Knowledge exploitation highlights the application of existing knowledge to improve performance utilising routinisation and effective implementation (Holmqvist, 2004). The effective management of exploitative and explorative knowledge strategies calls for quite distinct approaches (Grant & Baden-Fuller, 2004). Exploration is best undertaken across a wide range of possible sources, which facilitates novelty (Nooteboom, 2000). In contrast, exploitation of knowledge benefits from overlap and repeated experimentation (McEvily, Eisenhardt, & Prescott, 2004). For the global factory, this suggests a logical differentiation under which the focal firm, with its wider perspective, focuses on knowledge exploration, while specialist partner organisations emphasise the effective deployment of knowledge through exploitation.

Flexibility and Firm Performance

The pursuit of increased flexibility has important implications for firm performance. Because such initiatives impact on both cost and motivation, they influence performance (Valverde, Tregaskis, & Brewster, 2000). The extent of such costs and performance effects depends on the type of initiative adopted. Enhanced functional flexibility can contribute to greater performance where employees can be deployed to multiple tasks or skills are deepened. Employees enjoying job enlargement or increased responsibility may be more motivated. This could enable a reduction in resources committed to supervision or lower level management. The cost of functional flexibility is the need to ensure continuing employment relationships and the provision of employee development opportunities. As suggested above, these two may be incompatible.

Numerical flexibility seeks to reduce labour costs by better matching labour demand and supply through the use of variable hours and fixed term contracts. Such employees may also reduce costs if pay rates are lower or indirect costs (pension, sickness benefits) can be avoided. The costs of numerical flexibility revolve around the recruitment, retention, and effective deployment of such workers. This may necessitate increased managerial resources. Again, the global factory may find it more effective to synchronise labour demand and supply requirements through externalisation, effectively passing the costs and risks to an outside party. Rather than having to deal with labour as a factor of production, the focal firm sources products, intermediate components, and services from outside organisations in an embodied form.

Barriers to Flexibility

As well as the assessable costs of instituting flexibility, there are a number of barriers likely to impede the adoption of flexible strategies. The first of these is administrative heritage (Bartlett & Ghoshal, 1990; Collis, 1991). Administrative heritage is part of the accumulated assets of a firm and captures the ways in which an organisation's history determines its current strategy and structure. It influences a firm's strategy, generally constraining strategic choices. Administrative heritage is typically a source of organisational inertia reinforcing existing strategic and structural patterns and adversely impacting both the pace and direction of change. In the present context, we might expect traditional MNEs characterised by hierarchical internal exchange and coordination to be less inclined to adopt strategies of externalisation because of an entrenched organisational resistance (Liesch et al., 2012). Externalisation within a global factory network allows the lead firm to access a range of administrative heritages, some of which, such as new start-ups, can avoid historical inertia.

A second constraint is the existing level of external transactions that the global factory undertakes. Positive experience of outsourcing should encourage greater utilisation of this strategy, hence the higher the current level, the more likely is further externalisation (Liesch et al., 2012).

Product- and industry-specific characteristics are a third constraint on flexibility strategies based on externalisation. Where there are unique product characteristics such as the need for a high level of customisation, challenging logistics requirements, critical intellectual property protection needs or onerous quality standards, a strategy of internalisation offering enhanced control, may be preferred.

Conclusions

This paper examines the concept of flexibility within global factory systems. While a global factory is generally associated with higher levels of flexibility, the forms, and sources of this have not been clearly articulated. We offer a simple conception which links three forms of volatility with three sources of flexibility. We suggest that locational and governance differentiation characteristic of global factory systems offers more than lower cost and the benefits of specialisation. Differentiation also facilitates the pursuit of flexibility, a critical attribute for a customer-focused organisation operating in a volatile environment. Differentiation helps to mitigate many of the costs associated with pursuing labour flexibility enhancing strategies including conflict, commitment, learning, adverse reputational effects, and innovation.

Segmentation within the global factory may be based on task or activity, but it creates opportunities for accessing less regulated locations, for risk sharing, and for applying distinct management styles and practices. A domestic business, lacking these options, faces greater challenges when seeking increased flexibility. While mult-iplant operations do imply higher coordination costs, this is an area where the global factory enjoys competitive strength.

Our discussion has interesting implications for management within global factory systems. It highlights the importance of the focal firm in setting the intention of the business and shaping partner strategy around the overriding goal of customer satisfaction. The focal firm, drawing on the inputs of a multiplicity of contributor firms, needs to ensure cross-functional and cross-hierarchical coordination. What it does not need to do is engage in operational matters within partner organisations. Here, a strategy of minimal critical specification—focusing on cost, quality, and timeliness—may be the optimum approach.

The importance of flexibility also helps to explain a number of interesting characteristics of global firms. One is locational stickiness in the face of rising costs. For example, commentators have suggested that China could experience disinvestment if costs, particularly wage costs, continue to rise. We would argue that China's attractiveness to international business is built on much more than labour cost. Its relatively unregulated operating conditions, specialist suppliers, and fungible workforce bring advantages of flexibility which could offset declining cost competitiveness.

We acknowledge that our discussion is just a starting point in this important topic. More work on articulating how locational and governance choices influence flexibility is needed. This work needs to be embedded in the contextual reality of multiplant, cross-border operations rather than the firm- or plant-centric focus of labour dualism studies. Network studies, while providing useful insights, need to incorporate the directive role of lead firms within global factory systems. Research that considers regulatory and industry differences would be helpful. Industry characteristics seem to matter with, in some cases, idiosyncratic strategies being well established. An example is provided by 'industry crunch', the intensive work schedules expected before a product launch, apparently widely accepted in industries such as gaming.

References

Amsden, A. H. (1992). *Next giant: South Korea and late industrialization.* Oxford: Oxford University Press.

Atkinson, J. (1984). Manpower strategies for flexible organisations. *Personnel Management,* August, 28–31.

Balch, O. (2015). The women suffering for your valentine's day flowers. *The Guardian,* 12 February.

Baldwin, R. (2013). Global supply chains: Why they emerged, why they matter, and where they are going. In D. K. Elms & P. Low (Eds.), *Global value chains in a changing world* (pp. 3–59). Geneva: WTO Publications.

Bartlett, C. A., & Ghoshal, S. (1990). Administrative heritage. *McKinsey Quarterly,* Winter, 31–41.

Beer, M., Voelpel, S. C., Leibold, M., & Tekie, E. B. (2005). Strategic management as organizational learning: Developing fit and alignment through a disciplined. *Process Long Range Planning, 38*(5), 445–465.

Buckley, P. J. (2014). *The multinational enterprise and the emergence of the global factory.* Basingstoke: Palgrave Macmillan.

Buckley, P. J., & Carter, M. J. (1996). The economics of business process design: Motivation, information and coordination within the firm. *International Journal of Economics and Business, 3,* 5–25.

Buckley, P. J., & Carter, M. J. (2002). Process and structure in knowledge management practices of British and US multinational enterprises. *Journal of International Management, 8*, 29–48.

Buckley, P. J., & Casson, M. C. (1998). Models of the multinational enterprise. *Journal of International Business Studies, 29*(1), 21–44.

Burke, J. (2013). Bangladesh factory fires: Fashion industry's latest crisis. *The Guardian*, 8 December.

Chamberlain, G. (2013). Sore eyes, bad backs, low pay: The cost of false eyelash glamour. *The Guardian*, 28 December.

Collis, D. J. (1991). A resource-based analysis of global competition: The case of the bearings industry. *Strategic Management Journal, 12*, 49–68.

Cully, M., Woodland, S., O'Reilly, A., & Dix, G. (1999). *Britain at work: As depicted by the 1998 workplace employee relations survey*. London and New York: Routledge.

De Holan, P., Phillips, N., & Lawrence, T. B. (2004). Managing organizational forgetting. *Sloan Management Review, 45*(2), 45–51.

Dickson, P. R., Farris, P. W., & Verbeke, W. (2001). Dynamic strategic thinking. *Journal of the Academy of Marketing Science, 29*(3), 216–237.

Doeringer, P., & Piore, M. (1971). *Internal labor markets and manpower analysis*. Lexington, MA: D.C. Heath.

D'Souza, D., & Williams, F. (2000). Towards a taxonomy of manufacturing flexibility dimensions. *Journal of Operations Management, 18*(5), 577–593.

Duclos, L., Vokurka, R., & Lummus, R. (2003). A conceptual model of supply chain flexibility. *Industrial Management and Data Systems, 103*(6), 446–456.

Enderwick, P., & Buckley, P. J. (2015). *The distinctive nature of the global factory*. Unpublished paper.

FinancesOnline. (2013). *How and where iPhone is made: A surprising report on how much of Apple's top product is U.S.-manufactured*. FinancesOnline.com

Freeman, C., & Soete, L. (1997). *The economics of industrial innovation*. London: Pinter Press.

Geary, J. F. (1992). Employment flexibility and human resource management: The case of three American electronics plants. *Work, Employment and Society, 6*, 251–270.

Grant, R. M., & Baden-Fuller, C. (2004). A knowledge accessing theory of strategic alliances. *Journal of Management Studies, 41*(1), 61–84.

Grunwald, J., & Flamm, K. (1985). *The global factory: Foreign assembly in international trade*. Washington, DC: Brookings Institute.

Gupta, Y., & Somers, T. (1996). Business strategy, manufacturing flexibility, and organizational performance relationships: A path analysis approach. *Production and Operations Management, 5*(3), 204–231.

Hammond, M. M., Neff, N. L., Farr, J. L., Schwall, A. R., & Zhao, X. (2011). Predictors of individual-level innovation at work: A meta-analysis. *Psychology of Aesthetics, Creativity, and the Arts, 5*(1), 90–105.

Harrison, B. (1994). *Lean and mean.* New York: Basic Books.

Hiltrop, J.-M. (1996). Managing the psychological contract. *Employee Relations, 18*(1), 36–49.

Holmqvist, M. (2004). Experiential learning processes of exploitation and exploration within and between organizations: An empirical study of product development. *Organization Science, 15*(1), 70–81.

Hummels, D. (2007). Transportation costs and international trade in the second era of globalization. *Journal of Economic Perspectives, 21*(3), 131–154.

Jacoby, S. (1999). Are career jobs headed for extinction? *California Management Review, 42,* 123–145.

Jordan, W. C., & Graves, S. C. (1995). Principles on the benefits of manufacturing process flexibility. *Management Science, 41*(4), 577–594.

Kalleberg, A. L. (2001). Organizing flexibility: The flexible firm in a new century. *British Journal of Industrial Relations, 39*(4), 479–504.

Kandemir, D., & Hult, G. T. (2005). A conceptualization of an organizational learning culture in international joint ventures. *Industrial Marketing Management, 34*(5), 430–439.

Kantor, J., & Streitfeld, D. (2015). Inside amazon: Wrestling big ideas in a bruising workplace. *The New York Times,* 15 August.

Kenny, J. (2006). Strategy and the learning organization: A maturity model for the formation of strategy. *The Learning Organization, 13*(4), 353–368.

Leftwitch, A. (1995). Bringing politics back in: Towards a model of the developmental state. *Journal of Development Studies, 31*(3), 400–427.

Liesch, P. W., Buckley, P. J., Simonin, B. L., & Knight, G. (2012). Organizing the modern firm in the worldwide market for market transactions. *Management International Review, 52,* 3–21.

Lorenz, E., & Valeyre, A. (2005). Organisational innovation, human resource management and labour market structure: A comparison of the EU-15. *Journal of Industrial Relations, 47*(4), 424–442.

Lummus, R., Duclos, L., & Vokurka, R. (2003). Supply chain flexibility: Building a new model. *Global Journal of Flexible Systems Management, 4*(4), 1–13.

March, J. G. (1991). Exploration and exploitation in organizational learning. *Organization Science, 2,* 71–87.

Marglin, S. A., & Schor, J. B. (1992). *The golden age of capitalism: Reinterpreting the postwar experience.* Oxford: Oxford University Press.

McEvily, S. K., Eisenhardt, K. M., & Prescott, J. E. (2004). The global acquisition, leverage, and protection of technological competencies. *Strategic Management Journal, 25*(8-9), 713–722.

Metcalfe, J. (2004). The entrepreneur and the style of modern economics. *Journal of Evolutionary Economics, 14*(2), 157–175.

Michie, J., & Sheehan, M. (2003). Labour market deregulation, 'flexibility' and innovation. *Cambridge Journal of Economics, 27*, 123–143.

Morishima, M. (1995). Embedding HRM in a social context. *British Journal of Industrial Relations, 33*(4), 617–640.

Nooteboom, B. (2000). Learning by interaction: Absorptive capacity, cognitive distance and governance. *Journal of Management and Governance, 4*(1-2), 69–92.

Olhager, J., & West, B. (2002). The house of flexibility: Using the QFD approach to deploy manufacturing flexibility. *International Journal of Operations and Production Management, 22*(1), 50–79.

Osterman, P. (1999). *Securing prosperity*. Princeton: Princeton University Press.

Pieroni, L., & Pompei, F. (2007). Evaluating innovation and labour market relationships: The case of Italy. *Cambridge Journal of Economics, 32*(2), 325–347.

Probst, T. M., Stewart, S. M., Gruys, M. L., & Tierney, B. W. (2007). Productivity, counter productivity and creativity: The ups and downs of job insecurity. *Journal of Occupational and Organizational Psychology, 80*(3), 479–497.

Santos-Vijande, M. L., Lopez-Sanchez, J. A., & Trespalacios, J. A. (2012). How organizational learning affects a firm's flexibility, competitive strategy, and performance. *Journal of Business Research, 65*, 1079–1089.

Sauvant, K. P. (2016). *The evolving international investment law and policy regime: Ways forward*. E15 Task Force on Investment Policy—Policy Options Paper. E15Initiative. International Centre for Trade and Sustainable Development (ICTSD) and World Economic Forum, Geneva.

Shalley, C. E., Zhou, J., & Oldham, G. R. (2004). The effects of personal and contextual characteristics on creativity: Where should we go from here? *Journal of Management, 30*(6), 933–958.

Soper, S. (2011). Inside Amazon's warehouse. *The Morning Call*, 18 September.

Spiegelaere, S. D., Gyes, G. V., & Hootegem, G. V. (2013). Labour flexibility and innovation, complementary or concurrent strategies? A review of the literature. *Economic and Industrial Democracy, 35*(4), 653–666.

Storey, J., Quintas, P., Taylor, P., & Fowle, W. (2001). Flexible employment contracts and their implications for product and process innovation. *International Journal of Human Resource Management, 13*(1), 1–18.

Sverke, M., Hellgren, J., & Näswall, K. (2002). No security: A meta-analysis and review of job insecurity and its consequences. *Journal of Occupational Health Psychology, 7*(3), 242–264.

Teece, D., Pisano, G., & Shuen, A. (1997). Dynamic capabilities and strategic management. *Strategic Management Journal, 18*(7), 509–533.

Upton, D. (1994). The management of manufacturing flexibility. *California Management Review, 36*(1), 72–89.

Valverde, M., Tregaskis, O., & Brewster, C. (2000). Labor flexibility and firm performance. *International Advances in Economic Research, 6*(4), 649–661.

Volberda, H. W. (1998). *Building the flexible firm*. Oxford: Oxford University Press.

Williamson, O. E. (1975). *Markets and hierarchies: Analysis and anti-trust implications*. New York: The Free Press.

Williamson, O. E. (1996). *The mechanisms of governance*. Oxford: Oxford University Press.

World Bank (2009). *World Development Report 2009: Reshaping economic geography*. Washington, DC: World Bank.

Zhang, Q., Vonderembse, M. A., & Lim, J. S. (2003). Manufacturing flexibility: Defining and analyzing relationships among competence, capability and customer satisfaction. *Journal of Operations Management, 21*(2), 173–191.

Zhou, H., Dekker, R., & Kleinknecht, A. (2011). Flexible labor and innovation performance: Evidence from longitudinal firm-level data. *Industrial and Corporate Change, 20*(3), 1–28.

3

Leading for Innovation

Mohammad Haris Minai, Shailendra Singh, and Arup Varma

Introduction

Innovation is critical for organizations to not only thrive but survive in the competitive, ever-changing environment facing them (Dess & Picken, 2000; Tushman & O'Reilly, 2002). Globalization, the rapid changes in production technology, new consumer expectations, and increased rate of technological change have created conditions such that value is produced primarily by creativity and innovation in organizations (Florida, 2002). In such volatile environments, innovation is a critical ingredient by which organizations can gain and sustain a competitive advantage (Andriopoulos & Lewis, 2010). Earlier thought to be the domain

_____

M.H. Minai (✉) • S. Singh
Indian Institute of Management Lucknow, Lucknow, India

A. Varma
Loyola University Chicago, Chicago, IL, USA

© The Author(s) 2017
S. Kundu, S. Munjal (eds.), _Human Capital and Innovation_,
DOI 10.1057/978-1-137-56561-7_3

of smaller organizations, larger organizations are also now embracing the chaos that accompanies innovation (Quinn, 1985).

Organizations depend upon their human capital for the generation and implementation of new and useful ideas (Amabile, 1988; Scott & Bruce, 1994). Indeed, individual innovation is the cornerstone of several well-known management principles such as Total Quality Management (TQM), Kaizen, and organizational learning. Even within organizational literature, there is an appreciation of the role that individuals play in making organizations respond to the challenge of addressing both exploration and exploitation (Birkinshaw & Gibson, 2004). Though proper management is essential to increase the likelihood of success of a single innovation, an individual is usually the source of each new idea that results in innovation (Mumford, 2000).

Innovation at the individual and team level, where both the generation and initial prototype is developed by a single individual or a team, is contextually embedded (Amabile, Conti, Coon, Lazenby, & Herron, 1996; Woodman, Sawyer, & Griffin, 1993), and leadership is one of the most important contextual influences on innovative behaviours of employees (Mumford, Scott, Gaddis, & Strange, 2002; Oldham & Cummings, 1996). In fact, when supervisors are able to create a work environment conducive to innovation, even employees lacking a natural inclination may engage in innovative behaviours (Zhou & Hoever, 2014).

Ironically, the research on leading for innovation has often been criticized for not garnering its fair share of attention (Byrne, Mumford, Barrett, & Vessey, 2009). Though there have been some efforts to do so, as evidenced by the two part special issue on leading for innovation (Mumford & Licuanan, 2004), a clear view on how leaders influence the process of individual and team innovation is far from clear. The findings of the relationship between leadership and innovation have been inconsistent (Mumford et al., 2002; Rosing, Frese, & Bausch, 2011). Rosing et al. (2011), in a meta-analytic review of the relationship between leadership and innovation, have found that only transformational leadership and leader member-exchange (LMX) have been consistently found to have a positive relationship with innovation and the relationship with transformational leadership is also highly heterogeneous. Transformational leadership has been the most highly studied form of leadership for innovation and the findings suggest that it "… is not necessarily related to innovation under all circumstances, but some specific conditions need to be met" (Rosing, 2011). They suggest that current models of innovation do not adequately capture the role of leadership in the innovation process, as current models assume innovation to be a single "type" of activity and current evidence is against this conceptualization (Axtell et al., 2000; Caniëls, De Stobbeleir, & De Clippeleer, 2014) leading to calls for greater research on the links between leadership and innovation (Anderson, Potočnik, & Zhou, 2014).

Mainemelis, Kark, and Epitropaki (2015) have suggested that creative leadership can be broadly categorized as facilitating, directing, and integrating. The facilitating manifestation of creative leadership focuses on a leader's role in fostering creativity in others (primarily in the team and individuals they lead) within an organizational context, the directing creative leadership refers to the materialization of a leader's creative vision through the work of other people, while the integrating manifestation is conceptualized as the role of a leader in synthesizing their creative work with that of others. They further suggest that the facilitating manifestation is mainly based on the following three mainstream theories of creative behaviour: Amabile's (1988) componential model, Woodman et al.'s (1993) interactionist perspective, and Ford's (1996) theory of individual creative action.

The componential model of creativity (Amabile, 1988) allows for a motivational role of contextual factors. For the case of leadership, if leadership results in an increased intrinsic motivation, creative behaviours are expected to increase and vice versa for leadership that reduces intrinsic motivation. The interactionist perspective (Woodman & Schoenfeldt, 1990) of creative behaviour allows for more complex interplay between individual characteristics and the context, but does not provide specific directions on whether a certain behaviour would foster or hinder innovative behaviour. Ford's model of individual creative action (Ford, 1996) posits sense making by the employee as the mediator between leadership behaviours and the decision to undertake creative behaviour. All these approaches suggest that supportive leadership would have a positive impact on innovative behaviours via influence on the work environment (Amabile, Schatzel, Moneta, & Kramer, 2004). Support by the leader could be in the form of direct assistance, development of subordinate expertise, and enhancement of intrinsic motivation. Taking the componential model as a foundation, Amabile et al. (2004) found evidence for the role of subordinate perception of their environment, in particular the role of leader behaviours and its subsequent impact on the creativity of the subordinate. They, however, decry the lack of holistic views of how patterns of leader behaviour might impact subordinate creativity over time.

Rosing et al. (2011) on the other hand posit that the crucial feature of leading for innovation is the fostering of either explorative or exploitative behaviours in subordinates, the combination of which results in innovative behaviour. They frame ambidextrous leadership as the ability by a leader to demonstrate both behaviours that foster exploratory activities and behaviours that foster exploitative activities in their subordinates as well as switching between these two behaviours. Their model is based on a dialectical perspective on innovation (Bledow, Frese, Anderson, Erez, & Farr, 2009a, 2009b). This view is based on the understanding that innovation is composed of paradoxes and the resolution, synthesis, and integration of these paradoxes is what results in innovation. Therefore, it is useful to separate the components of innovative behaviour into those that foster exploration and those that foster exploitation and look for their antecedents independently, but jointly, as the presence of both these behaviours is essential for innovation to occur. Though Rosing et al. (2011) accept that motivation is an important antecedent of innovative behaviour, their theory concentrates on the specific activities of followers.

In this chapter, we try to build some degree of consensus about the relationship of leadership behaviours and individual innovation, by using a dialectical perspective on innovation (Bledow et al., 2009a), and incorporating the role of motivation and leader support that has received extensive evidence in literature (e.g. Eisenbeiss, van Knippenberg, & Boerner, 2008; Oldham & Cummings, 1996). We also address the possible substitution of leader behaviours by subordinate traits and integrate the decision-making concept from the theory of individual creative action (Ford, 1996). We couch our overall discussion in the context of globalization, since globalization and innovation are strongly inter-related, as demonstrated by the experience of countries like China (see Zhang & Roelfsema, 2014) and India (e.g. Jha & Krishnan, 2013).

Finally, we build testable propositions about the role of various established leader behaviours (Yukl, 2012a) in fostering innovative behaviour in the context of individuals and small teams.

This work is pertinent as a new look on leadership for innovation is required (Anderson, de Drew, & Nijstad, 2004), and studies examining exploration and exploitation at the microlevel are relatively scant (Gupta, Smith, & Shalley, 2006). Finally, we also answer the call for new models specifying how leadership influence tactics operate during both idea generation and implementation (Mumford & Licuanan, 2004; Yukl, 2009).

In the following sections, we discuss globalization, and how it affects innovation. This is followed by a discussion of innovation and the arguments for considering its paradoxical nature, whereby we also address the phases of innovation and how these phases differ from each other. We also look at the literature on how leadership influences innovative behaviour. Following this, we look at the current findings on leadership and innovation and we bring focus to those findings that inform our propositions. Subsequently, we elaborate on three approaches that leaders take to encourage innovative behaviour; the developmental approach, the ambidextrous approach, and the motivational approach. We finally conclude with a discussion on the contributions, limitations, and avenues for further research.

Globalization

While globalization is neither a new concept, nor a new occurrence, it has gained currency over the last two to three decades primarily due to the growth of emerging economies like China and India. In this connection, Gentry and Sparks (2012) have noted that, as a result of increasing foreign competition, organizations are sometimes forced to go global, whereby operating in a global context with a global mindset is an imperative, and not a choice. As these two economies have grown and become major exporters and also begun to attract foreign direct investment (FDI), innovation has played a critical role. Take the case of China, which has become a major exporter of all kinds of goods over the last two decades (Zhang & Roelfsema, 2014). In order to compete with the domestic producers of those goods, and exports from other nations, Chinese firms have naturally had to innovate, to ensure that their products meet global quality standards, while at the same time continuing to maintain low costs. Relatedly, the opening up of China's economy has also seen a rush by almost all major global corporations to set up manufacturing facilities in China. The resultant infusion of FDI has had significant positive impact on innovation (Cheung, 2010). Similarly, the opening up of the Indian economy in the early 1990s led to a huge influx of FDI into India, though the two Asian giants were seen as being different. While China became the "factory" of the world, India came to be known as the "back office." At least initially, many global corporations moved their service divisions to India, to capitalize on the English language ability of the workforce, and cheap labour costs. Indeed, India came to be known for BPOs (business process outsourcing), call centres, and software development work. However, this was soon followed by the establishment of research and development (R&D) facilities. As Jha and Krishnan (2013) have noted, "India has rapidly emerged as a hub of MNE innovation activity." In order to take advantage of the vast over-supply of intellectual capital, many multinationals (MNEs) started establishing R&D facilities in India, again confirming that there is a strong relationship between FDI flow and innovation. We started this section by discussing how globalization affects, and often causes, innovation. We want to conclude the section by noting that innovation was one of the prime factors that allowed globalization to grow and flourish (see, e.g. Josephine, 2014). Some of the earliest innovations like boats and ships allowed intrepid souls to set out in search of for-off lands, while the airplane made it possible to travel around the world in much shorter time spans. Over the last two decades or so, several technological innovations, including the invention of the world wide web, have revolutionized the world as we know it, leading to a much more connected globe. In the following sections, we present a discussion of the various facets and nuances of innovation, followed by a discussion of the interplay of innovation and leadership.

Innovation

Though there is a lack of consensus on what exactly constitutes innovation and how it is distinct from creativity, the integrative definition given by Anderson et al. (2014) seems to be closest to what would be generally agreeable. They delineate between an idea generation stage and an idea implementation stage with creativity research mostly concerned with the first stage and innovation concerned either with the second or with both stages. However, this clear delineation is not always apparent; for instance, it is rare that an idea can be communicated unless it takes on some tangible form, that is, it is implemented to some extent as a prototype or at least elaborated to make it easy to communicate. Similarly, it is rare for an idea which is novel to be implemented without recourse to further idea generation as the novelty of the idea itself implies that its implementation might not be straightforward. There is recognition that the innovation process is messy and involves forward, backward, and side steps (Anderson et al., 2014, p. 1299). Some scholars differentiate between creativity and innovation by arguing that creativity is the first step of innovation resulting in novel and useful ideas which when implemented result in innovation (Amabile, 1996a; Scott & Bruce, 1994). However, at the individual level of analysis, Sarooghi, Libaers, and Burkemper (2015) have found both to be highly correlated. Efforts by Janssen (2000) to distinguish between idea generation and its realization at the individual level have also not been supported in their analysis. For our purposes, we consider creativity and innovation to be related to a large extent and at the level of the individual and team when the implementation is encompassed within the boundary of the level being considered, the difference is irrelevant. In fact, since Wallas's (1926) early model of the creative process, all psychological models of the creative process have included some degree of idea elaboration, evaluation, and implementation within them. This is very similar to the stages that have been proposed for innovation discussed below (Mainemelis et al., 2015).

We do however consider pure implementation as an innovative behaviour as long as the idea is new to the unit under research. Hence, even if an idea has been promulgated elsewhere, its first implementation within a unit can still be considered an innovation (Anderson et al., 2004).

Innovation as Dialectical

Innovation and creativity is best understood as a balance between at least two, possibly conflicting constructs. These have been termed severally as follows: (1) novelty and usefulness (Amabile, 1996a), (2) idea generation and idea implementation (e.g. Anderson et al., 2004), and (3) exploration and exploitation (March, 1991). We discuss each of these means of partitioning innovation further.

Novelty and Usefulness

Amabile (1988) has suggested that creativity can be assessed in terms of its novelty and utility within a specific social domain. Leaning on Simonton's (1999) evolutionary thinking on innovation Amabile, Barsade, Mueller, and Staw (2005) argue that variation primarily contributes to idea novelty, whereas selection contributes to idea usefulness. Therefore, the more variation that can be introduced to an idea by an individual the more likely it is that the idea would be novel. Selection on the other hand is an evaluative activity, whereby an individual applies criteria depending upon the targeted social domain and selects the idea that is considered to be the most fruitful to pursue. Furthermore, initial selection is usually done by an individual proposer and subsequent selection happens when the idea is exposed to evaluation by the social group or community (Amabile et al., 2005).

From this view, we see that at least two distinct kinds of activities are envisaged that contribute towards an innovative product and which would constitute innovative behaviours. An ability to increase variation in the number and nature of ideas suggested and an ability to select an appropriate idea for further development.

Phases of Innovation

Similar to the duality of novelty and usefulness, innovation is considered to consist of at least two phases, that of idea generation and that of idea implementation. We use the term phases to account for the fact that idea generation and implementation might not necessarily be strictly ordered, and could be iterative and recursive (Anderson et al., 2004; King, 1992). This iterative nature is also emphasized by Mumford et al. (2002) when they talk about the progressive refinement and extension of the initial idea to permit successful implementation.

Idea generation is a free-flowing activity which identifies new variants by combining knowledge from various domains to come up with several alternatives that can be used to address the task at hand (Amabile, 1996a; Mumford, 2000). In contrast, after generation, an evaluative bent of mind is adopted by the parties concerned and ideas are winnowed down to the most useful ones which are elaborately refined. Not all ideas can be easily implemented in an organizational setting and the constraints placed by an organization might force parties involved in the implementation phase to look for means to make the implementation more useful or more cost-effective. Thus, idea implementation may call for as much creativity as idea generation (Mumford et al., 2002). These phases have also been referred to as initiation and implementation by innovation theorists; nevertheless, they contain elements (de Jong & Hartog, 2007) similar to the variation-selection duality that was discussed earlier. In an analysis of case studies, Caniëls et al. (2014) found that antecedents have differing roles in the stages of the creative process, and antecedents that are helpful in one stage might become hindrances in another. This strengthens our argument that there are at least two different types of activities that need to be undertaken in an innovative process.

Exploration and Exploitation

So far we have looked at literature that deals with the individual and group level processes. However, dual processes have also been proposed at the organizational level for innovation. These are referred to as exploration and exploitation. Exploration requires search, variation, experimentation, and discovery, whereas exploitation is linked to notions of refinement, efficiency, selection, implementation, and convergent thinking (Andriopoulos & Lewis, 2009; March, 1991). Strategy literature usually links exploration to the search for new products, processes or services and exploitation to incremental improvements in existing products, processes, and services (Yukl, 2009), this difference of target for exploration and exploitation is not contained in their original conceptualizations and we use these terms simply as short forms to the notions they are related to. This is also the way in which these terms have been used by Rosing et al. (2011). Therefore, explorative activities are those activities that entail search, variation, experimentation and discovery, whereas exploitative activities are those that entail refinement, selection, efficiency, and implementation.

Thus, we see that no matter what duality we concern ourselves with, whether novelty-usefulness, generation–implementation or exploration–exploitation. These constructs are linked to different activities that need to be undertaken by an individual or team that wishes to be innovative. We follow Rosing et al. (2011) and use the terms explorative and exploitative activities to refer to these activities.

These activities, however, do not follow a linear process as is implied by stage-based models of innovation. In the next section, we argue for the non-linear and iterative nature of the innovation process, such that there is no specific order in which these activities need to be undertaken.

Innovation as Dynamic

Research on innovation processes has unequivocally confirmed that these processes are iterative, non-linear, disjunctive, and cyclical (Anderson et al., 2004). The authors go on to criticize innovation research for the portrayal of innovation as linearly leading to a single outcome which is adjudged as innovative or not.

This lack of linearity makes it difficult to analyse the complex process of innovation by imposing an artificial structure or phases. For instance, in the creativity process proposed by Amabile (1996a), the stages are expected not to be linear and at the end of the process, it continues from any of the previous stages. In fact, Mumford (2000) suggests that planning for innovation should be opportunistic and incremental, rather than insisting that it adhere to a lock-step schedule. Even though the phases of innovation itself cannot be split into separate phases or stages

(Rosing et al., 2011), a finer level of granularity at the level of the individual or team that focuses on a single type of activity at a time can be instructive. We suggest that the analysis of the innovation process is most fruitful at a finer granularity, where we simply consider an innovation process to consist of multiple cycles of either explorative or exploitative activities undertaken by the concerned entities.

Given the necessity of both these activities to generate innovative outcomes and empirical support for interaction between exploration and exploitation leading to a positive impact on new product development (Katila & Ahuja, 2002), we come to our first proposition:

Proposition 1 Innovation is the result of an individual or team engaging in both explorative and exploitative activities over a period of time.

Leading for Innovation

The role of leadership in enhancing innovation is critical and important (Tierney, 2008). However, this has been found to be highly heterogeneous (Hammond, Neff, Farr, Schwall, & Zhao, 2011; Rosing et al., 2011). For instance, for follower creativity and innovation, Gong, Huang, and Farh (2009) and Shin and Zhou (2003) found a significant positive relationship with transformational leadership, whereas Jaussi and Dionne (2003) found a negative correlation which was not significant, whereas for team creative performance, it was negative and statistically significant. This heterogeneity extends to other leadership theories as well, Williams (2004) found an insignificant relationship between leader preference for initiating structure and follower creative performance, though Osborn and Marion (2009) found a positive relationship between initiating structure behaviours of leader on innovation performance of alliances. They also found a significant positive relationship between leader consideration behaviours and innovation performance though these two behaviours have been linked to differing outcomes by Judge, Piccolo, and Ilies (2004). Supervisor support was not found to be linked to creativity by Tierney and Farmer (2002) and Oldham and Cummings (1996) but was found to be linked to creativity and innovation by Ohly, Sonnentag, and Pluntke (2006). For transformational leadership, in particular, it is found to be related to explorative behaviours by followers but not to exploitative behaviours (Mainemelis et al., 2015). Kahai, Sosik, and Avolio (2003) go so far as to suggest that transactional leadership might have certain advantages in the leadership of creative efforts compared to transformational leadership. For team innovation, Eisenbeiß and Boerner (2010) found a curvilinear relationship between transformational leadership and team innovation.

This heterogeneity in the relationship between leadership and innovation has resulted in a search for moderators of the relationship. Herrmann and Felfe (2013) have explored task novelty and personal initiative, Keller (1989) consider employees that face an uncertain environment and are professional to place a higher value on leader-initiating structure behaviours, Gilmore, Hu, Wei, Tetrick, and Zaccaro (2013) have shown that positive trait affectivity substitutes for the influence of transformational leadership when considering creative performance, Pieterse, van Knippenberg, Schippers, and Stam (2010) found that transformational leadership was effective in encouraging innovative behaviour only when followers were psychologically empowered, and finally Rosing et al. (2011) suggest that different leader behaviours moderate each other.

Though Woodman et al. (1993) suggest that leadership (a contextual variable) would interact with personal characteristics to predict creative behaviour, there is no clear guidance on what interactions can be expected. Therefore, the interactionist perspective, though supported by current findings, needs to be enriched to create higher predictive value. Specific to the relationship of leader behaviours and innovation, Anderson et al. (2014) suggest that the heterogeneity could be due to different leadership styles and behaviours being important at different stages of the innovation cycle. In another recent review, Kesting, Ulhøi, Song, and Niu (2016) propose a similar argument of different stages of innovation placing differing demands on leadership. Amabile (1996b) suggest that certain tasks in the innovation cycle are *heuristic* whereas others are *algorithmic*. Heuristic tasks are those that cannot be solved by following a recipe, whereas as algorithmic tasks have a single process of solution. The differing nature of these tasks, suggests that different leadership behaviours may have differing effects during the innovation process and behaviours that facilitate one type of task might inhibit the other type, thus resulting in the overall effect being heterogeneous. As we argued in the previous section, the iterative and non-linear nature of innovation precludes us from insisting on a specific sequence of stages and conceptualizing follower behaviours at a finer level of granularity into explorative and exploitative behaviours would be a more beneficial approach. This is the approach taken by Rosing et al. (2011), and the approach that we build upon.

Leader Behaviours that Influence Innovation

Given that innovation places paradoxical demands on the individual, the explorative and exploitative activities that followers undertake to address these demands need to be integrated. Bledow et al. (2009a) suggest that the integration could occur at the level of the paradox itself, in our case—the individual, or team, or integration could be the task of higher management, which would include the immediate supervisor. As we have seen, it is necessary to engage in both of these activities in order to achieve an innovative outcome.

Leadership Behavioural Complexity

Leadership styles are too broad to work with when we analyse innovation at a granular level. Sarros, Cooper, and Santora (2008), in an exploration of transformational leadership and its impact on creating a climate for innovation found that only two of the six dimensions of transformational leadership, viz. visioning and individualized support were related to the perception of a climate for innovation. Similarly, Kesting et al. (2016) have also called for a decomposition of leadership styles to different elements in the study of this relationship. As noted earlier, different leadership elements appear to be related to the different activities required in the creative process. For example, by analysing case studies, Caniëls et al. (2014) found that a leader's facilitating attitude helps in the idea generation phase (which would mostly be explorative) and a hierarchical leadership style is beneficial during idea implementation (which in our conceptualization would be mostly exploitative).

Due to the paradoxical demands of innovation, leaders need to have a repertoire of behaviours that they can demonstrate with competence. In fact, Buijs (2007) styles them as "controlled schizophrenics" (p. 203). That managers can actually indulge in both searching, discovering and experimenting activities as well as selecting, improving, and refining activities is known (Mom, Van Den Bosch, & Volberda, 2007). However, they may differ in their excellence in each of these activities. Behavioural complexity on the part of leaders enables them to handle paradoxes (Denison, Hooijberg, & Quinn, 1995) enabling organizational ambidexterity (Carmeli & Halevi, 2009). Leaders of innovation must also find an optimal balance between autonomy (to encourage exploration) and structure (to encourage exploitation) (Mainemelis et al., 2015). For instance, Amabile et al. (2004) reports that while monitoring in the form of maintaining contact was beneficial for the perception of leader support, once this became excessive the effect became detrimental. Yuan and Zhou (2008) report that evaluation had differential effects on variation and retention, which roughly correspond to explorative and exploitative activities by followers. Therefore, leaders of innovation must fill multiple roles (Mumford et al., 2002), which are complex and make incompatible demands. How this behavioural complexity influences subordinate behaviour at various stages of the innovation process is not sufficiently clear in the current stage-based models of innovation and creativity. In line with Rosing et al. (2011), we agree that various leadership behaviours could be salient for different activities that an individual or team undertakes in the innovation process and could have facilitating or inhibiting effects on explorative and exploitative activities.

Leader Behaviour Taxonomies

Leadership behaviours conceptualized as two-factor models have been criticized for oversimplifying the complex phenomena of leadership (Yukl, 1999). Innovation research has also been criticized for using single leader behaviours as one factor among many while examining the relationship between leadership and innovation (de Jong & Hartog, 2007). As one of our concerns is in identifying individual impact of leader behaviours on explorative and exploitative activities, we need a more refined conceptualization of leader behaviours. Leaders take on many different roles in the process of leading (Mintzberg, 2007). They are able to do this by behaviours that can be categorized into the following meta-categories: task-oriented, relations-oriented, change-oriented, and external behaviours (Yukl, 2012b). The primary focus of task-oriented behaviours is efficiency that of change-oriented behaviours is to encourage learning and adaptation, relations-oriented behaviours are used by leaders to enhance member skills and the rapport with their subordinates, and finally external behaviours are directed outwards in getting relevant information and resources external to their immediate influence. Other researchers have also used the managerial practices scale (MPS) for looking at the effects of leadership on creativity and innovation (Amabile et al., 2004; de Jong & Hartog, 2007). In addition, the MPS categorizes leader behaviours into functional groups that are posited to have different effects on followers. This makes it eminently suitable for our framework. This is another departure in our work compared to Rosing et al. (2011), as they have defined a dichotomy of leader behaviours which are a priori expected to lead to explorative and exploitative activities in followers. By using a leader behaviour taxonomy that is comprehensive and well developed (Arnold, Arad, Rhoades, & Dragow, 2000), we hope to provide incremental evidence for a dialectical framework within which to look for relationships between leadership and innovation.

Approaches to Leading for Innovation

Taking this dialectical view of innovation as a starting point, we go on to suggest that in a team setting, leaders can influence the innovative behaviours of their followers in three ways. First their actions could result in increase in expertise of their subordinates in performing these activities which would result in better outcomes for the same amount of time spent in doing these activities. Secondly, leader behaviours could influence followers to engage in one of the two activities, either explorative or exploitative. Thus, the onus of deciding when explorative or exploitative activities is required is on the leader and the follower simply follows the cues provided by the leader, this is the model proposed by Rosing et al. (2011). Thirdly, leaders could empower and engage their followers such that the followers become adept at deciding when to engage in either explorative or exploitative activities. In this situation, leaders provide the support and followers are responsible for integrating the paradoxes of innovation. We discuss these approaches below as: (1) The developmental approach, (2) The ambidextrous approach, and (3) The motivational approach.

Developmental Approach

To excel in both explorative and exploitative activities, individuals must have different competencies. For instance looking at the competencies mentioned by Vila, Perez, and Coll-Serrano (2014) as relevant for innovating we can categorize them into abilities that are useful for explorative activities such as alertness to new opportunities, coming up with new ideas, straddling multiple fields of knowledge, and abilities that are useful for exploitative activities such as skill in presenting and preparing reports, ability to mobilize the capacity of others and ability to use computers. Amabile (1996a) sees them as *heuristic* and *algorithmic* and Andriopoulos and Lewis (2009) frame these are *passion* and *discipline*.

And indeed, the outcome of an activity would be dependent on the expertise with which the activity has been executed; therefore, individuals weak in creativity skills would find it difficult to get an innovative output even though they engage in explorative activities, similarly individuals with a less analytical bent of mind might have difficulty in delivering when required to carry out exploitative activities. In a study on goal conflict and creativity, James (1995) found that task conflict-enhanced creativity but only when individuals had sufficient expertise to manage the conflict. Leaders can expose their subordinates to training and development in these skills and therefore influence the innovative outcome indirectly. This is also one of the mechanisms by which leaders exert an influence on subordinate creativity within the componential model (Amabile et al., 2004). Informational–developmental feedback has also been found to generally foster employee creativity (Mumford, Gibson, Giorgini, & Mecca, 2014; Zhou, 2003, 2008). Thus, we come to our second proposition:

Proposition 2 Leaders can influence innovative outcomes of their subordinates by developing creative and domain relevant skills in their subordinates.

Ambidextrous Approach

Conceptualizing innovation as the interaction of both explorative and exploitative activities, we can explore the role of different leader behaviours on the follower's propensity to engage in either of these activities. In the context of learning processes, Yukl (2009) has called for more comprehensive models of leader influence in explaining exploration and exploitation by emphasizing specific types of relevant leadership behaviours. Explorative and exploitative activities are sufficiently disparate that different leadership behaviours would impact the propensity of a follower to engage in these activities differently. For instance, leader behaviour that emphasizes structure and task completion might be beneficial for exploitative activities such as refinement of idea under consideration, but might be detrimental for explorative activities such as generation of more alternatives for implementing an idea. Similarly, leader behaviour such as intellectual stimulation could be beneficial for explorative activities such as experimentation but might thwart exploitative activities such as applying rigid criteria to select between multiple alternatives.

Leader behaviours would influence subordinate actions via the perception that the followers have regarding what the best course of action would be. Černe, Jaklič, and Škerlavaj (2013) found that perceived authentic leadership had direct influence on follower creativity and team innovation but not so for self-ascribed leader authentic behaviour. Ford's (1996) theory also posits an important role for the sensemaking that an individual does before he decides on a course of action. The notion of follower perception about work environment being important for their creativity is also supported in the work of Amabile et al. (2004). Therefore, other aspects of the work environment apart from the leader behaviour could dynamically impact the perception that an individual and team has about which activity to undertake at that point in time. We consider the sum total of all contextual and personal factors that push towards exploitative or explorative activities as drivers for these activities and allow for the substitution of certain aspects of leadership (Kerr & Jermier, 1978; Nübold, Muck, & Maier, 2013) in creating these drivers in the perceptions of followers. With this lens, we look at the effect that various leader behaviours, as categorized in the MPS (Yukl, 2012a), have on innovation.

Leaders can influence innovation by exhibiting behaviours that foster explorative activities in their subordinates. Rosing et al. (2011) refers to these behaviours as "opening behaviours". These behaviours fall under change-oriented behaviours meta-category. These behaviours are used by leaders to "… increase innovation, collective learning and adaptation to external changes." (Yukl, 2012b, p. 72). However, as discussed earlier, the perception of drivers for exploration also need to be incorporated, we do this by proposing a mediational pathway, leading us to Propositions 3a and 3b:

Proposition 3a Leader change-oriented behaviours would be related to individual innovation via the engagement in explorative activities of the subordinate.

Proposition 3b The relationship of leader change-oriented behaviours to explorative activities undertaken by a subordinate is mediated by the drivers for exploration that are perceived by the subordinate.

Other factors in the work environment or personality of the individual could also create these drivers. Björn Michaelis, Ralf Stegmaier, and Karlheinz Sonntag (2010) found that perceived climate for initiative moderated the relationship between leadership and innovation implementation. Feist and Gorman (1998) found that successful creative scientists has certain consistent personality traits, such as openness which could have a role to play in making them more successful at innovation. Job characteristics, such as job challenge, (Shalley, Zhou, & Oldham, 2004) might also drive exploration. This leads us to Proposition 3c:

Proposition 3c Personal and organizational factors that push for explorative activities, such as openness to experience, job challenge, and climate for initiative can substitute for leader change-oriented behaviours in creating drivers for exploration.

Leaders can also influence innovation by exhibiting behaviours that foster exploitative activities. First, by directly applying pressure on an individual by active goal setting, close monitoring, and so on, which are referred to as "closing behaviours" by Rosing et al. (2011). Second, leaders could create a climate of accountability and narrow focus, which emphasizes the achievement of goals and closure of projects. These actions by themselves would be beneficial for innovation, if there are other contextual or personal factors that foster explorative activities as well, or could be dysfunctional for innovation in the absence of such factors. Within Yukl's (2012b) meta-categories these could be classified as task-oriented behaviours. The primary objective of which is to accomplish work in an efficient and reliable way. We also suggest that this effect is mediated by drivers for exploitation, along similar lines as we made for exploration. This leads to Propositions 4a and 4b:

Proposition 4a Leader task-oriented behaviours would be related to individual innovation via the engagement in exploitative activities of the subordinate.

Proposition 4b The relationship of leader task-oriented behaviours to exploitative activities undertaken by a subordinate are mediated by the drivers for exploitation that are perceived by the subordinate.

For exploitation as well, personal and contextual factors not related to leadership could act as drivers for exploitation. The nearness of a deadline for instance could cause individuals to focus on finishing off tasks rather than looking for more alternatives (Vancouver, Weinhardt, & Schmidt, 2010). Output expectations and work pressure have also been found to be effective when involvement support and autonomy are already present (Ekvall & Ryhammar, 1999). This leads to Proposition 4c:

Proposition 4c Personal and organizational factors that push for exploitative activities, such as output expectations, work pressure, and imminent deadlines can substitute for leader task-oriented behaviours in creating drivers for exploitation.

Motivational Approach

Till now we have considered employees as simply reacting to the behaviours of leaders and their work environment. However, employees might also take a proactive approach to addressing the challenges of innovation. In fact, Bledow et al. (2009a) suggest that it is beneficial for paradoxes to be resolved at the level that they exist, in our case, the individual or team. Employees could self-regulate themselves in determining whether to undertake explorative or exploitative activities, this builds upon Ford's (1996) theory of individual creative action, where individuals decide based on environmental cues and their abilities as to whether to engage in innovative behaviour or routine behaviour. Personal initiative has been found to be important for innovative behaviour (Frese & Fay, 2001). Apart from the influence leaders have in creating drivers for exploration and exploitation, leaders can also influence innovation by affecting the motivational and psychological states of their followers.

In the context of ethical leadership, individual and group motivations are important mediators of the relationship between leadership and innovative behaviour (Yidong & Xinxin, 2013). The componential theory of creativity also places emphasis on the role leader behaviours play in increasing or reducing the intrinsic motivations of their followers

(Amabile, 1996a). One reason for the important role of motivation is that innovation is difficult and can be demanding and time-consuming; therefore, innovators need to be highly motivated (Mumford et al., 2002). And Ruscio, Whitney, and Amabile (1998, Amabile et al., 2004) suggest that motivation leads to deeper engagement in work and therefore greater creative performance. Another way in which engagement with one's task could lead to more proactive selection between explorative and exploitative activities is via psychological safety. Palanski and Vogelgesang (2011), in an online experiment demonstrated that leader behavioural integrity affected creative thought by the perception of psychological safety, and psychological safety was also proposed to be the mechanism by which leader playfulness impacts intrinsic motivation (Kark, 2011). And psychological safety is an important condition for engagement in work (Kahn, 1990), which is defined as a positive, fulfilling, work-related state of mind characterized by vigour, dedication and absorption (Schaufeli, Salanova, González-Romá, & Bakker, 2002). An engaged worker is energized, resilient and highly involved in his work (Schaufeli, 2013).

Apart from engagement another active work-related state of mind is psychological empowerment, which is characterized by the motivational cognitions of meaning, impact, competence, and self-determination (Spreitzer, 1995). Psychological empowerment has also been linked to creative process engagement, and empowering leadership was found to lead to increases in psychological empowerment (Zhang & Bartol, 2010). Apart from leader behaviours, the effect of structural empowerment on creativity is also mediated by psychological empowerment (Sun, Zhang, Qi, & Chen, 2012).

Apart from engagement and empowerment, self-efficacy has also been posited to be an important part of self-regulation (Bandura, 1997). In particular reference to innovation, creative self-efficacy (Tierney & Farmer, 2002) was found to incrementally predict creative performance beyond job self-efficacy.

In light of the above arguments, we frame Proposition 5a:

Proposition 5a Individuals and teams can self-regulate themselves such that their decision to undertake explorative or exploitative activities is dependent not only on the drivers for the same but also on their motivation for the task, their degree of empowerment, their degree of engagement, and their feelings of efficacy.

Therefore, leaders can influence innovation by delegating the decision of which activity to pursue to the individual, thereby creating an environment of contextual ambidexterity (Gibson & Birkinshaw, 2004). Pieterse et al. (2010) show that transformational leadership is positively related to innovative behaviour only when psychological empowerment is also high. Atwater and Carmeli (2009) found that LMX was related to employee's feeling of energy, which in turn was related to high level of involvement in creative work. Tierney and Farmer (2004) found creative self-efficacy to mediate the effect of leadership on creative performance in R&D employees. This was further confirmed by Gong et al. (2009) in a study of insurance agents.

Relational behaviours are employed by leaders to enhance leader–member relationship, identification and commitment (Yukl, 2012b). These, should therefore have a role in innovative behaviour via their effect on motivation, empowerment, engagement, and efficacy. In particular, LMX has been found to be consistently and positively related with innovation (Rosing et al., 2011). Tierney, Farmer, and Graen (1999) also found that LMX was positively related to indices of intrinsic motivation and creativity ratings and disclosures. Janssen and Van Yperen (2004) explored the role of relationship quality on the broader construct of innovative behaviour and found a positive relationship. This effect of relationship quality was also supported meta-analytically by Hammond et al. (2011). This leads us to Proposition 5b:

Proposition 5b The effect of LMX and leader relational behaviours on innovation would be mediated by intrinsic motivation, psychological empowerment, engagement and feelings of efficacy.

The complete proposed model is shown in Fig. 3.1.

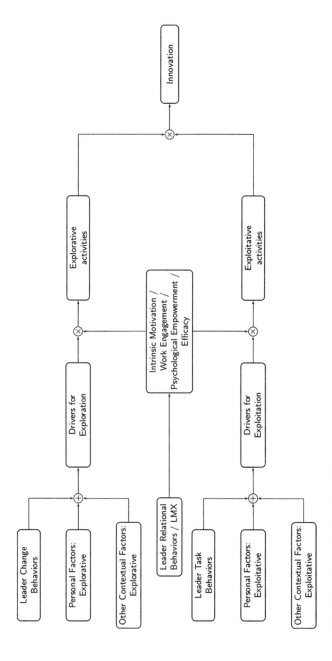

Fig. 3.1 Hypothesized model

Discussion and Conclusion

Over the last three decades or so, the world has witnessed two major developments—the fast pace of globalization, whereby corporations from around the world have expanded operations into various parts of the world. Initially, we witnessed Western MNEs selling their products to the rest of the world, or establishing manufacturing and/or service operations in emerging economies, in order to capitalize on cheap labour and the availability of highly skilled professionals. However, the last 15–20 years have seen many corporations from emerging economies spreading their wings and establishing operations in the so-called developed world (see, e.g. Tung & Varma, 2008). Furthermore, many of these emerging economy MNEs have gone on to buy western corporations to establish a foothold in those countries. The cornerstone of these moves has been innovation and the concomitant leadership skills available within the organization.

Our contribution lies in using a standardized taxonomy for leadership behaviours, suggesting that these behaviours could be substituted by framing drivers for exploitative and explorative activities, and incorporating the role of motivational and developmental pathways. This allows us to cater to the heterogeneous relationship found between leadership and individual innovation and also helps explain how the presence of just one type of leader behaviour could also result in innovative work behaviour due to the presence of personal and environmental factors that compensate for the missing leader behaviours. With all other factors remaining the same, leaders need to balance task-oriented and change-oriented behaviours in order to encourage innovation at the individual and team level.

Further, other contextual and personal factors apart from leadership could substitute for leader behaviours that are lacking. Therefore, unless the entire gamut of behaviours is explored together and relevant personal and contextual factors are included, studies could show diverse and heterogeneous effects of leadership on innovation.

Another means by which leaders could affect innovation at the team and organizational levels, could be by segregating exploitative and explorative activities to different people, teams, or divisions, a form of structural ambidexterity (Tushman & O Reilly, 1996). The role of integrating the outputs would then lie with higher management. At the level of the individual, such a separation would not be possible.

Some inconsistent findings can be explained using the model and the outline given earlier. Transformational leadership, for instance, is known to have all of change-oriented, task-oriented, and relationship-oriented behaviours (Derue, Nahrgang, Wellman, & Humphrey, 2011); therefore, it would influence innovation through all of the approaches discussed above, and thus, the somewhat consistent (though heterogeneous) finding of the relationship between transformational leadership and innovation.

LMX is a relational form of leadership and characterized by trust, respect and liking of subordinate, increasing engagement. Apart from these a good LMX relationship provides employees the ability to modify their job roles to some extent (Rousseau, Ho, & Greenberg, 2006). And engaged employees could also use job crafting (Bakker, Tims, & Derks, 2012). Thus, LMX affects innovation through the motivational approach. Without the complications of the first two approaches which could be dysfunctional in certain cases, LMX has consistently (and homogeneously) been found to relate to innovation (Rosing et al., 2011).

Leader-initiating structure behaviour by itself would foster only exploitative activities and explorative activities would be neglected, in these cases leader preference for initiating structure behaviour would not be expected to lead to innovation as found by Williams (2004). However, in the presence of external factors which foster explorative activities, leader-initiating structure behaviour provides the impetus for exploitative activities, thus the presence of both results in innovative outcomes as found by Osborn and Marion (2009). Leader consideration behaviours might be acting via the suggested motivational approach, thus being relatively immune to other contextual and personal factors.

By taking a more nuanced view of leader behaviours and the activities involved in individual innovation, it is possible to account for the impact that leadership has on innovation. Given that leadership is one of the most important contextual factors (Tierney et al., 1999) on individual creativity, it stands to reason that leading for innovation requires a balance between behaviours that foster exploitative and explorative activities. Though, via the motivational approach, leaders can empower employees to arrive at this balance themselves, at times it might still be necessary for the leader to step in and make any adjustments necessary.

Leading for innovation is a tightrope act that requires skilful management of a wide repertoire of leadership behaviours. In this chapter we have tried to put forward certain propositions about how various leader behaviours could affect innovation and how other contextual and personal factors could compensate for some deficiencies by leaders in achieving a perfect balance.

References

Amabile, T. M. (1988). A model of creativity and innovation in organizations. In B. M. Staw & L. L. Cummings (Eds.), *Research in organizational behavior* (Vol. 10, pp. 123–167). Greenwich, CT: JAI Press.

Amabile, T. M. (1996a). *Creativity in context: Update to the social psychology of creativity*. Boulder, CO: Westview Press.

Amabile, T. M. (1996b). *Creativity and innovation in organizations*. Cambridge, MA: Harvard University Press.

Amabile, T. M., Barsade, S. G., Mueller, J. S., & Staw, B. M. (2005). Affect and creativity at work. *Administrative Science Quarterly, 50*(3), 367–403.

Amabile, T. M., Conti, R., Coon, H., Lazenby, J., & Herron, M. (1996). Assessing the work environment for creativity. *Academy of Management Journal, 39*(5), 1154–1184.

Amabile, T. M., Schatzel, E. A., Moneta, G. B., & Kramer, S. J. (2004). Leader behaviors and the work environment for creativity: Perceived leader support. *The Leadership Quarterly, 15*(1), 5–32.

Anderson, N., de Drew, C. K. W., & Nijstad, B. A. (2004). The routinization of innovation research: A constructively critical review of the state-of-the-science. *Journal of Organizational Behavior, 25*(2), 147–173.

Anderson, N., Potočnik, K., & Zhou, J. (2014). Innovation and creativity in organizations a state-of-the-science review, prospective commentary, and guiding framework. *Journal of Management, 40*(5), 1297–1333.

Andriopoulos, C., & Lewis, M. W. (2009). Exploitation-exploration tensions and organizational ambidexterity: Managing paradoxes of innovation. *Organization Science*, 20(4): 696–717, 829–830.

Andriopoulos, C., & Lewis, M. W. (2010). Managing innovation paradoxes: Ambidexterity lessons from leading product design companies. *Long Range Planning, 43*(1), 104–122.

Arnold, J. A., Arad, S., Rhoades, J. A., & Drasgow, F. (2000). The empowering leadership questionnaire: The construction and validation of a new scale for measuring leader behaviors. *Journal of Organizational Behavior, 21*(3), 249–269.

Atwater, L., & Carmeli, A. (2009). Leadermember exchange, feelings of energy, and involvement in creative work. *The Leadership Quarterly, 20*(3), 264–275.

Axtell, C. M., Holman, D. J., Unsworth, K. L., Wall, T. D., Waterson, P. E., et al. (2000). Shopfloor innovation: Facilitating the suggestion and implementation of ideas. *Journal of Occupational and Organizational Psychology, 73*(3), 265–285.

Bakker, A. B., Tims, M., & Derks, D. (2012). Proactive personality and job performance: The role of job crafting and work engagement. *Human Relations, 65*(10), 1359–1378.

Bandura, A. (1997). *Self-efficacy: The exercise of control.* New York: Freeman Press.

Birkinshaw, J., & Gibson, C. (2004). Building ambidexterity into an organization. *MIT Sloan Management Review, 45*(4), 47–55.

Bledow, R., Frese, M., Anderson, N., Erez, M., & Farr, J. (2009a). A dialectic perspective on innovation: Conflicting demands, multiple pathways, and ambidexterity. *Industrial and Organizational Psychology, 2*(3), 305–337.

Bledow, R., Frese, M., Anderson, N., Erez, M., & Farr, J. (2009b). Extending and refining the dialectic perspective on innovation: There is nothing as practical as a good theory; nothing as theoretical as a good practice. *Industrial and Organizational Psychology, 2*(3), 363–373.

Buijs, J. (2007). Innovation leaders should be controlled schizophrenics. *Creativity and Innovation Management, 16*(2), 203–210.

Byrne, C. L., Mumford, M. D., Barrett, J. D., & Vessey, W. B. (2009). Examining the leaders of creative efforts: What do they do, and what do they think about? *Creativity and Innovation Management, 18*(4), 256–268.

Caniëls, M. C., De Stobbeleir, K., & De Clippeleer, I. (2014). The antecedents of creativity revisited: A process perspective. *Creativity and Innovation Management, 23*(2), 96–110.

Carmeli, A., & Halevi, M. Y. (2009). How top management team behavioral integration and behavioral complexity enable organizational ambidexterity:

The moderating role of contextual ambidexterity. *The Leadership Quarterly, 20*(2), 207–218.

Černe, M., Jaklič, M., & Škerlavaj, M. (2013). Authentic leadership, creativity, and innovation: A multilevel perspective. *Leadership, 9*(1), 63–85.

Cheung, K. Y. (2010). Spillover effects of FDI via exports on innovation performance of China's high-technology industries. *Journal of Contemporary China, 19*(65), 541–557.

de Jong, J. P., & Hartog, D. N. D. (2007). How leaders influence employees' innovative behaviour. *European Journal of Innovation Management, 10*(1), 41–64.

Denison, D. R., Hooijberg, R., & Quinn, R. E. (1995). Paradox and performance: Toward a theory of behavioral complexity in managerial leadership. *Organization Science, 6*(5), 524–540.

Derue, D. S., Nahrgang, J. D., Wellman, N., & Humphrey, S. E. (2011). Trait and behavioral theories of leadership: An integration and meta-analytic test of their relative validity. *Personnel Psychology, 64*(1), 7–52.

Dess, G. G., & Picken, J. C. (2000). Changing roles: Leadership in the 21st century. *Organizational Dynamics, 28*(3), 18–34.

Eisenbeiß, S. A., & Boerner, S. (2010). Transformational leadership and R&D innovation: Taking a curvilinear approach. *Creativity and Innovation Management, 19*(4), 364–372.

Eisenbeiss, S. A., van Knippenberg, D., & Boerner, S. (2008). Transformational leadership and team innovation: Integrating team climate principles. *Journal of Applied Psychology, 93*(6), 1438–1446.

Ekvall, G., & Ryhammar, L. (1999). The creative climate: Its determinants and effects at a Swedish University. *Creativity Research Journal, 12*(4), 303–310.

Feist, G. J., & Gorman, M. E. (1998). The psychology of science: Review and integration of a nascent discipline. *Review of General Psychology, 2*(1), 3–47.

Florida, R. (2002). *The rise of the creative class: And how it's transforming work, leisure, community and everyday life*. New York: Basic Books.

Ford, C. M. (1996). A theory of individual creative action in multiple social domains. *Academy of Management Review, 21*(4), 1112–1142.

Frese, M., & Fay, D. (2001). Personal initiative: An active performance concept for work in the 21st century. *Research in Organizational Behavior, 23*, 133–187.

Gentry, W., & Sparks, T. (2012). A convergence/divergence perspective of leadership competencies managers believe are most important for success in organizations: A cross-cultural multilevel analysis of 40 countries. *Journal of Business & Psychology, 27*(1), 15–30.

Gibson, C. B., & Birkinshaw, J. (2004). The antecedents, consequences, and mediating role of organizational ambidexterity. *Academy of Management Journal, 47*(2), 209–226.

Gilmore, P. L., Hu, X., Wei, F., Tetrick, L. E., & Zaccaro, S. J. (2013). Positive affectivity neutralizes transformational leadership's influence on creative performance and organizational citizenship behaviors. *Journal of Organizational Behavior, 34*(8), 1061–1075.

Gong, Y., Huang, J.-C., & Farh, J.-l. (2009). Employee learning orientation, transformational leadership, and employee creativity: The mediating role of employee creative self-efficacy. *Academy of Management Journal, 52*(4), 765–778.

Gupta, A. K., Smith, K. G., & Shalley, C. E. (2006). The interplay between exploration and exploitation. *Academy of Management Journal, 49*(4), 693–706.

Hammond, M. M., Neff, N. L., Farr, J. L., Schwall, A. R., & Zhao, X. (2011). Predictors of individual-level innovation at work: A meta-analysis. *Psychology of Aesthetics, Creativity, and the Arts, 5*(1), 90–105.

Herrmann, D., & Felfe, J. (2013). Moderators of the relationship between leadership style and employee creativity: The role of task novelty and personal initiative. *Creativity Research Journal, 25*(2), 172–181.

James, K. (1995). Goal conflict and originality of thinking. *Creativity Research Journal, 8*(3), 285–290.

Janssen, O. (2000). Job demands, perceptions of effort-reward fairness and innovative work behaviour. *Journal of Occupational and Organizational Psychology, 73*(3), 287–302.

Janssen, O., & Van Yperen, N. W. (2004). Employees' goal orientations, the quality of leader-member exchange, and the outcomes of job performance and job satisfaction. *Academy of Management Journal, 47*(3), 368–384.

Jaussi, K. S., & Dionne, S. D. (2003). Leading for creativity: The role of unconventional leader behavior. *The Leadership Quarterly, 14*(45), 475–498.

Jha, S. K., & Krishnan, R. T. (2013). Local innovation: The key to globalisation. *IIMB Management Review, 25*(4), 249–256.

Josephine, N. D. (2014). Implication of globalization on organization culture, Kenyan experience. *International Journal of Academic Research in Business and Social Sciences, 4*(4), 285–290.

Judge, T. A., Piccolo, R. F., & Ilies, R. (2004). The forgotten ones? The validity of consideration and initiating structure in leadership research. *Journal of Applied Psychology, 89*(1), 36–51.

Kahai, S. S., Sosik, J. J., & Avolio, B. J. (2003). Effects of leadership style, anonymity, and rewards on creativity-relevant processes and outcomes in an electronic meeting system context. *The Leadership Quarterly, 14*(45), 499–524.

Kahn, W. A. (1990). Psychological conditions of personal engagement and disengagement at work. *Academy of Management Journal, 33*(4), 692–724.

Kark, R. (2011). Games managers play: Play as a form of leadership development. *Academy of Management Learning & Education, 10*(3), 507–527.

Katila, R., & Ahuja, G. (2002). Something old, something new: A longitudinal study of search behavior and new product introduction. *Academy of Management Journal, 45*(6), 1183–1194.

Keller, R. T. (1989). A test of the path-goal theory of leadership with need for clarity as a moderator in research and development organizations. *Journal of Applied Psychology, 74*(2), 208–212.

Kerr, S., & Jermier, J. M. (1978). Substitutes for leadership: Their meaning and measurement. *Organizational Behavior & Human Performance, 22*(3), 375–403.

Kesting, P., Ulhøi, J. P., Song, L. J., & Niu, H. (2016). The impact of leadership styles on innovation—A review. *Journal of Innovation Management, 3*(4), 22–41.

King, N. (1992). Modelling the innovation process: An empirical comparison of approaches. *Journal of Occupational and Organizational Psychology, 65*(2), 89.

Mainemelis, C., Kark, R., & Epitropaki, O. (2015). Creative leadership: A multi-context conceptualization. *Academy of Management Annals, 9*(1), 393–482.

March, J. G. (1991). Exploration and exploitation in organizational learning. *Organization Science, 2*(1), 71–87.

Michaelis, B., Stegmaier, R., & Sonntag, K. (2010). Shedding light on followers' innovation implementation behavior: The role of transformational leadership, commitment to change, and climate for initiative. *Journal of Managerial Psychology, 25*(4), 408–429.

Mintzberg, H. (2007). *Mintzberg on management.* New York: Simon & Schuster.

Mom, T. J. M., Van Den Bosch, F. A. J., & Volberda, H. W. (2007). Investigating managers' exploration and exploitation activities: The influence of top-down, bottom-up, and horizontal knowledge inflows. *Journal of Management Studies, 44*(6), 910–931.

Mumford, M. D. (2000). Managing creative people: Strategies and tactics for innovation. *Human Resource Management Review, 10*(3), 313–351.

Mumford, M. D., & Licuanan, B. (2004). Leading for innovation: Conclusions, issues, and directions. *The Leadership Quarterly, 15*(1), 163–171.

Mumford, M. D., Gibson, C., Giorgini, V., & Mecca, J. (2014). Leading for creativity: People, products, and systems. In D. V. Day (Ed.), *The Oxford handbook of leadership and organizations* (pp. 754–779). New York, NY: Oxford University Press.

Mumford, M. D., Scott, G. M., Gaddis, B., & Strange, J. M. (2002). Leading creative people: Orchestrating expertise and relationships. *The Leadership Quarterly, 13*(6), 705–750.

Nübold, A., Muck, P. M., & Maier, G. W. (2013). A new substitute for leadership? Followers' state core self-evaluations. *The Leadership Quarterly, 24*(1), 29–44.

Ohly, S., Sonnentag, S., & Pluntke, F. (2006). Routinization, work characteristics and their relationships with creative and proactive behaviors. *Journal of Organizational Behavior, 27*(3), 257–279.

Oldham, G. R., & Cummings, A. (1996). Employee creativity: Personal and contextual factors at work. *Academy of Management Journal, 39*(3), 607–634.

Osborn, R. N., & Marion, R. (2009). Contextual leadership, transformational leadership and the performance of international innovation seeking alliances. *The Leadership Quarterly, 20*(2), 191–206.

Palanski, M. E., & Vogelgesang, G. R. (2011). Virtuous creativity: The effects of leader behavioural integrity on follower creative thinking and risk taking. *Canadian Journal of Administrative Sciences/Revue Canadienne Des Sciences de L'Administration, 28*(3), 259–269.

Pieterse, A. N., van Knippenberg, D., Schippers, M., & Stam, D. (2010). Transformational and transactional leadership and innovative behavior: The moderating role of psychological empowerment. *Journal of Organizational Behavior, 31*(4), 609–623.

Quinn, J. B. (1985). Managing innovation: Controlled chaos. *Harvard Business Review, 63*(3), 73–84.

Rosing, K. (2011). *Dynamics of the innovation process: The linear-recursive model of innovation and the implications for leadership and self-regulation.* PhD, Leuphana University, Luneburg.

Rosing, K., Frese, M., & Bausch, A. (2011). Explaining the heterogeneity of the leadership-innovation relationship: Ambidextrous leadership. *The Leadership Quarterly, 22*(5), 956–974.

Rousseau, D. M., Ho, V. T., & Greenberg, J. (2006). I-deals: Idiosyncratic terms in employment relationships. *Academy of Management Review, 31*(4), 977–994.

Ruscio, J., Whitney, D. M., & Amabile, T. M. (1998). Looking inside the fishbowl of creativity: Verbal and behavioral predictors of creative performance. *Creativity Research Journal, 11*(3), 243–263.

Sarooghi, H., Libaers, D., & Burkemper, A. (2015). Examining the relationship between creativity and innovation: A meta-analysis of organizational, cultural, and environmental factors. *Journal of Business Venturing, 30*(5), 714–731.

Sarros, J. C., Cooper, B. K., & Santora, J. C. (2008). Building a climate for innovation through transformational leadership and organizational culture. *Journal of Leadership & Organizational Studies, 15*(2), 145–158.

Schaufeli, W. B. (2013). What is engagement? In C. Truss, K. Alfes, R. Delbridge, A. Shantz, & E. Soane (Eds.), *Employee engagement in theory and practice* (pp. 15–35). New York, NY: Routledge.

Schaufeli, W. B., Salanova, M., González-Romá, V., & Bakker, A. B. (2002). The measurement of engagement and burnout: A two sample confirmatory factor analytic approach. *Journal of Happiness Studies, 3*(1), 71–92.

Scott, S. G., & Bruce, R. A. (1994). Determinants of innovative behavior: A path model of individual innovation in the workplace. *Academy of Management Journal, 37*(3), 580–607.

Shalley, C. E., Zhou, J., & Oldham, G. R. (2004). The effects of personal and contextual characteristics on creativity: Where should we go from here? *Journal of Management, 30*(6), 933–958.

Shin, S. J., & Zhou, J. (2003). Transformational leadership, conservation, and creativity: Evidence from Korea. *Academy of Management Journal, 46*(6), 703–714.

Simonton, D. K. (1999). *Origins of genius: Darwinian perspectives on creativity* (1st ed.). New York: Oxford University Press.

Spreitzer, G. M. (1995). Psychological empowerment in the workplace: Dimensions, measurement, and validation. *Academy of Management Journal, 38*(5), 1442–1465.

Sun, L.-Y., Zhang, Z., Qi, J., & Chen, Z. X. (2012). Empowerment and creativity: A cross-level investigation. *The Leadership Quarterly, 23*(1), 55–65.

Tierney, P. (2008). Leadership and creativity. In J. Zhou & C. E. Shalley (Eds.), *Handbook of organizational creativity* (1st ed., pp. 95–124). New York: Psychology Press.

Tierney, P., & Farmer, S. M. (2002). Creative self-efficacy: Its potential antecedents and relationship to creative performance. *Academy of Management Journal, 45*(6), 1137–1148.

Tierney, P., & Farmer, S. M. (2004). The pygmalion process and employee creativity. *Journal of Management, 30*(3), 413–432.

Tierney, P., Farmer, S. M., & Graen, G. B. (1999). An examination of leadership and employee creativity: The relevance of traits and relationships. *Personnel Psychology, 52*(3), 591–620.

Tung, R. L., & Varma, A. (2008). Expatriate selection and evaluation. In P. B. Smith, M. F. Peterson, & D. C. Thomas (Eds.), *Handbook of cross-cultural management research* (pp. 367–378). London: Sage.

Tushman, M. L., & O'Reilly, C. A. I. (1996). Ambidextrous organizations: Managing evolutionary and revolutionary change. *California Management Review, 38*(4), 8–30.

Tushman, M., & O'Reilly, C. A. (2002). *Winning through innovation: a practical guide to leading organizational change and renewal.* Boston, MA: Harvard Business Press.

Vancouver, J. B., Weinhardt, J. M., & Schmidt, A. M. (2010). A formal, computational theory of multiple-goal pursuit: Integrating goal-choice and goal-striving processes. *Journal of Applied Psychology, 95*(6), 985–1008.

Vila, L. E., Perez, P. J., & Coll-Serrano, V. (2014). Innovation at the workplace: Do professional competencies matter? *Journal of Business Research, 67*, 752–757.

Wallas, G. (1926). *The art of thought.* New York, NY: Harcourt Brace.

Williams, S. D. (2004). Personality, attitude, and leader influences on divergent thinking and creativity in organizations. *European Journal of Innovation Management, 7*(3), 187–204.

Woodman, R. W., Sawyer, J. E., & Griffin, R. W. (1993). Toward a theory of organizational creativity. *Academy of Management Review, 18*(2), 293–321.

Woodman, R. W., & Schoenfeldt, L. F. (1990). An interactionist model of creative behavior. *The Journal of Creative Behavior, 24*(4), 279–290.

Yidong, T., & Xinxin, L. (2013). How ethical leadership influence employees' innovative work behavior: A perspective of intrinsic motivation. *Journal of Business Ethics, 116*(2), 441–455.

Yuan, F., & Zhou, J. (2008). Differential effects of expected external evaluation on different parts of the creative idea production process and on final product creativity. *Creativity Research Journal, 20*(4), 391–403.

Yukl, G. A. (1999). An evaluative essay on current conceptions of effective leadership. *European Journal of Work and Organizational Psychology, 8*(1), 33–48.

Yukl, G. A. (2009). Leading organizational learning: Reflections on theory and research. *The Leadership Quarterly, 20*(1), 49–53.

Yukl, G. A. (2012a). *Leadership in organizations* (8th ed.). Boston: Prentice Hall.

Yukl, G. A. (2012b). Effective leadership behavior: What we know and what questions need more attention. *Academy of Management Perspectives, 26*(4), 66–85.

Zhang, X., & Bartol, K. M. (2010). Linking empowering leadership and employee creativity: The influence of psychological empowerment, intrinsic motivation, and creative process engagement. *Academy of Management Journal, 53*(1), 107–128.

Zhang, Y., & Roelfsema, H. (2014). Globalization, foreign direct investment, and regional innovation in China. *Journal of International Commerce, Economics and Policy, 05*(03), 1440007.

Zhou, J. (2003). When the presence of creative coworkers is related to creativity: Role of supervisor close monitoring, developmental feedback, and creative personality. *Journal of Applied Psychology, 88*(3), 413–422.

Zhou, J. (2008). Promoting creativity through feedback. In J. Zhou & C. E. Shalley (Eds.), *Handbook of organizational creativity* (1st ed.). New York, NY: Lawrence Erlbaum Associates.

Zhou, J., & Hoever, I. J. (2014). Research on workplace creativity: A review and redirection. *Annual Review of Organizational Psychology and Organizational Behavior, 1*(1), 333–359.

4

The Microfoundations of Global Innovation: Disrupting the Balance Between Centripetal and Centrifugal Forces

Juan I. Sanchez and Yasmina Lazrak

Whereas the dominant conceptualization of human capital refers to the knowledge and abilities that facilitate actions leading to economic growth (Coleman, 1988; Dakhli & De Clercq, 2004), a more fine-grained understanding of how these individual attributes emerge across individuals to produce global innovation is warranted. In this chapter, we aim to isolate the microlevel attributes and capabilities that underlie the individual actions that stimulate global innovation. In addition, we advance a series of arguments explaining how these attributes basically respond to the ability to balance two sets of challenges: (1) assimilation pressures emanating from headquarters, and (2) differentiation pressures emanating from local factors.

J.I. Sanchez (✉)
Department of Management and International Business, Florida International University, Miami, FL, USA

Y. Lazrak
Skiversity, Inc., Miami, FL, USA

© The Author(s) 2017
S. Kundu, S. Munjal (eds.), *Human Capital and Innovation*,
DOI 10.1057/978-1-137-56561-7_4

Microfoundations of Global Human Capital

What are the individual attributes underlying the actions that spur global innovation? It is reasonable to assume that, although some of those attributes may respond to innate predispositions, they are also likely to be at least partly forged in the process of adapting to different cultures. The literature on international assignments has been understandably passionate about the need to develop a global mindset to succeed in international markets (see Levy, Beechler, Taylor, & Boyacigiller, 2007 for a review). A theme that runs through this literature is that international executives need to undergo a constant metamorphosis by adopting the local ways in a variety of cultural contexts (e.g., Kefalas, 1998). The purpose of the reflection to be presented herein is not to minimize the contributions of prior research and thought on international assignments, but to alert about a common misconception inspired by a less than careful reading of this literature, namely that innovative breakthroughs in an international assignment require that one becomes an accommodating "cosmopolitan chameleon" willing to give up whatever is necessary to succeed locally.

As in physics, international assignments can be said to be ruled by both "centrifugal" and "centripetal" forces. Whereas centrifugal forces, such as local and institutional pressures, pull international assignees toward localization, centripetal forces pull the international assignee towards headquarters' strategic goals. We argue here that the secret to global innovation lies not on finding a proverbial equilibrium between local (i.e., centrifugal) and global (i.e., centripetal) forces. That is, managing the global–local dilemma does not necessarily involve giving up a bit of the global imperative for the sake of local concerns. On the contrary, in many cases, truly innovative management of international operations requires true "glocalization." That is, international managers should refuse to mimic the old advice to "act locally" and, instead, stick to certain aspects that one deems strategically critical for achieving innovative breakthroughs and, therefore, are not subject to compromise.

The manager's ability to ascertain the strategic value of certain aspects of the business is at least as important as the ability to understand the nuances embedded in a different culture. In fact, cultural intelligence, which has been defined as "the capability to function effectively in situations characterized by cultural diversity" (Ang et al., 2007) does not necessarily imply that individuals merely emulate local usages. On the contrary, effective international executives would sometimes purposefully decide against changing certain aspects of the business simply because they do not conform with local norms at face value. In doing so, these executives do not ignore warnings that such aspects oppose local norms; instead, their solid understanding of the host culture, together with a deep understanding of the firm's strategic imperative, lead them to promote the strategic value added by such distinct innovations, in spite (and often because) of their deviation from local norms.

As an example of the primary argument advanced here, consider the case of fast food American outlets in North African nations like Morocco. In these countries, these hamburger restaurants are often located in prime real estate enjoying the best views of the city and include spacious and luxurious outdoor patios covered with delicate canvas where patrons slowly enjoy their meals and spend time together after finishing them. Management of these chains certainly knows that their positioning in these markets differs markedly from its positioning in the USA. These locales are frequented by entire families seeking to share not only a meal, but also time together, rather than by hurried consumers with a relatively short time to grab something to eat at a convenient place, as it is characteristic in the USA and other developed markets. Nevertheless, these outlets feature hamburgers that have undergone relatively minor modifications in relation to these same products in the USA. The hamburger bun might be slightly larger and shinier and also slightly adapted to local taste, but the essential ingredients and their appearance makes it undeniable that these are hamburgers that conform to how a hamburger looks and tastes like in the USA. Clearly, these operations have been localized, but they still conserve the essence of the brand that they represent or, better, the brand that they represent in the locals' mind.

The central premise of this manuscript is that advising international managers to "think globally, act locally" (Grauer, 1989) is at least partly misguided, because it suggests that one should give up to local usages as much as needed and as long as the "global" firm benefits from it. This notion of the whole as something that is not affected by the parts ignores current thinking on strategic management, which advocates the creation of a strongly shared corporate climate that signals the importance of certain strategic or core competencies across the board (Bowen & Ostroff, 2004; Sanchez & Levine, 2009). Thus, international managers sometimes need to both think and act globally, which of course does not exclude the fact that, at times, they need to think and act locally too.

The arguments to be introduced herein expand those concerning the need to manage the dualities of the expatriate's role that were already formulated more than 15 years ago (Sanchez, Spector & Cooper, 2000). Our contention that innovatively managing an international venture requires learning to live with the contradictions that come with the role of expatriate, however, differs from the traditional advice to "balance" global and local concerns. We argue here that truly innovative "glocalization" often implies taking advantage of the asymmetries—or even disrupting the balance—between global and local forces. Unlike the bipolar model that has dominated this field to date, this bidimensional model maintains that managing the dualities of an international role does not imply finding a proverbial point of equilibrium between centripetal (global) and centrifugal (local) forces (Fig. 4.1). On the contrary, true innovations arise from exacerbating rather than reducing the tension between local and global forces, such as for instance ignoring pressures to localize certain aspects of the business which one deems strategically critical and therefore not subject to compromise. Consider for instance the case of a fast-moving consumer goods multinational corporation that, when

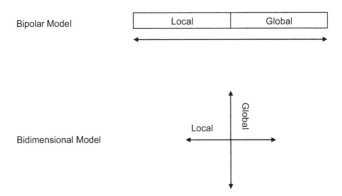

Fig. 4.1 Bipolar versus bidimensional models of international assignments

launching its orange-favored soda in a North African market, chose to keep the sugar level lower than market research preferences. This decision to lower sugar level in their flavored drinks was predicated on the multinational brand's claim for healthy products, which was thought to trump local preferences, at least in the long term.

In summary, the widely heard advice to "glocalize" is not achieved by simply giving up a bit to local demands, so that one can find a "happy medium." Quite the opposite, finding the mid-point between the two vectors representing local and global forces can kill innovation, because the global aspects that were sacrificed for the sake of balance may be the ones that conferred the business its uniqueness and competitiveness. As pointed out by Rhinesmith (2005), the global paradox, like any other paradox, cannot be solved, but needs to be managed.

Of course, it is also true that stubborn, parochial resistance to localize marginal aspects of the business may accelerate failure, but being too quick to localize may give up the essence of one's innovative advantage. After all, there is nothing less innovative, less sustainable, and easier to imitate than the mere replication of the same old and traded local formula. The aspects of the firm's business model that drive its novelty, innovation, and competitiveness often stem from the uniqueness associated with its global brand, its economies of scale, or other characteristics associated with its global operations, rather than from localization. Excessive localization may dilute such competitive advantage, thereby turning the business into a watered-down, unoriginal replica of better-known, and better-established local enterprises.

The importance of sticking to certain global standards is evidenced by the success of global brands in emerging markets which, in the words of Nigerian consumers, are often "brand-crazy." As an executive of a US-based firm put it, "in China, if you can brand it, you can sell it." Therefore, any attempt at localizing a product or service that somehow degrades its brand name is likely to fail. In fact, prior research on the so-called "liability of foreignness" highlights the difficulties of doing business in an unknown environment, but it also points out that simply copying local practices is an ill-advised way to overcome such a liability (Zaheer, 1995). Sticking to the strategic aspects of one's business model, especially when such model significantly deviates from local usages, undoubtedly represents taking the hard road, but it may prove to be the only way to develop an innovative competitive advantage over time.

The advice to "localize breakfast, globalize lunch," provides a valid metaphor for what we believe marks a largely overlooked requirement for succeeding abroad. This metaphor is inspired by our interactions with top management of a multinational corporation in the fast food industry whose primary product is American-style hamburgers. This corporation has wisely chosen to internationalize by localizing their breakfast menu with popular breakfast items in each culture (e.g., "Johnny cakes" in Jamaica, "Tajine" in Morocco, "Mallorcas" in Puerto Rico, and "Gallo Pinto" in Costa Rica, to cite a few examples) as a means of attracting customers to consume their core product (i.e., American-style hamburgers) for lunch and dinner. The international managers of this fast food corporation clearly understood the need to stand by their primary, value-added menu item, namely the American-style hamburger which, if replaced by a local delicacy, would have diluted their innovative advantage by turning them into just another local chain.

Arguing in favor of preserving the truly strategic aspects of the firm's business model does not imply that headquarters' espoused values are superior to those of host countries. There is no need to revive the debate about cultural relativism, which has questioned the merits of one set of cultural values over the others. Instead, we do advocate a primarily strategic approach to international assignments and, as such, we endorse the view of international executives as the primary decision makers charged with innovative deployment of the global strategy. As part of their strategy-deployment role, international managers should be aware of not only local issues to which they need to adjust, but equally (if not more) important strategically key issues that, in spite of their apparent opposition to local usages, should be kept intact or at least minimally changed. Indeed, these strategically key issues constitute the true innovations that the organization brings to other markets.

The next sections provide further insight into the competencies that international managers require in order to capitalize on the innovative potential that lies behind the apparent conflict between the local and global demands impinging on their role. In the next few pages, we have divided our discussion of these managerial competencies in three major types: cognitive, emotional, and "glocalized entrepreneurship." We have deliberately chosen the first two terms because they provide a parallel to the constructs of *cognitive complexity* and *cosmopolitanism* that are thought to underlie the notion of "global mindset" (Levy et al., 2007; Rhinesmith, 1992). Our position is that discussions of these two constructs have often tilted the balance in favor of "centrifugal" forces, thereby emphasizing the need to adopt local ways to the detriment of the "centripetal" forces calling for the retention or at least minimal modification of strategically critical innovation drivers. The third term, which we have termed glocalized entrepreneurship, introduces the idea that a successful international manager is by definition a risk taker, but one that takes calculated risks based on a solid understanding of the how the organization's strategic core competencies can be combined with knowledge of local voids to form asymmetries that confer the business a competitive advantage.

Cognitive Competencies

Discussions of the cognitive requirements of international assignments tend to emphasize the need to absorb and process a great deal of information from a variety of sources, and to revise one's conception of the world accordingly. An underlying theme in this literature is that international managers are reluctant to change their ways, and that as a result they are often inattentive to and even dismissive of local aspects that are critical to their business. Clearly, the assumption that runs through these discussions is that, if left to their own devices, international managers tend to be ethnocentric and to miss opportunities in their new environment. This line of thinking accords to the post-World War II international expansion of MNCs. In such preglobalized times, the main concern was that many home-country nationals were unprepared to conduct business in culturally different settings, that they would ethnocentrically replicate what they did at home and that, as a result, they would fail.

This view of expatriates subscribes to the same premises that characterize research on diversity management, which advocates a series of means (e.g., diversity training) designed to increase executives' awareness of the nuances inherent in today's culturally diverse workforce, even within the same country (Sanchez & Brock, 1996; Sanchez & Medkik, 2004). Notwithstanding the importance of cross-cultural understanding and cultural intelligence in today's heterogeneous workplace (Ang et al., 2007), the primary roots of expatriates' failure may lie elsewhere. First, globalization has significantly reduced cultural distances and increased awareness of how people live and do business in other countries. Even if an international executive is feeling lost or displaced (or perhaps because of it), she/he may be too quick to adopt local usages, which can be as strategically deadly as ignoring them. Therefore, we would argue for a moratorium on calls for further study of cognitive complexity as a requirement for international assignments, because even though it is true that the world is increasingly complex and interconnected, international management failures often arise not from failing to understand a complex global environment, but from failing to discern the core, fundamentally innovative aspects of one's own business model whose localization may threaten its very foundation.

Current thinking on the cognitive requirements of international managers often ignores that a solid understanding of how things work elsewhere, no matter how complex such network of relationships is, should not necessarily lead to significant localization of one's business practices. In fact, we would argue that it is possibly more important to ensure that international managers possess a strategic understanding of their business, which coupled with their understanding of the global environment will ensure that they do not localize those core aspects of their business model that account for its innovative advantage. In other words, there is a difference between understanding the local terrain and acting locally. Armed with an understanding of local norms, international executives are best positioned to realize that working differently, as their global, strategic imperative dictates, may confer them unique potential for innovation.

It is possible that discussions of cognitive complexity in the context of international management place too much emphasis on differentiation to the detriment of integration (Gupta & Govindarajan, 2002). Admittedly, understanding and changing one's cognitive schemata to suit a variety of different contexts is important, but such differentiation does not ensure international success. On the contrary, it is the integration of such varied elements and, perhaps more importantly, their subordination to the global imperative represented by the firm strategy that is truly innovativel (Kedia & Mukherji, 1999). In other words, we contend that managers need to have the ability to simplify complex environments while understanding which aspects of their business are strategically important and cannot be sacrificed to local concerns. In simpler terms, managers should not get lost in surface differences among cultures, but should instead have the ability to "separate the figure from the background" by understanding the extent and scope of contextualization that the local environment requires and, more importantly, the threshold of such localization efforts beyond which the innovative advantage of one's model would be diluted or entirely lost.

As an example, consider the go-to-market strategy of still another orange-flavored soda in the same North African market mentioned earlier. The multinational corporation's attempt to make this product as popular as possible drove its choice to make the product available in even the most remote rural locations. This decision, together with a low-pricing strategy that deviated from the global platform, created the impression of a b-level brand that was rejected by consumers from premium market segments.

The pressure to give up to local forces might be augmented by heeding the advice of those who seek to skew the so-called "liability of foreignness." This liability seemingly emanates from the incremental costs involved in acquiring legitimacy, local knowledge, and government contacts (Kostova & Zaheer, 1999; Zaheer, 1995). However, prior research has also demonstrated that such a liability is far from monolithic, because foreignness does at times confer an advantage in areas such as talent recruitment (Newburry, Gardberg, & Sanchez, 2014). In any case, foreignness should not be confused with the global imperative of a multinational corporation. Indeed, the core competencies of the organization are capable of crossing boundaries and do not constitute a liability. On the contrary, they represent a unique set of forces that can fill a void in the local market and, as such, they should be intelligently adapted to the local context rather than abandoned.

Emotional Competencies

The concept of cosmopolitanism seems to dominate discussions of the cultural requirements of a global mindset (Levy et al., 2007). The focus of this debate seems to be the need to be sensitive to a number of different cultural norms. Granted, respect for local norms and values are a necessary condition for international management, but such respect does not exclude the recognition that, in many cases, the firm's innovative advantage stems from being different. For instance, the success of global brands emanates from awakening the consumption habits of local consumers in emerging economies, as such consumers choose to model their consumption habits after those of their at least partly aspirational societies. In a way, the innovative potential of global brands is to some extent determined by their ability to replicate a true and tested model that has already been endorsed by consumers in their host country. If localization efforts of such a product or service dilute the brand to the point where it does no longer represent the aspirational society, success may be compromised.

The commonly held belief that international assignees fail primarily due to their inability to cope with local usages or "localize" is not backed by empirical evidence. Indeed, even though a great deal of research (Bhaskar-Shrinivas, Harrison, Shaffer, & Luk, 2005; Bolino, 2007; Mezias & Scandura, 2005; Takeuchi, Lepak, Marinova, & Yun, 2007) has suggested that maladjustment is a core contributor to expatriate failure, such research has not demonstrated that failure can be necessarily traced to the fact that international assignees erred on the side of failing to adopt local usages. Instead, we argue that failure often stems not from the inability to act locally, but from failing to implement or, possibly more frequently, from failing to understand how certain global standards provide a competitive advantage in spite of their apparent opposition to local usages. Consider for instance the case of an Italian manager working for a Swiss multinational specialized in manufacturing commercial elevators and lifts in India. Concerned about the fact that local employees did not understand the Swiss identity of their employer, the manager organized a visit to the local Swiss embassy, where employees were encouraged to take note of how the place looked like, including its sober furnishings and neatly arranged spaces. The manager felt that familiarity with its Swiss identity would help employees understand the values of reliability and practicality that their company represented, and to communicate such values to customers.

A different stream of research has explored the role of prior cross-cultural experiences as an antecedent of adjustment to international assignments (Takeuchi, Shay, & Li, 2008; Takeuchi, Tesluk, Yun, & Lepak, 2005). Less thought, however, has been dedicated to why such experiences facilitate the adjustment process. In my opinion, an unwarranted conclusion often drawn from such evidence is that cross-cultural experience allows individuals to resolve the tension between global and local forces by simply accepting and adopting local usages. We would argue that prior cross-cultural experience becomes a precursor of adjustment through a different mechanism. Undoubtedly, cross-cultural experience allows the individual to experience the tension between local and global forces. Those who truly learn from this experience, however, are not the ones who quickly adopted the local ways, but those who learned to respect local norms without rejecting their underlying core values. That is, adoption of local ways constitutes thoughtless imitation, and it cannot be equated to intelligent adaptation.

The literature on acculturation and cultural identity has revealed that maladjustment does not necessarily come from rejecting the host culture, but from trying to assert the home culture as the "true" and opposite way of the host culture (Sanchez & Fernandez, 1993). Thus, when the manager perceives the host and home identities as mutually exclusive s/he fails to realize that an individual can indeed develop multiple identities and simultaneously fit into various groups and sets of norms.

In short, managers who learn to reconcile the tension between home and host cultures do so by recognizing that global and local forces are two sets of distinct forces that can coexist, rather than being opposite poles of the same continuum. In other words, the process of acculturation in which the international executive is immersed is best represented by a two-factor model, where identification with the host culture proceeds along a different continuum than identification with the home country (Fig. 4.1). This bidimensional model contrasts with the bipolar one where local is the opposite pole of global in either a "thinking" or an "acting" continuum (Kefalas, 1998). As a result, managing the tension between local and global forces does not necessarily mean "balancing" them by finding a proverbial mid-point where such forces neutralize each other and attain equilibrium, but often learning to live with such dualities rather than trying to solve them by shortcutting one in favor of the other.

The literature has long warned international executives about the perils of "going native," which involves breaking all ties with headquarters and, instead, becoming an ardent defendant of the local approach to doing business. Clearly, this approach is likely to infuriate the corporate headquarters, whose insistence on preserving certain global standards seems ignored. Such a process of "psychological naturalization" pushes the international manager away from his/her boundaryless role, whose nature is precisely to maintain a dual identity and preserve dual loyalties to both the home and host countries (Sanchez et al., 2000).

Going native represents the opposite pole of refusing any form of localization, and both approaches are ineffective ways of managing the tension between centripetal and centrifugal forces, because they both assume that these forces should be balanced—the strength of one should be counterbalanced by the other, so that a proverbial equilibrium may be achieved. We maintain that balancing these forces is not a necessarily effective way to manage them, because quite often one's innovative advantage resides in the asymmetries that exist between these forces such as, for instance, in preserving certain global standards in the face of local opposition. Once again, consider the example of the multinational specializing in fast-moving consumer goods that insisted in keeping sugar at lower levels than those preferred by local customers in a North African market because their core brand was associated with a happy and healthy lifestyle. Indeed, business is not politics, and a "centrist" approach does not necessarily bring a wider range of potential consumers.

"Glocalized" Entrepreneurship

The work of Buckley et al. on how innovation takes place in the "global factory" is key to understanding how international executives are uniquely equipped with knowledge of local and global factors to exercise judgment in the face of uncertainty (Buckley, 2016; Buckley & Prashantham, 2016). Buckley calls for a division of entrepreneurial labor between multinationals and their local collaborators, so that a solid understanding of how centripetal and centrifugal factors can be innovatively combined begins to emerge.

Armed with an understanding of the institutional voids and associated market inefficiencies that characterize local markets, risk-taking international executives are ideally positioned to make local adjustments to the global brand. These calculated adjustments capitalize on the strengths of the multinational brand, but also on the executives' knowledge of local nuances that reveals the necessary tweaks for a successful local adaptation.

The international executive plays a central role in creating a dialog among international settings, which should reveal new opportunities to capitalize on the brand's strengths that become obvious solely when one understands the local voids that such strengths can fill. This type of capability, which Buckley and Prashantham (2016) refer to as "complementary entrepreneurship," signifies the need to understand that global innovation often equates to smart local adaptations. Such adaptations take advantage of synergies that only those who are familiar with both sets of forces—centripetal and centrifugal—understand.

This kind of "glocalized" entrepreneurship meets the criteria of causal ambiguity and social complexity that define difficult to imitate assets leading to competitive advantage (Teece, 2007; Teece, Pisano, & Shuen, 1997). Prior research also suggests that CEO experience in an international assignment combines with organizational characteristics to create rare, socially complex resources that facilitate the appropriation of a greater proportion of performance in CEO pay (Carpenter, Sanders, & Gregersen, 2001). In support of the argument advanced here, the positive effects of international assignment experience were boosted by having a strong global strategic posture, thereby suggesting that the combination of difficult to imitate resources with the appropriate contextual factors further enhances their utility.

Implications for Executive Education

Still another facet of the in our view excessive emphasis on localization in the international business domain is illustrated by the abundance of teaching cases describing the failure of cross-culturally insensitive, almost xenophobic "expatriates" who refused to localize. For instance, consider the case of the American expatriate in Chile who refused to try local food and even local beer, being uninterested in learning from or mingling with locals. Although his refusal to show an interest in local customs might have contributed to this expatriate's failure abroad, this type of cases do not prove that successful adaptation equates to full localization. In our opinion, these cases fail to illustrate an equally important phenomenon; that is the case of expatriates who, in their desire to accommodate to local norms, failed to preserve core elements of the global business model, which in turn would have prevented their failure. Very few cases talk about how expatriates who easily gave up their standards because they did not conform to counterproductive local norms such as lax deadlines, lack of accountability, bribes, and a going with the flow mentality, ended up paying a high price for their hurried and thoughtless localization. Unfortunately, classroom discussions of the need to achieve a balance between global and local concerns are often biased, because they unduly emphasize the need to be flexible, which is frequently pictured as the need to adjust one's practices to local usages. Much less common are cases that pinpoint the failure of firms that, obsessed with the need to localize, ended up losing their innovative advantage, or cases where a strategically insightful executive understood the importance of sticking to certain global practices in spite of local opposition.

Consider for instance the case of the marketing director working for a fast-moving consumer goods multinational in charge of relaunching a soft drink that had not been initially successful in an emerging market. This executive refused internal pressures from local managers to change the contents of a new cartoon-based advertising strategy for this soft drink. Internal critics of the advertising campaign argued against it on the grounds that using cartoons represented an extreme deviation from the type of advertising that local consumers were used to for this type of product, and hence it will confuse consumers. The marketing director insisted on keeping the advertising campaign in sync with the global platform calling for cartoon-based ads, because she understood how these ads represented an aspirational society associated with the brand, as well as the synergies that result from such global efforts. Within one year, the soft drink in question has exceeded the sales goal by 14%, and gained a 2.4% marketshare.

Among instructors of international business courses and seminars, the roots of the preference for content that advises executives to localize are understandable. Undoubtedly, instructors who encourage executives to become well-traveled, worldly, and sophisticated "cosmopolitans" who can seamlessly mingle in today's multicultural business environment are likely to become popular. After all, becoming a cosmopolitan, world-traveling James Bond-like executive is a charming proposition. The downside of this approach is that, by ignoring the less appealing but probably more critical need to stick to the innovative drivers of the firm's strategy, we may be doing a disservice to those whom we claim to be training for an international assignment.

After all, even James Bond stood by some cultural norms of his home country when on assignment, as attested by his preference for a tuxedo over local clothing on most social occasions… Humor aside, tipping the balance in favor of cosmopolitanism overlooks the fact that success on an international assignment is often determined not only by the willingness to accommodate to a different culture, but precisely by the refusal to relax certain, innovative aspects of one's business strategy simply because they do not conform to local norms. The ability to discern the truly innovative aspects of the global strategy that should not be compromised is a must amongst international executives, who should tirelessly hold on to these innovative aspects in spite of the losses in local popularity that they these executives are likely to endure.

In other words, training executives to manage global and local concerns should not be equated to an exercise in physics where the goal is to calculate the mid-point of perfect equilibrium between two vectors. Specifically, managing the global–local dilemma does not always require tipping the balance in favor of the local side. Because much of this literature emphasizes the need to adopt local usages, preparation for international assignments should probably emphasize the global side, which includes strengthening the need to preserve the innovative potential of a global-platform strategy that would otherwise succumb to the inertia of local forces.

Conclusion

We have contended here that the laws of physics are not applicable to the global–local dilemma, which is not solved by simply identifying a suitable mid-point between centripetal (global) and centrifugal (local) forces, but by learning to live with the tension between them. In fact, innovative breakthroughs in international assignments often necessitate solutions that elevate rather than lower the local *versus* global tension, as it occurs in instances where the executive understands the importance of retaining key innovation drivers in spite of their apparent opposition to local ways. We hope the preceding discussion steers further thinking on global human capital away from the accommodation paradigm represented by the adage "when in Rome, do as the Romans do." Indeed, much of the innovation potential in international ventures stems from holding on to the global imperatives that define the corporate brand, even when (or precisely because of) such imperatives appear to pull the business in a different direction than that exerted by local forces.

References

Ang, S., Van Dyne, L., Koh, C., Ng, K. Y., Tampler, K. J., Tay, C., & Chandrasekar, N. A. (2007). Cultural intelligence: Its measurement and effects on cultural adjustment and decision making, cultural adaptation, and task performance. *Management and Organization Review, 3*(3), 335–371.

Bhaskar-Shrinivas, P., Harrison, D. A., Shaffer, M. A., & Luk, D. M. (2005). Input-based and time-based models of international adjustment: Meta-analytic evidence and theoretical extensions. *Academy of Management Journal, 48*(2), 257–280.

Bolino, M. C. (2007). Expatriate assignments and intra-organizational career success: Implications for individuals and organizations. *Journal of International Business Studies, 38*, 819–835.

Bowen, D. E., & Ostroff, C. (2004). Understanding HRM-firfm performance linkages: The role of the "strength" of the HRM system. *Academy of Management Review, 29*(2), 203–221.

Buckley, P. J. (2016). The contribution of internalisation theory to international business: New realities and unanswered questions. *Journal of World Business, 51*(1), 74–82.

Buckley, P., & Prashantham, S. (2016). Global interfirm networks: The division of entrepreneurial labour between MNEs and SMEs. *The Academy of Management Perspectives, 30*(1), 40–58.

Carpenter, M. A., Sanders, W. G., & Gregersen, H. B. (2001). Bundling human capital with organizational context: The impact of international assignment experience on multinational firm performance and CEO pay. *Academy of Management Journal, 44*(3), 493–511.

Coleman, J. S. (1988). Social capital in the creation of human capital. *American Journal of Sociology, 94*, S95–S120.

Dakhli, M., & De Clercq, D. (2004). Human capital, social capital, and innovation: A multi-country study. *Entrepreneurship & Regional Development, 16*(2), 107–128.

Grauer, S. (1989). *Think globally, act locally: A delphi study of educational leadership through the development of international resources in the local community.* San Diego: University of San Diego.

Gupta, A. K., & Govindarajan, V. (2002). Cultivating a global mindset. *Academy of Management Executive, 16*(1), 116–126.

Kedia, B., & Mukherji, A. (1999). Global managers: Developing a global mindset for global competitiveness. *Journal of World Business, 34*(3), 230–251.

Kefalas, A. G. (1998). Think globally, act locally. *Thunderbird International Business Review, 40*(6), 547–562.

Kostova, T., & Zaheer, S. (1999). Organizational legitimacy under conditions of complexity: The case of the multinational enterprise. *Academy of Management Review, 24*(1), 64–81.

Levy, O., Beechler, S., Taylor, S., & Boyacigiller, N. A. (2007). What we talk about when we talk about "global mindset": Managerial cognition in multinational corporations. *Journal of International Business Studies, 38*, 231–258.

Mezias, J. M., & Scandura, T. A. (2005). A needs-driven approach to expatriate adjustment and career development: A multiple-mentoring perspective. *Journal of International Business Studies, 36*, 519–538.

Newburry, W., Gardberg, N. A., & Sanchez, J. I. (2014). Employer attractiveness in Latin America: The association among foreignness, internationalization and talent recruitment. *Journal of International Management, 20*(3), 327–344.

Rhinesmith, S. H. (1992, October). Global mindsets for global managers. *Training & Development, 46*(10), 63–68.

Rhinesmith, S. H. (2005). *How can you manage global paradox?* Mercer Delta Executive Learning Center.

Sanchez, J. I., & Brock, P. (1996). Outcomes of perceived discrimination among Hispanic employees: Is diversity management a luxury or a necessity? *Academy of Management Journal, 39*(3), 704–719.

Sanchez, J. I., & Fernandez, D. M. (1993). Acculturative stress among Hispanics: A bidimensional model of ethnic identification. *Journal of Applied Social Psychology, 23*(8), 654–668.

Sanchez, J. I., & Levine, E. L. (2009). What is (or should be) the difference between competency modeling and tradicional job analysis? *Human Resource Management Review, 19*(2), 53–63.

Sanchez, J. I., & Medkik, N. (2004). The effects of diversity awareness training on differential treatment. *Group & Organization Management, 29*(4), 517–536.

Sanchez, J. I., Spector, P. E., & Cooper, C. L. (2000). Adapting to a boundaryless world: A developmental expatriate model. *Academy of Management Executive, 14*(2), 96–106.

Takeuchi, R., Lepak, D. P., Marinova, S. V., & Yun, S. (2007). Nonlinear influences of stressors on general adjustment: The case of Japanese expatriates and their spouses. *Journal of International Business Studies, 38,* 928–934.

Takeuchi, R., Shay, J. P., & Li, J. (2008). When does decision autonomy increase expatriate managers' adjustment? An empirical test. *Academy of Management Journal, 51*(1), 45–60.

Takeuchi, R., Tesluk, P. E., Yun, S., & Lepak, D. P. (2005). An integrative view of international experience. *Academy of Management Journal, 48*(1), 85–100.

Teece, D. J. (2007). Explicating dynamic capabilities: The nature and microfoundations of (sustainable) enterprise performance. *Strategic Management Journal, 28*(13), 1319–1350.

Teece, D. J., Pisano, G., & Shuen, A. (1997). Dynamic capabilities and strategic management. *Strategic Management Journal, 18*(7), 509–533.

Zaheer, S. (1995). Overcoming the liability of foreignness. *Academy of Management Journal, 38*(2), 341–363.

5

Managing Non-traditional Human Capital in International Assignments: A Qualitative Analysis of the Talent and Innovation Gaps

Kowoon Kim and Mary Ann Von Glinow

Introduction

Talent Gaps in International Assignments: Non-traditional Expatriates

As businesses globalize, companies continue to rely on expatriates for their expertise, since it is often relatively difficult to find qualified local candidates even though local talent pools are widening. As a result, the success of expatriates during the international assignment (IA) has long been seen as a crucial part of the multinational enterprise (MNE)'s performance (Tung, 1981).

The overwhelming majority of MNE expatriates have typically been married white males with accompanying female spouses and children

K. Kim (✉) • M.A. Von Glinow
Department of Management & International Business, Florida International University, Miami, FL, USA

© The Author(s) 2017
S. Kundu, S. Munjal (eds.), *Human Capital and Innovation*,
DOI 10.1057/978-1-137-56561-7_5

(Adler, 1979; Hutchings, French, & Hatcher, 2008; Tung, 1993), sent on IAs of three or more years (Meyskens, Von Glinow, Werther, & Clarke, 2009). Therefore, previous studies on expatriates have mostly focused on traditional "white," "male" expatriates (Takeuchi, 2010).

However, as global mobility and talent seeking have increased significantly over the past few decades, the workforce is overwhelmingly more diverse in terms of age, gender, race, culture, religion, and sexual orientation (Chatman & O'Reilly, 2004; Dovidio, Kawakami, & Gaertner, 2002; Islam & Hewstone, 1993; Kunze, Böhm, & Bruch, 2011; Ragins, Cornwell, & Miller, 2003; Reskin, 1993; Toossi, 2012) despite the fact that talent trumps diversity. Accordingly, the expatriate population has become more talented and diverse simultaneously (Inkson, Arthur, Pringle, & Barry, 1998; McNulty, 2015; McNulty & Hutchings, 2016). Not only women (Brookfield Global Relocation Services, 2015) but also other non-traditional groups have entered into IAs (McNulty, 2015; McPhail, McNulty, & Hutchings, 2016). In fact, there has been an explosive growth of self-initiated expatriates (SIEs) with vastly different skill sets (Kim, Halliday, Zhao, Wang, & Von Glinow, 2016) who tend to be less male, younger, single, and often looking for specific assignments in a culture of interest to them (Andresen, Biemann, & Pattie, 2015; Biemann & Andresen, 2010; Suutari & Brewster, 2001).

Halliday, Kim, Zhao, and Von Glinow (2015) introduced three broad types of non-traditional expatriates: *LGBT* expatriates (e.g., lesbian, gay, bisexual, transgender), *religious* expatriates (e.g., Christians, Muslims, Jews), and expatriates from *non-traditional family compositions* (e.g., single parents, female breadwinners, multi-generational families, semi-retirees, and those with special needs children).

Bell, Özbilgin, Beauregard, and Sürgevil (2011) asserted that LGBTs represent an increasing proportion of the workforce in the USA, composing nearly 8.8 million potential employees. Similarly, several studies have reported a rising number of LGBT expatriates in recent years (Collins, 2009; Gedro, 2010; Gedro, Mizzi, Rocco, & van Loo, 2013; McNulty & Hutchings, 2016; Paisley & Tayar, 2016). Nonetheless, to date, LGBT employees appear to be less likely to be selected for IAs (Collins, 2009; Gedro, 2010; McNulty & Hutchings, 2016; Paisley & Tayar, 2016) despite the fact that they may possess the appropriate talent and skill set for IAs. Additionally, even if chosen, LGBT expatriates often do not receive sufficient support from their home MNE; and as a result, they face greater challenges during the IA (Mercer, 2014).

Religious expatriates, who do not share the same religion with the host country's predominant or official religion, have also been under-researched. In some parts of the world, particularly conservative Muslim countries, religion is central to the host's daily life, having a significant effect on non-Muslim expatriates (Selmer, 1995). Deviation from the host country's religion can make life difficult for such non-Muslim expatriates. For instance, there are arrests and deportations of non-Muslim expatriates in Saudi Arabia due to non-Muslim worship, even though non-Muslim expatriates are permitted to worship in private by law (U.S. Commission on International Religious Freedom, 2010).

Beck and Beck-Gernsheim (2002) argued that over the past few decades, there have been rapid changes in family structures with an increase in divorced families, unmarried families, and homosexual families. In particular, traditional families have been dramatically transformed to "post-familial families," reflecting a wide variety of forms. Along with their argument, a new form of non-traditional family, the female bread-winner family, is growing quickly, representing 35 percent of dual-career families (U.S. Department of Labor, 2010). According to a recent survey by Brookfield Global Relocation Services (2014), approximately 18 percent of expatriates represent female breadwinner families with accompanying male spouses.

Expatriates with accompanying elderly parents constitute relatively low proportions (two percent of total expatriates); therefore, this may not be too problematic at present. Not surprisingly, 92 percent of MNEs currently do not have a formal policy for them (Brookfield Global Relocation Services, 2015). However, it is noteworthy that elder care will continue to rise worldwide and pose an issue for MNEs wishing to recruit top talent.

Despite these recent and upcoming changes in global talent pools, many MNEs still maintain a traditional "one-size fits all" strategy to manage non-traditional expatriates. However, "one-size" does not fit all; rather, it is bound to have severe limitations in managing non-traditional expatriates (Hipsher, 2008). This is because non-traditional expatriates differ not only from their traditional counterparts, but also from each other in diversity attributes (e.g., religion, sexual orientation, and family structure) as discussed above. Hence, instead of using a "one-size fits all" approach, inclusive and differentiated human capital management will enable non-traditional expatriates to reach their full potential in IAs. Moreover, inclusive talent management attracts not only top non-traditional expatriates, but also other top talents who advocate diversity in the workplace (Cox & Blake, 1991; Hewlett & Yoshino, 2016). Indeed, according to a recent industry survey (Center for Talent Innovation, 2016), 72 percent of respondents prefer to work for the MNE that is supportive of LGBT employees than one that is not. Consequently, understanding non-traditional expatriates' international work experiences is essential for maximizing the talent pipeline and achieving successful international human resource management (IHRM).

Innovation Gaps: Workforce Diversity and Innovation

As MNEs face greater uncertainty and risk in the era of "the new normal," the need for innovation becomes more salient (McNamee, 2004; Mike, 2013). This is due to the fact that the new normal in the business environment challenges the status quo or business-as-usual; instead, it requires new approaches or different perspectives to deal with uncertainty. In this regard, diverse workforces, rather than just limited to traditional homogeneous expatriates, can bring thinking beyond the status quo and diverse perspectives to IAs that encourage innovation (Gossling & Rutten, 2007; Niebuhr, 2010; Nieto & Santamaría, 2007; Nelson & Winter, 1982, Schumpeter, 1934).

Diversity not only can promote innovation itself, but also accelerate the diffusion of innovation with its rich networks. Over the past few decades, innovation researchers have consistently demonstrated that innovations spread through interpersonal communication networks (Rogers, 1962, 2010; Valente & Rogers, 1995). In this regard, diverse workforces can bring a wide range of diffusion chains to IAs. Indeed, according to the Corporate Equality Index from the Human Rights Campaign Foundation (HRCF, 2016), an increasing number of MNEs have formally recognized business networks (or employee resource groups) for their diverse workforces, including women, LGBT, and so on. In particular, 78 percent of respondent MNEs have business networks across the globe for diverse workforces, and 85 percent have them for LGBT employees; as a result, MNEs increase the probability of broader and more rapid innovation spurts. Moreover, the diffusion of the innovation, in turn, leads to continuous innovations, such as incremental improvements and complementary investments.

With respect to workforce diversity in IAs as a significant driver of innovation, Miralles-Vazquez and McGaughey (2016) pointed out the importance of organizational contexts. Nevertheless, while there is significant research on traditional expatriate management and adjustment, little research addresses the experiences of non-traditional talents in the IA. To date, even fewer attempts to describe non-traditional expatriates have relied on sound conceptual frameworks and thus much research is needed (Gedro, 2012).

While discussing non-traditional expatriates' international work experiences, this paper emphasizes the need to broaden our lens from a rather narrowly focused view of traditional expatriates to include non-traditional expatriates. The need for worldwide talent demands no less. Two decades ago, Mamman and Richards (1996) insisted that expatriate research should be broadened to embrace more diverse expatriate characteristics; the time has now come with urgency since MNEs worldwide experience talent shortage. Given global talent gaps in today's innovation-based economy, we assert that non-traditional expatriates will be a valuable source of talent for MNEs that promote both innovation and productivity.

Among diverse groups of non-traditional expatriates, this study focuses particularly on LGBT expatriates, because sexual orientation diversity is a provocative issue transcending expatriation into talent acquisition and filtering through all aspects of societies today from legal, social, and identity diversity; it has taken on center stage in the quest for talent, yet it remains under-researched (Bell et al., 2011). Therefore, we believe this study is timely and important.

LGBT Expatriates

As noted, the term "diversity" has taken on an expanded meaning with widely recognized importance, particularly since a large number of studies have revealed its positive relationship with innovation (Bassett-Jones, 2005; O'Reilly, Williams, & Barsade, 1998; Østergaard, Timmermans, & Kristinsson, 2011). In addition, innovation is broadly deemed as an integral component of a firm's competitiveness (Bassett-Jones, 2005; Gunday, Ulusoy, Kilic, & Alpkan, 2011). With growing attention on diversity, many studies now include sexual orientation as a diversity attribute (Harvey & Allard, 2002; McNulty, 2015; Ragins et al., 2003; Rumens & Broomfield, 2012; Rumens & Kerfoot, 2009), despite the fact that few explicitly empirically investigate the phenomenon, particularly as it relates to talent.

There are many different ways that diversity might be classified, however, it is usually divided into visible diversity and invisible diversity based on different attributes (Barak & Levin, 2002; Jackson, May, & Whitney, 1995). *Visible diversity*, such as race and gender, refers to characteristics that are more external and observable and that are different from the majority of others in the organization or social network, whereas *invisible diversity* refers to those differences that are not readily seen (Barak, 1999) by even those in the same culture. In this regard, sexual orientation is one of the invisible attributes of diversity (Özbilgin & Woodward, 2004). Due to its nature, visible diversity involves more overt and direct discrimination, while invisible diversity involves subtle and covert forms of discrimination (Bell et al., 2011). To wit, Ragins and Cornwell (2001) found that LGBT employees indirectly experience discrimination through the existence of a hostile work environment directed toward them. As a result, MNEs may not see such invisible sexual orientation discrimination as a problem because it is invisible. What makes matters worse is that LGBT employees often remain silent, or are forced to be quiet for fear of being thought of as abnormal in their MNEs (Bell et al., 2011). Supporting this point of view, Bowen and Blackmon (2003) noted that fear of discrimination appears stronger for those with invisible diversity attributes.

Levine and Leonard (1984) identified formal and informal discrimination against LGBT employees. Formal discrimination includes disadvantages for employment, promotions, rewards, and even firing. On the other hand, informal discrimination includes lack of trust, acceptance, and respect either by coworkers or by supervisors, which can have equally negative employment outcomes.

Sexual orientation discrimination at work has a substantially detrimental effect both on LGBT employees and MNEs. Not only actual discrimination, but also perceived discrimination, can create negative work outcomes. Ragins and Cornwell (2001) found that perceived sexual orientation discrimination in the workplace is negatively related to job attitudes and job satisfaction. Consequently, knowing and understanding its antecedents and what can be done by the MNE about sexual orientation discrimination is important for MNEs wishing to retain their human capital regardless of sexual orientation.

Despite the fact that same sex marriage has become legal in all 50 states in the USA and other countries, there has been a growing worldwide effort to prevent sexual orientation discrimination in the workplace, LGBTs are often overlooked in business practices as well as in IAs. LGBT expatriates carry a stigma related to their invisible diversity (McNulty, 2015) and oftentimes face institutional discrimination within a dominant heterosexual organizational culture, exacerbated by a homophobic host country environment. We now turn to theoretical backdrops against which we discuss diverse human capital and innovation.

Theoretical Background

Social identity theory (Tajfel & Turner, 1979), uncertainty identity theory, similarity-attraction paradigm (Byrne & Lamberth, 1971), and attraction-selection-attrition framework (Schneider, 1987) explain why traditional expatriates are so homogeneous contextually that they exclude other diversities regardless of talent. With respect to human capital and innovation, details of how a homogeneous group impacts innovation will be further discussed later in this section.

Social Identity Theory and Uncertainty Identity Theory

Social identity theory (Tajifel, 1982) states that people tend to identify themselves as members of a social group (i.e., demographic characteristics are likely to be used as bases for social categorization such as gender, social class, marital status, nationality, etc.) and differentiate their own group (us) from other groups (them). To increase their positive distinctiveness, people unconsciously or automatically have more favorable views of "in-group" rather than the "out-group" (Ashforth & Mael, 1989). This human tendency to favor "in-group," known as "in-group favoritism," triggers bias and discrimination against the "out-group," and this bias is quite independent of talent.

The Second World War was highly influential in the formation and development of social identity theory. Having a strong connection to a certain group identity was said to buffer the stress of uncertainty. As a response to prevailing uncertainties during the war, collective identification was inspired while limiting individualistic approaches to the study of intergroup relations (Oyserman, 2007).

With the emphasis on its resolving uncertainties, social identity theory has been subsequently extended to uncertainty identity theory (Hogg, 2007). According to uncertainty identity theory, people fundamentally want to reduce uncertainty and an uncertain environment motivates such basic needs of uncertainty reduction by means of reinforcing group identification (Grieve & Hogg, 1999; Hogg & Grieve, 1999; Hogg & Mullin, 1999).

Uncertainty is an integral part of expatriation; living abroad, working in a multinational environment, and dealing across cultures are fraught with uncertainty. To the MNE, sending an expatriate overseas entails uncertainty. Aside from the loss of key global talent, the financial costs of expatriate failure, either direct or indirect, and its underperformance implications are usually formidable (Collings, Scullion, & Morley, 2007; Harzing & Christensen, 2004; Meyskens et al., 2009). Given the number of uncertainties related to expatriation, MNEs are attracted to those who are more similar to the traditional expatriate when it comes to selection. In other words, MNEs tend to opt for the safer choice, which is generally the white male.

Similarity-Attraction Paradigm and Attraction-Selection-Attrition Framework

All of these points are consistent with the key argument of the similarity-attraction paradigm. Byrne and Lamberth (1971) posited that as the saying goes "birds of a feather flock together" so too do people inherently prefer others who are similar, rather than dissimilar, to themselves. Adding to this, Schneider's attraction-selection-attrition framework (1987) postulated that companies are more likely to select those who are similar to their existing employees. Owing to these factors, demographic characteristics of employees in an MNE tend to become more similar over time.

Taken together, social identity theory, uncertainty identity theory, similarity-attraction paradigm, and attraction-selection-attrition framework commonly argue that people have a tendency to exaggerate the similarities between in-group members and the differences between in-group members and out-group members, especially under conditions of uncertainty. This is due to the fact that similarity, in general, has been believed to generate attraction, loyalty, mutual support, trustworthiness, and cohesion within the group (Byrne, 1997; Byrne & Nelson, 1965; Harrison, Price, & Bell, 1998); and in turn, in-group similarity is positively associated with various group-level outcomes, such as organization tenure, group functioning, and organizational behavior (Byrne, 1971; Day & Bedeian, 1995; Jackson et al., 1995; Turban & Jones, 1988).

Subsequent studies, however, have pointed out that similarity evokes these positive outcomes, particularly in a relationship with a stranger or in the beginning of a relationship. In other words, the effect of in-group similarity on work-related outcomes varies considerably depending on the context. Similarly, numerous scholars have noted that the positive association between in-group similarity and outcomes becomes trivial in ongoing relationships (Montoya & Horton, 2004; Sunnafrank, 1991, 1992) and long-term relationships (White & Hatcher, 1984), which share a historical context in either the past or the present (Bochner, 1991). In this view, expatriate relationships are hardly considered relationships among strangers or relationships in the nascent stage; rather, they are more likely to be classified as existing and continuous relationships, since international assignments, in most cases, require a certain period of time and ongoing efforts. In sum, the positive consequences of similarity will be reduced, or even cancelled, in the expatriate context.

Furthermore, based on the attraction-selection-attrition theory, Jackson et al. (1991) argued that similarity decreases the likelihood of conflict; yet at the same time, the lack of group conflict can lead to groupthink. The term groupthink was first introduced by Janis in 1972 and refers to an absence of critical thinking in groups (Cox, 1994). Homogeneous groups are often subject to groupthink, because they typically tend to ensure higher levels of group cohesiveness, seek an extreme consensus, and as a consequence, lack divergent ideas; in other words, they do not want to "rock the boat" (Herring & Henderson, 2014). Given the fact that innovation often requires thinking "outside the box," groupthink, as a tendency to remain "inside the box", can stifle innovation (Weisberg, 2009).

In contrast, diverse groups oftentimes provide different frames of reference, which offer rich and unique insights into the work; as a result, it reduces the probability of groupthink and creates more opportunities for innovation (Cox & Blake, 1991). Similarly, Basset-Jones (2005) insisted that innovation is enhanced by the existence of diversity. Nonetheless, diversity is the least understood force for innovation (Page, 2007). In this regard, we assert that non-traditional talents, particularly LGBT expatriates, will make international assignments more diverse and multifaceted and eventually more innovative.

However, diversity enhances innovation not simply because it generates more ideas, but because innovation emerges through communication-friendly environments in the diverse group. Findler, Wind, and Barak (2007) have found evidence that workforce diversity demonstrates a willingness to accept the differences and encompass divergent ideas, even conflicting ideas; as a result, it fosters mutual respect and creates more inclusive and tolerant communications for the diversity of opinion. In other words, diverse and inclusive contexts in the workplace enrich communications and enhance idea sharing; by doing so, it leverages differences and allows everyone to reach his/her full potential. As a natural consequence, it provokes greater innovation. In addition, according to a recent report by McKinsey & Co. (2015), MNEs with more diverse workforces financially outperform their rivals, and therefore, diversity, including sexual orientation, produces greater competitive advantages for MNEs. As such, we believe that diverse and inclusive expatriate environments make MNEs more acceptable, more marketable, and ultimately more competitive.

Methodology

Case Studies

When a phenomenon is under-researched, a case study can be particularly appropriate, providing a valuable source of insight, theory, and data about the phenomenon (Eisenhardt, 1989; Marshall & Rossman, 2014). As mentioned earlier, non-traditional expatriates have not received sufficient research attention. The case study is capable of a holistic perspective and a deeper exploration of non-traditional expatriates' international work experiences. In this regard, the purpose of this case study is to develop a clearer understanding of how human capital management influences job-related outcomes, such as talent development and innovation.

Cases are selected based on purposeful and theoretical sampling. Each case was reported by a combination of written answers and in-depth clinical interviews. Interview questions (see Appendix 1) were provided to each participant in advance of the interview. Then participants were interviewed with follow-up questions based on respondent answers. The interview was conducted over a two-month period (August to September, 2015) and the length of interviews ranged from 40 to 70 minutes. The first two interviews were conducted via Skype due to distance. The use of Skype allows participants to carry out interviews in their personal location, so that participants feel comfortable (Hanna, 2012; Lev, 2007). This is important, especially when the research focuses on a "private" and "sensitive" issue. The remaining two interviews were conducted face-to-face. All interviews were conducted in English, audiotaped with the participant's permission, and were transcribed verbatim.

The interview transcripts were analyzed manually and narrative analysis was used to help capture how participants define and construct their experiences, providing rich descriptions and hidden perspectives (Abbott, 1992; Bossard & Peterson, 2005; Orbuch, 1997; Yoddumnern-Attig, Attig, & Boonchalaksi, 1991). In other words, its focus lies on the "actor's point of view" (Hannabuss, 1996). To illustrate this, we focus on an emic approach in cross-cultural research. Since the terms "etic and emic approaches" were coined by Pike (1967), these two different approaches have been frequently used in studying cultures (Berry,

1969, 1989; Peterson & Pike, 2002). While an etic approach observes a culture by imposing a set of universal values (i.e., external or outsiders' viewpoint) onto that culture being studied, an emic approach takes a native or insider's point of view as its starting point (Malinowski, 1922). In other words, the emic approach is driven by how insiders sort their stories with a "thick description" (i.e., which means, not just describing the event itself but explaining its social context as well) (Geertz, 1973). In taking an emic approach, we can better understand and contextualize individuals in their daily lives, including their attitudes and motives (Berry, 1989) and eventually rewrite and resituate reality for the future (Mott-Stenerson, 2008). This paper focuses in detail on participants' stories at the emic level of narrative analysis.

Although narrative analysis has been frequently used in the social sciences (Czarniawska, 2004), there has been an increased interest in the use of narration across other disciplines including business research (Boje, 2001; Czarniawska, 1998; Gedro et al., 2013; Gertsen & Søderberg, 2010; Søderberg, 2006; Von Glinow, Shapiro, & Brett, 2004; Watson, 2009). Soin and Scheytt (2006) highlighted the importance of a narrative analysis in cross-cultural research. Similarly, Glanz (1993) insisted that stories told by existing employees to the newcomer can lead to more effective and valuable learning than formal training programs.

Participants

Four case participants were recruited through snowball sampling. Participants were invited to participate in the study by email and personal contact.

Participants were expatriates self-identified as LGBTs. This study included both organizational expatriates (OEs), those who are sent by their home MNEs on IAs and self-initiated expatriates (SIEs), those who themselves make the decision to work abroad (Peltokorpi & Jintae Froese, 2009). Participants represented a wide range of expatriation from academia to the agricultural industry (see Appendix 2).

Although bisexual and transgender expatriates were not intentionally excluded, due to the researchers' limited access, they were left out of the current study. Three gay expatriates and one lesbian expatriate were interviewed in total.

Each participant was informed that the research would be conducted following the university's ethical protocols and all responses would be treated in confidence.

Case Findings

Case 1 Work is work and sexual orientation really does not have anything to do with your talents or your work or whatever per se.

Bert Cotreau is a dual citizen of the USA and Hungary. He was brought up in the mid-west USA, which was according to him a very homophobic environment. Bert is well-educated, holding his PhD degree in Psychology. He has been in business since the 1970s, working for a number of MNEs. Now, he is approaching retirement age.

In the 70s, when Bert was working with Native-American groups for promotion of gambling in California; he had Native-American clients that became aware of his sexual orientation due to the fact that he attended a special event with his partner. When it came time to renew the contracts, they chose not to work with Bert and he was laid off from his job. Since then, Bert has gone by himself to most special events. "Other people brought their girlfriends and I brought my partner," he says, "It was never said or established that my partner was my life-partner, but anyone with any intelligence would draw that conclusion."

In the Native-American culture, the term "two spirits" (i.e., the French word "Berdache") refers to a person who adopts the roles of the opposite gender, as the contemporary label of LGBT (Callender et al., 1983). This was most common among Native Americans living in the western region of the USA. Nonetheless, "They [were] very conservative and anti-gay," said Bert.

Although he faced this challenge in the USA, he thinks discrimination is standard worldwide. "That was then in the '80s and '90s and I find it still true today I think," Bert says, "It is changing but it will not change dramatically unless (open-minded and diverse) young people come into leadership positions. It will not change as long as people in my age group are in my position [leadership], because it is a cultural thing. The issue is not as important as it was 10 years ago. Gay rights have changed dramatically. I never thought it would be."

Consistent with his arguments, based on upper echelon theory (Hambrick & Mason, 1984), several scholars have demonstrated that top management team (TMT) diversity, such as demographic diversity (Jiménez, Ruiz-Arroyo, & Pulles, 2014; Zhu & Yin, 2016), educational diversity (Wiersema & Bantel, 1992), functional diversity (Bantel & Jackson, 1989; Qian, Cao, & Takeuchi, 2013), task-related diversity (Li, Liu, Lin, & Ma, 2016), and tenure diversity (Boeker, 1997; Elenkov, Judge, & Wright, 2005), has a strong positive effect on firm innovation performance (Hambrick, Cho, & Chen, 1996; Pitcher & Smith, 2001). This is primarily due to the fact that TMT diversity increases the level of cognitive diversity, which is a necessary element of innovation (Bantel & Jackson, 1989; Miller, Burke, & Glick, 1998; Wiersema & Bantel, 1992); besides, it enhances the level of commitment to R&D (Talke, Salomo, & Kock, 2011).

Bert developed a non-profit organization himself, because of his interest in human rights and women's rights issues. It is a human rights program with a church affiliation. With the church affiliation, homosexuality is not exactly an open topic for them, because Bert's workers are quite conservative. "Even though we are doing human rights, it is sort of odd. We are doing such a big thing on human rights and women's rights and [other rights] but not gay rights," he says.

As a business partner, Bert started working with his Chinese female friend in the packaging industry in Beijing, China. Then Bert, as cofounder, owned the education company for 10 years, having offices in Seoul, Korea, and Beverly Hills, California.

Bert never intended to work internationally. He just evolved into the international assignment. "As I met these people, the opportunity presented itself to expand the business and go into different [international] areas," explains Bert.

He has been running a plant nursery business in Estonia since 2009, living in an agriculturally based culture in Southern Estonia. His company is becoming the leading producer in his geographical market. As

Ragins and Cornwell (2001) argued that gay supervisors are also vulnerable to discrimination, Bert, as an employer who owns a company, has been discriminated against at work by his employees because of his sexual orientation. "My gayness to this day is not an outward expression in Estonia. It is not outwardly expressed nor accepted here," he explains, because "it is possible for community members to act adversely." "I live a private life where my home is my castle. My partner and I can be ourselves in our house," he says. "I have the means to go places and do things where I am accepted," said Bert.

Even though "organizational culture regarding LGBT was prohibited in China and would not have been acceptable in Korea," for his personal well-being, he felt much more relaxed and much more part of the environment in Asia. He has more concerns and worries in Europe.

Numerous studies have argued that national culture is a key determinant of innovation (Ulijn & Weggeman, 2001; Van Everdingen & Waarts, 2003; Waarts & Van Everdingen, 2005; Westwood & Low, 2003). This is because national culture not only influences people's tendency to take risks/opportunities, but also shapes people's values and beliefs on diversity. Florida (2004) argued that the national culture that displays high levels of tolerance, diversity, and open-mindedness attracts more top creative talents.

Except for his Chinese business partner who was Bert's heterosexual friend, Bert never brought up his sexual orientation with other business partners with whom he met on a business level. Even when people asked him about it, "I would deny it," he said. "I do not think it is wise in our business environment to do that." Researchers (Bell et al., 2011; Kurdek, 2004; Özbilgin & Woodward, 2004) found that some LGBT employees strategically construct hypothetical heterosexual partners and bring them as "pretend" partners to company events to avoid discrimination at work. Similarly, once Bert and another lesbian friend falsely announced their engagement at the company party.

His recommendations for MNEs are: "Anytime someone either hires, or chooses not to work with someone other than because of his or her skill level or talents, it is a disservice to the company. [MNEs] are in business to do business. In a world where competition [for talent] is getting greater and greater, discriminating against anyone should be out of the question. It is bad business. It happens and it exists, but it should not be tolerated much less supported," he says, "not business smart."

His advice for other LGBT expatriates is: "It is critical to be understanding and knowledgeable of the culture and environment that one is placed into or is to be part of," he says. "They should strongly think about the ramifications before making the final decision," said Bert "If they are skeptical about going to, or becoming a part of an environment that may be hostile to them."

Also, Bert refers to expatriates as "guests." "If my partner and I would go out and hold hands and kiss in public and perhaps violate [host] cultural norms or standards, they in turn would make me an unwelcomed guest. If we go out and we do not show our affection in public, we are more welcome," he says, "Like-minded people like like-minded people."

Case 2 I do not think being gay had a massive impact on my performance.

James Fleck is a young Irish gay man in his mid-20s. Ireland now has legalized same sex marriage, however, when James worked in Ireland, he perceived a tone of insensitivity from a general conversation at work. "Ireland in some sense is very forward-looking in the newer generation, but … in the work environment, there is still a strong attachment to concepts like masculinity," he says. Rumens and Broomfield (2012) revealed that masculine culture in the workplace often delays or impedes disclosure. Such barriers to disclosure restrain the full potential of human capital, and eventually, undermine their potential for innovation.

James worked at a social media platform company as an intern for six months in Munich, Germany. He felt a lot freer and a lot easier on a day-to-day basis in Germany. "The Irish are more masculine in terms of perception of what a man should be," James says. "Germans are serious in work, but once they are out, they are great people. They are really fun and they are really accepting of modern fashion," says James, "I did not know it about the Germans before I went there."

"One of the main reasons I went to Germany was because I loved the country," he says, but "I [really] fell in love [with the country] when I got there." Additionally, James was seeking new career opportunities through his IA.

It was a small startup company (i.e., 8 years old now) with fewer than 60 employees. "The company was so new and was [entrepreneurial] not 'faceless', as many companies become when they grow in age and size," James says, "We were so small that everybody knew each other and it was hard not to bring out that side of yourself and not to let people know exactly who you are in many different senses."

According to James, in Munich, a big international city, the company would never have "a strong attachment to traditional concepts like masculinity." The MNE considers diversity to be an integral part of employment. As a result, the company is extraordinarily heterogeneous.

Employees came from all over the world. There were 30–40 different ethnic backgrounds (e.g., Polish, Lithuanian, Pakistani, Brazilian, Serbian, American, Australian, Portuguese, Colombian, and Russian). "Almost everybody was from a different place," he says, "It was a melting pot." Furthermore, he noted there are multiple staff members in varying degrees of seniority who are gay.

Despite the fact that the company did not have any written guiding principles or rules in place for LGBT employees, they consciously supported them in their company culture. "A company culture is a major aspect of safeguarding LGBT employees from discrimination in that sense," said James. "Their acceptance of and their promotion of LGBT employees as [traditional employees] is the way future international assignments will become," James says.

"We had a lot of staunch Catholics, Christians, Hindus, and Muslims. And there was never a bit of discrimination in them either," he says, "They were younger and [represented] a newer generation, but they are more used to seeing these things and the concept of live and let live … People within the power structures in the company were more modern and it bolsters [an inclusive company culture]."

Ancona and Caldwell (1992) argued that team diversity fosters external communications, and in turn, it leads to higher levels of innovation. Furthermore, Dahlin, Weingart, and Hinds (2005) found that team diversity is positively associated with the range and depth of information use. Considering the fact that the information is the basis of innovation (Cohen & Levinthal, 1990), team diversity accelerates innovation.

Although he had to leave earlier than expected because of family reasons, he did very well on his assignment and he loved the life he had. "My experience was, while a rare one, a place where many companies will [move] toward in the future. I worked for an excellent, modern startup company, [which] honestly believed in the health and well-being of their staff," he comments, "Great efforts were made by upper management for everyone to know each other from team days to a 'lunch-lottery'."

James plans to work abroad again, largely owing to his positive work experience in Germany. During the past few months, he has had several interviews. "The hostility of another country toward LGBT would not deter me as much," James says.

Case 3 Why do I have to hide myself even though I am still a good employee?

Paolo Tiraboschi is an Italian researcher in his 20s. As a research assistant, Paolo worked for two years in the department of public administration at a private university in Milan. He was consulting on public administration projects and also teaching classes.

While working there, Paolo concealed his sexual orientation, because it was not an LGBT-friendly workplace. "It was a very homogenous group of people. They were all Italians (i.e., except one foreigner), white, and Catholic," he explains. "Most of them [were] married with kids, just like a traditional Italian family. Being different was not accepted." In the past, gay employees had to quit their job because of a hostile work environment after coming out as gay. "That was apparently not a good move," Paolo says, "That is why I did not want to disclose my sexual orientation at work. Only one person knew I was gay, because he was gay as well. He had been working there for ten years, but he never said he was gay. He told me that if I want to survive working in that department, I have to shut up."

When his coworkers asked Paolo if he had a girlfriend, he answered, "I do not have a girlfriend. I am single." "Technically, I did not have a girlfriend, so that was not a lie. But I had a boyfriend at that time, so it was not fully true," Paolo says, "I was feeling upset about it. As a researcher, I can write, I can teach and I can do the exact same thing as others do.

But why can [I] not be who I am and why [do] I have to pretend being somebody else?"

Paolo came to the USA to study in 2012. Since then, he has been pursuing his PhD in public administration. When he was accepted, his department was unaware of his sexual orientation. "When I first moved here, I was afraid [of finding] a situation similar to the one in Italy. However, when I realized that people do not care if I am straight, gay or whatever, well, I said [to] them [that] I am gay," he says. It did not take him long (i.e., a month) to share his sexual orientation with the department. Nothing changed after his disclosure. "The relationship with some cohorts even improved a lot, because I do not have to pretend [to be] somebody I am not. I am more myself," he says, "As a gay, I have never had a problem while working here." Some professors have a "safe zone" sticker on the office door, which means that they accept diversity. "I felt accepted for who I am and no need to cover my identity," said Paolo.

The diversity of the department itself in terms of race (e.g., American, Asian, Indian, Latin, etc.) and religion (e.g., Christian, Jewish, Hindu, etc.) may increase the level of tolerance and inclusion. In addition to an open-minded work environment, his current school has well-developed and proactive HR policies against discrimination of any kind as to race, gender, and sexual orientation. Additionally, the LGBT community is active on campus.

A large number of studies have highlighted the importance of organizational guidelines and regulations in regard to diversity inclusion, as well as diverse resource groups/communities, on innovation (Forbes, 2011; HRCF, 2016). Given the fact that exclusion and discrimination inhibit innovation, creating a more inclusive workplace is key to successful innovation.

Paolo volunteered in Africa for three months. "I went there in 2010," he recalls, "They were pretty homophobic, but that did not stop me [from going to Africa]. They were just not ready for this thing. Perhaps in 2030, they [will] be ready and it [will] be fine. We need to give people time to accept these differences. It is not to be done in a day."

Paolo's advice for other LGBT expatriates is: "Just be yourself and work hard to prove that your diversity does not affect your work performance.

Being gay always pushes me forward to the limit. I always need to prove myself," Paolo says. As a graduate student, his performance is outstanding with a 4.0 GPA and several publications at his current school.

Case 4 My difference is getting almost invisible.

Leona Tobar, in her early 30s, grew up in Bogota, the capital city of Colombia, and she has been with her wife for six years. Leona, as a researcher, worked for a year at a public institution in Bogota. She has bad memories from the time she worked there, because of the homophobic work environment. "It was not only homophobic, but also macho. Gender roles were well established and I did not like it," she says. When Leona brought up the subject of her partner with her coworkers, everyone assumed she had a husband. She said to them "I have never said that my partner is my husband. You have to ask first." "They did not like me, because I am different," Leona says. Her coworkers left her out of social meetings and conversations.

Leona, as a Fulbright scholar, came to the USA in 2013. As a pre-orientation for the Fulbright scholarship program, Leona was in Virginia for two weeks and it was a traumatic experience for her where there were numerous homophobic slurs or sexist jokes.

Substantial evidence indicates that workplace harassment or discrimination not only violate human rights, but also waste or lose the human talent needed, and eventually, stifle innovation (Gao & Zhang, 2015; USAID, 2014). Furthermore, previous empirical studies (Silverschanz, Cortina, Konik, & Magley, 2008; Waldo, 1999) found that LGBT employees who are exposed to anti-gay jokes or heterosexism have greater organizational withdrawal and lower satisfaction with work, coworkers, and supervisors.

"Young boys tend to show off their masculinity, making silly jokes about women or gays. The program has to correct it," said Leona. Indeed, she wrote a letter to the Fulbright organization arguing that the orientation program should cover not only the topic of racial and cultural diversity but also sexual orientation diversity. Leona believes that education and awareness help people understand diversity. In the same vein, Bell, Connerley, and Cocchiara (2009) demonstrated that diversity training within the workplace should also include sexual orientation diversity. Bell et al. (2009) also asserted that diversity training would prevent discrimination by increasing empathy, awareness, and knowledge while reducing stereotypes.

Now, Leona is studying for her PhD in Florida. "I feel very lucky, because I never have felt any discrimination here. I feel accepted by my program, my classmates, and my professors," she says, "Also, my department (public administration) is serious about jokes." Her current school embraces diversity providing several programs for LGBTs. For instance, in a school-based mentoring program, senior LGBT students mentor LGBT newcomers helping startups, offering advice, and sharing their experiences. "I met my mentor who gives me a lot advice. Everything (i.e., the adaptation process) was smooth," said Leona. "Always look for help and try to build a support net," Leona recommended to other LGBT expatriates.

On a personal note, Leona mentioned that she will not go to a closed or homogeneous country because she may be at higher risk of being discriminated against. "I [will] never put myself in danger. I am never going to be in an environment where something represents a threat to me due to my sexual orientation," said Leona. In order for LGBT expatriates to feel safe in the IA and reach their full potential, a feeling of security and acceptance of their sexual orientation needs to be ensured.

Discussion and Conclusion

Knowledge and innovation are highly related to human talent since, after all, humans are the ones who directly possess knowledge, and innovation is mostly a group activity. In this regard, although many non-traditional talents hold great potential for leading innovation, to date, the majority of MNEs have preferred traditional talent and impeded the development of their own innovative capacity. In other words, MNEs have been hesitant to recognize and value non-traditional expatriates' talents when it comes to selecting expatriates for IAs (Hewlett, Luce, & West, 2005). With social identity theory, uncertainty identity theory, similarity-attraction paradigm, and attraction-selection-attrition framework as backdrops, we discuss why non-traditional talents have been excluded in IAs and what relationships between diverse human capital and innovation might exist.

As the global economy has become more knowledge- and innovation-based, the demand for talented expatriates has grown continuously (Scullion, 1994); this results in a *global talent shortage* that is one of the biggest challenges facing MNEs at present. Increasing talent shortages across the globe pose a significant threat to MNEs; yet simultaneously, they increase the recruiting opportunity for talent with non-traditional backgrounds, including sexual orientation. Indeed, in recent years, there has been a growing number of MNEs that are coming forward to include more diverse talent in their IAs. In support of this trend, we address that MNEs should cast nets beyond traditional talent pools, particularly taking LGBT talents into consideration to fill expatriate positions.

Diversity has long been overlooked in innovation research, albeit with increasing recognition of its importance as a key driver of innovation. According to a study conducted by the Center For Talent Innovation (Center For Talent Innovation, 2013), MNEs embracing inherent diversity, such as sexual orientation and religious background in the workplace, have much greater possibilities for innovation. This is not only because of an influx of diverse inputs that diverse talent generates, but also because diversity triggers more open, frequent, and creative information processing that is oftentimes lacking in homogeneous groups (Milliken & Martins, 1996). Consistent with this, several scholars have demonstrated that homogeneous groups may hinder innovative thoughts and ideas (Bantel & Jackson, 1989; Cox, 1993; Nijstad & De Dreu, 2002).

Innovation is not a single level of matter. In other words, neither individual-level factors nor organizational-level factors alone can fully explain innovation (Van Everdingen & Waarts, 2003; Waarts & Van Everdingen, 2005); rather, including multilevel factors provides a richer understanding and a clearer direction for innovation. In short, as four case findings have shown, innovation hinges on various levels, including individual-level (micro), organizational-level (meso), and national-level (macro). Table 5.1 provides details of contextual factors at three levels affecting innovation. In addition, Fig. 5.1 depicts a model for integrating multilevel sources on innovation.

Table 5.1 Three levels of innovation factors

Levels	Key factors affecting innovation
Individual level (Micro)	• Perceived fairness of the equality
	• Perceived organizational support
Organizational level (Meso)	• Open discussion
	• Diversity training
	• Organizational diversity
	• Inclusive corporate culture
	• Diversity-friendly workplace
	• Equal employment opportunity
	• Diverse employee resource groups
	• Organizational guidelines and regulations
	• TMT's favorable attitudes toward diversity
National level (Macro)	• Culture of tolerance and acceptance
	• LGBT-related legislation (e.g., non-discrimination laws, equal rights, marriage equality)

The Center For Talent Innovation study (2013) reported further that diverse and innovative MNEs are highly correlated with market growth. More specifically, 75 percent of respondents who work for MNEs with diversity are more likely to have a marketable idea implemented. Similarly, Gunday et al. (2011) found positive effects of innovations on firm performance.

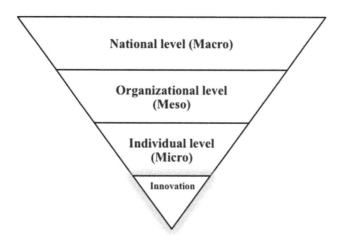

Fig. 5.1. Innovation model

On balance, with increasing needs for MNEs to promote innovation in order to compete in today's global business environment (Subramaniam & Youndt, 2005), the more an MNE values non-traditional diversity, the greater the innovation and productivity (Cox, Lobel, & McLeod, 1991; McLeod, Lobel, & Cox, 1996).

Implications

Up until recently, few qualitative studies have been conducted and very little is known about non-traditional talents. In this sense, this paper contributes to advance the state of our empirical understanding of non-traditional human capital, particularly LGBT expatriates in IAs.

Besides, the present study attempts to address some of the theoretical gaps in the extant literature on diverse human capital and innovation. Although an increasing number of MNEs began supporting the inclusion of LGBT employees largely due to the substantial social progress that has been made by LGBT activities in recent years, this is not simply because of moral and legal imperatives; rather, this is because of the innovation and productivity that MNEs can gain from non-traditional talents (particularly in this paper, LGBT expatriates in IAs). Therefore, the findings of this paper have implications for MNEs sending expatriates on IAs. Although all four LGBT expatriates reported successful outcomes in their IAs, it is also clear that many of them struggled with discrimination based on sexual orientation during the years abroad. Their angst is clearly articulated.

Discrimination at work has a profoundly detrimental effect on the MNE, contributing to low morale, reduced productivity, and high conflict (Barclay & Scott, 2006). Furthermore, innovation suffers when all talents are not valued. Therefore, discrimination against LBGT expatriates in the IA jeopardizes not only LGBT expatriates themselves, but also the entire MNE's competitiveness and sustainability.

To reduce discrimination based on sexual orientation, first and foremost, MNEs should initiate and enforce zero-tolerance policies and practices toward sexual orientation discrimination. The ethical codes and guidelines on LGBT expatriates are part and parcel of IHRM policies. Beyond simply implementing policies and practices, more fundamentally, MNEs should create a diversity-friendly workplace environment. Training expatriates, including LGBT expatriates, is critical, because education fosters tolerance and acceptance (Vogt, 1997). According to Cox and Blake (1991), savvy MNEs are successful in embracing diversity and managing diversity properly; as a consequence, they enjoy greater innovation and productivity.

Future Directions

Intersectionality

Further research on non-traditional expatriates, especially LGBT expatriates, should aim to explore the impact of LGBT expatriates' "intersectionality" (Ali, Malik, Pereira, & Al Ariss, 2016). In other words, LGBT expatriates may also differ from each other in terms of gender, age, race, marital status, and talent; and therefore, what difficulties gay expatriates experienced in their international assignment might not be the same as those experienced by lesbian expatriates. Consequently, the ways to protect gay expatriates might not work for lesbian expatriates. Indeed, Gedro (2010) found that lesbian expatriates face far more discrimination in the international environment, because they face discrimination for their gayness and their femaleness in addition to their foreignness (Olsen & Martins, 2009). Similarly, Thorpe-Moscon and Pollack (2014) presented that lesbian employees are more likely to lower their aspirations to contribute to the company (42 percent) than their gay counterparts (29 percent) due to their additional "otherness."

In the same vein, LGBT expatriates with their same sex spouses may have complex challenges, including obtaining a marriage certificate. Despite the fact that same sex married expatriates compose four percent of total expatriates according to a survey by Brookfield Global Relocation Services (2015), Mercer's Worldwide Survey (2011) reported that only 38 percent of the company had broadened the definition of spouse regardless of their sex.

Limitations

Like any research study, this study has limitations. The first limitation of the current study is the small number of cases; hence, the generalizability and replicability of the case findings are limited. Yet, as Stake (1995) stated, the real business of case study is particularization, not generalization. The main purpose of case study research is not necessarily to generalize hypotheses, but to observe phenomena richly and develop a better understanding of each case. Further limitations include the fact that participants were somewhat biased; in particular, all participants are highly educated with graduate degrees and bisexual and transgender expatriates are not included. Therefore, future cases need to have greater demographic variance.

Appendix 1: Interview Questions

Part 1
1. What is your nationality?
2. How long have you been at this company?
3. Describe international assignments you've been on.
   a. List countries and cities you've been assigned to.
   b. For how long?
   c. Describe the main motives for accepting international assignments.
   d. Describe the type of training you received, either pre-departure or overseas.

Part 2
1. Explain the type of diversity you have (e.g., sexual orientation, religion, and family structure).
   a. Was your company aware of your diversity at the time of recruiting expatriates for international assignment?
   b. Given your diversity, describe your company's organizational culture (e.g., HR policies, workplace climate).
2. Describe in detail any and every challenge you've encountered based on your diversity in international assignments.
   a. How did you deal or overcome such challenges?
   b. How did these challenges impact on the success or failure (both real and perceived) of your assignment?
   c. Describe how your company helped you deal or overcome these challenges.
   d. What recommendations would you have for organizations regarding reducing such challenges (e.g., HR policies, diversity training program)?
   e. What recommendations would you have for other future non-traditional expatriates?

Part 3
1. Describe what expatriate success or failure in an international assignment means in your home and host culture, respectively.
2. Describe what expatriate success or failure in an international assignment means to you, personally.
a. Did the company encourage you or discourage you from taking the assignment? Explain.
b. How do you evaluate your performance in international assignments? Explain.
3. Describe how your employers or company evaluated your performance in international assignments.
4. Before we finish, please leave any final comments if you have.

Appendix 2: Participant Details

	Sexual orientation	Age	Type of expatriation	Role	Industry	Length of interview
Bert Cotreau	Gay	Retiring age	SIE	Employer	Agriculture, NGO, Education	50 min
James Fleck	Gay	20s	OE	Intern	Social media	30 min
Paolo Martien	Gay	20s	SIE	Employee	Academia	45 min
Leona Tobar	Lesbian	30s	SIE	Employee	Academia	60 min

References

Abbott, A. (1992). From causes to events notes on narrative positivism. *Sociological Methods and Research, 20*(4), 428–455.

Adler, N. J. (1979). Women as androgynous managers: A conceptualization of the potential for American women in international management. *International Journal of Intercultural Relations, 3*(4), 407–436.

Ali, F., Malik, A., Pereira, V., & Al Ariss, A. (2016). A relational understanding of work-life balance of Muslim migrant women in the west: Future research agenda. *The International Journal of Human Resource Management*, 1–19.

Ancona, D. G., & Caldwell, D. F. (1992). Bridging the boundary: External activity and performance in organizational teams. *Administrative Science Quarterly, 37*, 634–665.

Andresen, M., Biemann, T., & Pattie, M. W. (2015). What makes them move abroad? Reviewing and exploring differences between self-initiated and assigned expatriation. *The International Journal of Human Resource Management, 26*(7), 932–947.

Ashforth, B. E., & Mael, F. (1989). Social identity theory and the organization. *Academy of Management Review, 14*(1), 20–39.

Bantel, K. A., & Jackson, S. E. (1989). Top management and innovations in banking: Does the composition of the top team make a difference? *Strategic Management Journal, 10*(S1), 107–124.

Barak, M. E. M. (1999). Repositioning occupational social work in the new millennium. *Administration in Social Work, 23*(3-4), 201–210.

Barak, M. E. M., & Levin, A. (2002). Outside of the corporate mainstream and excluded from the work community: A study of diversity, job satisfaction and well-being. *Community, Work and Family, 5*(2), 133–157.

Barclay, J. M., & Scott, L. J. (2006). Transsexuals and workplace diversity: A case of "change" management. *Personnel Review, 35*(4), 487–502.

Bassett-Jones, N. (2005). The paradox of diversity management, creativity and innovation. *Creativity and Innovation Management, 14*(2), 169–175.

Beck, U., & Beck-Gernsheim, E. (2002). *Individualization: Institutionalized individualism and its social and political consequences*. London, England: Sage.

Bell, M. P., Connerley, M. L., & Cocchiara, F. K. (2009). The case for mandatory diversity education. *Academy of Management Learning and Education, 8*(4), 597–609.

Bell, M. P., Özbilgin, M. F., Beauregard, T. A., & Sürgevil, O. (2011). Voice, silence, and diversity in 21st century organizations: Strategies for inclusion of gay, lesbian, bisexual, and transgender employees. *Human Resource Management, 50*(1), 131–146.

Berry, J. W. (1969). On cross-cultural comparability. *International Journal of Psychology, 4*(2), 119–128.

Berry, J. W. (1989). Imposed etics-emics-derived etics: The operationalization of a compelling idea. *International Journal of Psychology, 24*(6), 721–735.

Biemann, T., & Andresen, M. (2010). Self-initiated foreign expatriates versus assigned expatriates: Two distinct types of international careers? *Journal of Managerial Psychology, 25*(4), 430–448.

Bochner, A. P. (1991). On the paradigm that would not die. *Communication Yearbook, 14*, 484–491.

Boeker, W. (1997). Strategic change: The influence of managerial characteristics and organizational growth. *Academy of Management Journal, 40*(1), 152–170.

Boje, D. M. (2001). *Narrative methods for organizational and communication research*. London, England: Sage.

Bossard, A. B., & Peterson, R. B. (2005). The repatriate experience as seen by American expatriates. *Journal of World Business, 40*(1), 9–28.

Bowen, F., & Blackmon, K. (2003). Spirals of silence: The dynamic effects of diversity on organizational voice. *Journal of Management Studies, 40*(6), 1393–1417.

Brookfield Global Relocation Services. (2014). *Global Mobility Trends Survey.* Retrieved August 5, 2015, from http://www.brookfieldgrs.com

Brookfield Global Relocation Services. (2015). *Global Mobility Trends Survey.* Retrieved August 5, 2015, from http://www.brookfieldgrs.com

Byrne, D. (1997). An overview (and underview) of research and theory within the attraction paradigm. *Journal of Social and Personal Relationships, 14*(3), 417–431.

Byrne, D., & Lamberth, J. (1971). Cognitive and reinforcement theories as complementary approaches to the study of attraction. In B. I. Murstein (Ed.), *Theories of attraction and love* (pp. 59–84). New York, NY: Springer.

Byrne, D., & Nelson, D. (1965). Attraction as a linear function of proportion of positive reinforcements. *Journal of Personality and Social Psychology, 1*(6), 659–663.

Byrne, D. E. (1971). *The attraction paradigm* (Vol. 11). New York: Academic Press.

Callender, C., Kochems, L. M., Bleibtreu-Ehrenberg, G., Broch, H. B., Brown, J. K., Datan, N., et al. (1983). The North American Berdache [and comments and reply]. *Current Anthropology, 24*, 443–470.

Center for Talent Innovation. (2013). *Innovation, diversity, and market growth.* Retrieved August 5, 2015, from http://www.talentinnovation.org/

Center for Talent Innovation. (2016). *Out in the world: Securing LGBT rights in the global marketplace*. Retrieved August 5, 2015, from http://www.talentinnovation.org/

Chatman, J. A., & O'Reilly, C. A. (2004). Asymmetric reactions to work group sex diversity among men and women. *Academy of Management Journal, 47*(2), 193–208.

Cohen, W. M., & Levinthal, D. A. (1990). Absorptive capacity: A new perspective on learning and innovation. *Administrative Science Quarterly, 35*(1), 128–152.

Collings, D. G., Scullion, H., & Morley, M. J. (2007). Changing patterns of global staffing in the multinational enterprise: Challenges to the conventional expatriate assignment and emerging alternatives. *Journal of World Business, 42*(2), 198–213.

Collins, D. (2009). "We're there and queer" homonormative mobility and lived experience among gay expatriates in Manila. *Gender and Society, 23*(4), 465–493.

Cox, T. (1993). *Cultural diversity in organizations: Theory, research & practice.* San Francisco, CA: Berrett-Koehler.

Cox, T. (1994). *Cultural diversity in organizations: Theory, research and practice.* San Francisco, CA: Berrett-Koehler Publishers.

Cox, T., & Blake, S. (1991). Managing cultural diversity: Implications for organizational competitiveness. *The Executive, 5*(3), 45–56.

Cox, T., Lobel, S. A., & McLeod, P. L. (1991). Effects of ethnic group cultural differences on cooperative and competitive behavior on a group task. *Academy of Management journal, 34*(4), 827–847.

Czarniawska, B. (1998). *Qualitative research methods series: A narrative approach to organizational studies.* Thousand Oaks, CA: Sage.

Czarniawska, B. (2004). *Narratives in social science research.* London, England: Sage.

Dahlin, K. B., Weingart, L. R., & Hinds, P. J. (2005). Team diversity and information use. *Academy of Management Journal, 48*(6), 1107–1123.

Day, D. V., & Bedeian, A. G. (1995). Personality similarity and work-related outcomes among African-American nursing personnel: A test of the supplementary model of person-environment congruence. *Journal of Vocational Behavior, 46*(1), 55–70.

Dovidio, J. F., Kawakami, K., & Gaertner, S. L. (2002). Implicit and explicit prejudice and interracial interaction. *Journal of Personality and Social Psychology, 82*(1), 62–68.

Eisenhardt, K. M. (1989). Building theories from case study research. *Academy of Management Review, 14*(4), 532–550.

Elenkov, D. S., Judge, W., & Wright, P. (2005). Strategic leadership and executive innovation influence: An international multi-cluster comparative study. *Strategic Management Journal, 26*(7), 665–682.

Findler, L., Wind, L. H., & Barak, M. E. M. (2007). The challenge of workforce management in a global society: Modeling the relationship between diversity, inclusion, organizational culture, and employee well-being, job satisfaction and organizational commitment. *Administration in Social Work, 31*(3), 63–94.

Florida, R. (2004). *The rise of the creative class.* New York, NY: Basic Books.

Forbes. (2011, July). *Global diversity and inclusion: Fostering innovation through a diverse workforce.* Retrieved August 5, 2015, from https://images.forbes.com/forbesinsights/StudyPDFs/Innovation_Through_Diversity.pdf

Gao, H., & Zhang, W. (2015). *Does workplace discrimination impede innovation?* Retrieved August 5, 2015, from www3.ntu.edu.sg/home/hsgao/GaoZhang20150307.pdf

Gedro, J. (2012). *A critical examination of the cosmopolitan manager.* Retrieved August 5, 2015, from www.ufhrd.co.uk/wordpress/wp-content/uploads/2012/10/UFHRD2012Critical7revised.pdf

Gedro, J. (2010). The lavender ceiling atop the global closet: Human resource development and lesbian expatriates. *Human Resource Development Review, 9*(4), 385–404.

Gedro, J., Mizzi, R. C., Rocco, T. S., & van Loo, J. (2013). Going global: Professional mobility and concerns for LGBT workers. *Human Resource Development International, 16*(3), 282–297.

Geertz, C. (1973). Thick description: Toward an Interpretive theory of culture. In C. Geertz (Ed.), *In the interpretation of cultures: Selected essay* (pp. 1–32). New York, NY: Basic Books.

Gertsen, M. C., & Søderberg, A. M. (2010). Expatriate stories about cultural encounters: A narrative approach to cultural learning processes in multinational companies. *Scandinavian Journal of Management, 26*(3), 248–257.

Glanz, J. (1993). *Bureaucracy and professionalization.* State College, PA: Penn State University Press.

Gössling, T., & Rutten, R. (2007). Innovation in regions. *European Planning Studies, 15*(2), 253–270.

Grieve, P. G., & Hogg, M. A. (1999). Subjective uncertainty and intergroup discrimination in the minimal group situation. *Personality and Social Psychology Bulletin, 25*(8), 926–940.

Gunday, G., Ulusoy, G., Kilic, K., & Alpkan, L. (2011). Effects of innovation types on firm performance. *International Journal of Production Economics, 133*(2), 662–676.

Halliday, C. S., Kim, K. W., Zhao, Y., & Von Glinow, M. A. (2015, June). *Non-traditional managers in international assignments.* Paper presented at the Academy of International Business, Bangalore, India.

Hambrick, D. C., & Mason, P. A. (1984). Upper echelons: The organization as a reflection of its top managers. *Academy of Management Review, 9*(2), 193–206.

Hambrick, D. C., Cho, T. S., & Chen, M. J. (1996). The influence of top management team heterogeneity on firms' competitive moves. *Administrative Science Quarterly, 41*, 659–684.

Hanna, P. (2012). Using internet technologies (such as Skype) as a research medium: A research note. *Qualitative Research, 12*(2), 239–242.

Hannabuss, S. (1996). Research interviews. *New Library World, 97*(5), 22–30.

Harrison, D. A., Price, K. H., & Bell, M. P. (1998). Beyond relational demography: Time and the effects of surface-and deep-level diversity on work group cohesion. *Academy of Management Journal, 41*(1), 96–107.

Harvey, C. P., & Allard, M. J. (2002). *Understanding and managing diversity: Readings, cases, and exercises.* Upper Saddle River, NJ: Prentice Hall.

Harzing, A. W., & Christensen, C. (2004). Expatriate failure: Time to abandon the concept? *Career Development International, 9*(7), 616–626.

Herring, C., & Henderson, L. (2014). *Diversity in organizations: A critical examination.* New York, NY: Routledge.

Hewlett, S. A., Luce, C. B., West, C., Chernikoff, H., Samalin, D., & Shiller, P. (2005). *Invisible lives: Celebrating and leveraging diversity in the executive suite.* New York: Center for Work-Life Policy.

Hewlett, S. A., & Yoshino, K. (2016). *LGBT-inclusive companies are better at 3 big things.* Retrieved August 5, 2015, from https://hbr.org/2016/02/lgbt-inclusive-companies-are-better-at-3-big-things#

Hipsher, S. (2008). *Expatriates in Asia: Breaking free from the colonial paradigm.* Oxford, England: Chandos Publishing.

Hogg, M. A. (2007). Uncertainty–identity theory. *Advances in Experimental Social Psychology, 39*, 69–126.

Hogg, M. A., & Grieve, P. (1999). Social identity theory and the crisis of confidence in social psychology: A commentary, and some research on uncertainty reduction. *Asian Journal of Social Psychology, 2*(1), 79–93.

Hogg, M. A., & Mullin, B. A. (1999). Joining groups to reduce uncertainty: Subjective uncertainty reduction and group identification. In D. Abrams & M. A. Hogg (Eds.), *Social identity and social cognition* (pp. 249–279). Oxford: Blackwell.

Human Rights Campaign Foundation (HRCF). (2016). *Corporate equality index: Rating american workplaces on lesbian, gay, bisexual and transgender equality.* Washington, DC: Author. Retrieved March 5, 2016, from http://www.hrc.org/campaigns/corporate-equality-index

Hutchings, K., French, E., & Hatcher, T. (2008). Lament of the ignored expatriate: An examination of organisational and social network support for female expatriates in China. *Equal Opportunities International, 27*(4), 372–391.

Inkson, K., Arthur, M. B., Pringle, J., & Barry, S. (1998). Expatriate assignment versus overseas experience: Contrasting models of international human resource development. *Journal of World Business, 32*(4), 351–368.

Islam, M. R., & Hewstone, M. (1993). Dimensions of contact as predictors of intergroup anxiety, perceived out-group variability, and out-group attitude: An integrative model. *Personality and Social Psychology Bulletin, 19*(6), 700–710.

Jackson, S. E., Brett, J. F., Sessa, V. I., Cooper, D. M., Julin, J. A., & Peyronnin, K. (1991). Some differences make a difference: Individual dissimilarity and group heterogeneity as correlates of recruitment, promotions, and turnover. *Journal of Applied Psychology, 76*(5), 675.

Jackson, S. E., May, K. E., & Whitney, K. (1995). Understanding the dynamics of diversity in decision-making team. In R. A. Guzzo, E. Salas, & Associates (Eds.), *Team effectiveness and decision making in organizations* (pp. 204–261). San Francisco, CA: Jossey-Bass.

Jiménez, J. M. R., Ruiz-Arroyo, M., & Pulles, D. C. (2014, January). Gender diversity, knowledge combination and innovation in the technological context. *Academy of Management Proceedings, 2014*(1), 16531. Academy of Management.

Kim, K. W., Halliday, C. S., Zhao, Y., Wang, C., & Von Glinow, M. A. (2016). Rewarding self-initiated expatriates: A skills-based approach. *Thunderbird International Business Review*, doi:10.1002/tie.21832.

Kunze, F., Böhm, S. A., & Bruch, H. (2011). Age diversity, age discrimination climate and performance consequences: A cross organizational study. *Journal of Organizational Behavior, 32*(2), 264–290.

Kurdek, L. A. (2004). Are gay and lesbian cohabiting couples really different from heterosexual married couples? *Journal of Marriage and Family, 66*(4), 880–900.

Lev, A. I. (2007). Transgender communities: Developing identity through connection. In K. J. Bieschke, R. M. Perez, & K. A. DeBord (Eds.), *Handbook of counseling and psychotherapy with lesbian, gay, bisexual, and transgender clients* (pp. 147–175). Washington, DC: American Psychological Association.

Levine, M. P., & Leonard, R. (1984). Discrimination against lesbians in the work force. *Signs, 9*(4), 700–710.

Li, C. R., Liu, Y. Y., Lin, C. J., & Ma, H. J. (2016). Top management team diversity, ambidextrous innovation and the mediating effect of top team decision-making processes. *Industry and Innovation*, 1–16.

Malinowski, B. (1922). *Argonauts of the western Pacific*. London, England: Routledge and Kegan Paul.

Mamman, A., & Richards, D. (1996). Perceptions and possibilities of intercultural adjustment: Some neglected characteristics of expatriates. *International Business Review, 5*(3), 283–301.

Marshall, C., & Rossman, G. B. (2014). *Designing qualitative research* (6th ed.). Thousands Oaks, CA: Sage.

McKinsey & Co. (2015, January). *Why diversity matters*. Retrieved August 5, 2015, from http://www.mckinsey.com/business-functions/organization/our-insights/why-diversity-matters

McLeod, P. L., Lobel, S. A., & Cox, T. (1996). Ethnic diversity and creativity in small groups. *Small Group Research, 27*(2), 248–264.

McNamee, R. (2004). *The new normal: Great opportunities in a time of great risk*. New York, NY: Penguin.

McNulty, Y. (2015). Acculturating non-traditional expatriates: A case study of single parent, overseas adoption, split family, and lesbian assignees. *International Journal of Intercultural Relations, 49*, 278–293.

McNulty, Y., & Hutchings, K. (2016). Looking for global talent in all the right places: A critical literature review of non-traditional expatriates. *The International Journal of Human Resource Management, 27*(7), 699–728.

McPhail, R., McNulty, Y., & Hutchings, K. (2016). Lesbian and gay expatriation: Opportunities, barriers and challenges for global mobility. *The International Journal of Human Resource Management, 27*(3), 382–406.

Mercer. (2011). *Worldwide Survey of International Assignment Policies and Practices (WIAPP)*. Retrieved August 5, 2015, from www.imercer.com/products/2011/worldwideIAPP.aspx

Mercer. (2014). *North America LGBT global mobility pulse survey*. Retrieved August 5, 2015, from https://info.mercer.com/Talent_Mobility-LGBT-Global-Mobility-Survey.html

Meyskens, M., Von Glinow, M. A., Werther Jr., W. B., & Clarke, L. (2009). The paradox of international talent: Alternative forms of international assignments. *The International Journal of Human Resource Management, 20*(6), 1439–1450.

Mike, M. (2013, January). *Leadership and the new normal*. Retrieved August 5, 2015, from http://www.ceo.com/leadership_and_management/leadership-and-the-new-normal/

Miller, C. C., Burke, L. M., & Glick, W. H. (1998). Cognitive diversity among upper-echelon executives: Implications for strategic decision processes. *Strategic Management Journal, 19*(1), 39–58.

Milliken, F. J., & Martins, L. L. (1996). Searching for common threads: Understanding the multiple effects of diversity in organizational groups. *Academy of Management Review, 21*(2), 402–433.

Miralles-Vazquez, L., & McGaughey, S. L. (2016). Non-traditional international assignments, knowledge and innovation: An exploratory study of women's experiences. *Prometheus, 27*(7), 1–27.

Montoya, R. M., & Horton, R. S. (2004). On the importance of cognitive evaluation as a determinant of interpersonal attraction. *Journal of Personality and Social Psychology, 86*(5), 696–712.

Mott-Stenerson, B. (2008). Integrating qualitative and quantitative theoretical perspectives in applied advertising research. *Journal of Business Research, 61*(5), 431–433.

Nelson, R. R., & Winter, S. G. (1982). The Schumpeterian tradeoff revisited. *The American Economic Review, 72*(1), 114–132.

Niebuhr, A. (2010). Migration and innovation: Does cultural diversity matter for regional R&D activity? *Papers in Regional Science, 89*(3), 563–585.

Nieto, M. J., & Santamaría, L. (2007). The importance of diverse collaborative networks for the novelty of product innovation. *Technovation, 27*(6), 367–377.

Nijstad, B. A., & De Dreu, C. K. (2002). Creativity and group innovation. *Applied Psychology, 51*(3), 400–406.

Olsen, J. E., & Martins, L. L. (2009). The effects of expatriate demographic characteristics on adjustment: A social identity approach. *Human Resource Management, 48*(2), 311–328.

Orbuch, T. L. (1997). People's accounts count: The sociology of accounts. *Annual Review of Sociology, 23*, 455–478.

O'Reilly, C. A., Williams, K. Y., & Barsade, S. G. (1998). Group demography and innovation: Does diversity help? In E. Mannix & M. Neale (Eds.), *Research on managing groups and teams* (pp. 183–207). Greenwich, CT: JAI Press.

Østergaard, C. R., Timmermans, B., & Kristinsson, K. (2011). Does a different view create something new? The effect of employee diversity on innovation. *Research Policy, 40*(3), 500–509.

Oyserman, D. (2007). Social identity and self-regulation. In A. W. Kruglanski & E. T. Higgins (Eds.), *Social psychology: Handbook of basic principles* (pp. 432–453). New York, NY: Guilford.

Özbilgin, M. F., & Woodward, D. (2004). 'Belonging' and 'otherness': Sex equality in banking in Turkey and Britain. *Gender, Work and Organization, 11*(6), 668–688.

Page, S. (2007, January). *Diversity powers innovation*. Retrieved August 5, 2015, from http://americanprogress.org/issues/economy/news/2007/01/26/2523/diversity-powers-innovation/

Paisley, V., & Tayar, M. (2016). Lesbian, gay, bisexual and transgender (LGBT) expatriates: An intersectionality perspective. *The International Journal of Human Resource Management, 27*(7), 766–780.

Peltokorpi, V., & Jintae Froese, F. (2009). Organizational expatriates and self-initiated expatriates: Who adjusts better to work and life in Japan? *The International Journal of Human Resource Management, 20*(5), 1096–1112.

Peterson, M. F., & Pike, K. L. (2002). Emics and etics for organizational studies: A lesson in contrast from linguistics. *International Journal of Cross Cultural Management, 2*(1), 5–19.

Pike, K. L. (1967). *Language in relation to a unified theory of the structure of human behavior*. The Hague, Netherlands: Mouton and Co.

Pitcher, P., & Smith, A. D. (2001). Top management team heterogeneity: Personality, power, and proxies. *Organization Science, 12*(1), 1–18.

Qian, C., Cao, Q., & Takeuchi, R. (2013). Top management team functional diversity and organizational innovation in China: The moderating effects of environment. *Strategic Management Journal, 34*(1), 110–120.

Ragins, B. R., & Cornwell, J. M. (2001). Pink triangles: Antecedents and consequences of perceived workplace discrimination against gay and lesbian employees. *Journal of Applied Psychology, 86*(6), 1244–1261.

Ragins, B. R., Cornwell, J. M., & Miller, J. S. (2003). Heterosexism in the workplace do race and gender matter? *Group and Organization Management, 28*(1), 45–74.

Reskin, B. (1993). Sex segregation in the workplace. *Annual Review of Sociology, 19*(1), 241–270.

Rogers, E. M. (1962). *Diffusion of innovations*. New York, NY: Free Press.

Rogers, E. M. (2010). *Diffusion of innovations*. New York, NY: Simon and Schuster.

Rumens, N., & Broomfield, J. (2012). Gay men in the police: Identity disclosure and management issues. *Human Resource Management Journal, 22*(3), 283–298.

Rumens, N., & Kerfoot, D. (2009). Gay men at work: (Re) constructing the self as professional. *Human Relations, 62*(5), 763–786.

Schneider, B. (1987). The people make the place. *Personnel Psychology, 40*(3), 437–453.

Schumpeter, J. A. (1934). *The theory of economic development: An inquiry into profits, capital, credit, interest, and the business cycle* (Vol. 55). New York, NY: Transaction Publishers.

Scullion, H. (1994). Staffing policies and strategic control in British multinationals. *International Studies of Management and Organization, 24*(3), 86–104.

Selmer, J. (1995). *Expatriate management: New ideas for international business.* Westport, CT: Greenwood Publishing Group.

Silverschanz, P., Cortina, L. M., Konik, J., & Magley, V. J. (2008). Slurs, snubs, and queer jokes: Incidence and impact of heterosexist harassment in academia. *Sex Roles, 58*(3-4), 179–191.

Søderberg, A. M. (2006). Narrative interviewing and narrative analysis in a study of a cross-border merger. *Management International Review, 46*(4), 397–416.

Soin, K., & Scheytt, T. (2006). Making the case for narrative methods in cross-cultural organizational research. *Organizational Research Methods, 9*(1), 55–77.

Stake, R. E. (1995). *The art of case study research.* Thousand Oaks, CA: Sage.

Subramaniam, M., & Youndt, M. A. (2005). The influence of intellectual capital on the types of innovative capabilities. *Academy of Management Journal, 48*(3), 450–463.

Sunnafrank, M. (1991). Interpersonal attraction and attitude similarity: A communication-based assessment. *Communication Yearbook, 14*, 451–483.

Sunnafrank, M. (1992). On debunking the attitude similarity myth. *Communications Monographs, 59*(2), 164–179.

Suutari, V., & Brewster, C. (2001). Making their own way: International experience through self-initiated foreign assignment. *Journal of World Business, 35*(4), 417–436.

Tajfel, H. (1982). Social psychology of intergroup relations. *Annual Review of Psychology, 33*(1), 1–39.

Tajfel, H., & Turner, J. C. (1979). An integrative theory of intergroup conflict. In W. G. Austin & S. Worchel (Eds.), *The social psychology of intergroup relations* (pp. 33–47). Monterey, CA: Brook/Cole.

Takeuchi, R. (2010). A critical review of expatriate adjustment research through a multiple stakeholder view: Progress, emerging trends, and prospects. *Journal of Management, 36*(4), 1040–1064.

Talke, K., Salomo, S., & Kock, A. (2011). Top management team diversity and strategic innovation orientation: The relationship and consequences for innovativeness and performance. *Journal of Product Innovation Management, 28*(6), 819–832.

Thorpe-Moscon, J., & Pollack, A. (2014). *Feeling different: Being the "other" in US workplaces.* Retrieved August 5, 2015, from www.catalyst.org

Toossi, M. (2012). Labor force projections to 2020: A more slowly growing workforce. *Monthly Laboratory Review, 135*, 43–64.

Tung, R. L. (1981). Selection and training of personnel for overseas assignments. *Columbia Journal of World Business, 16*(1), 68–78.

Tung, R. L. (1993). Managing cross-national and intra-national diversity. *Human Resource Management, 32*(4), 461–477.

Turban, D. B., & Jones, A. P. (1988). Supervisor-subordinate similarity: Types, effects, and mechanisms. *Journal of Applied Psychology, 73*(2), 228–234.

U.S. Commission on International Religious Freedom. (2010). *Annual report of the United States Commission on International Religious Freedom.* Retrieved August 5, 2015, from http://www.uscirf.gov/countries/saudi-arabia

U.S. Department of Labor (2010). *Bureau of labor statistics.* Washington, DC: US Government Printing Office.

Ulijn, J. M., & Weggeman, M. C. D. P. (2001). Towards an innovation culture: What are it's national, corporate, marketing and engineering aspects, some experimental evidence. In C. L. Cooper, P. C. Earley, & S. Cartwright (Eds.), *Handbook of organizational culture and climate* (pp. 487–517). London, England: Wiley.

USAID. (2014, May). *LGBT vision for action: Promoting and supporting the inclusion of lesbian, gay, bisexual, and transgender individuals.* Retrieved August 5, 2015, from https://www.google.com/url?sa=t&rct=j&q=&esrc=s&source =web&cd=1&ved=0ahUKEwjvrMHpo7DMAhWEWh4KHTC6BtIQFggc MAA&url=https%3A%2F%2Fwww.usaid.gov%2Fsites%2Fdefault%2Ffile s%2Fdocuments%2F1874%2FLGBT%2520Vision.pdf&usg=AFQjCNEp XzLAzYtVxt7AP32jPCCz1AeXVA&bvm=bv.120853415,d.dmo&cad=rja

Valente, T. W., & Rogers, E. M. (1995). The origins and development of the diffusion of innovations paradigm as an example of scientific growth. *Science Communication, 16*(3), 242–273.

Van Everdingen, Y. M., & Waarts, E. (2003). The effect of national culture on the adoption of innovations. *Marketing Letters, 14*(3), 217–232.

Vogt, W. P. (1997). *Tolerance and education: Learning to live with diversity and difference.* Thousand Oaks, CA: Sage.

Von Glinow, M. A., Shapiro, D. L., & Brett, J. M. (2004). Can we talk, and should we? Managing emotional conflict in multicultural teams. *Academy of Management Review, 29*(4), 578–592.

Waarts, E., & Van Everdingen, Y. (2005). The influence of national culture on the adoption status of innovations: An empirical study of firms across Europe. *European Management Journal, 23*(6), 601–610.

Waldo, C. R. (1999). Working in a majority context: A structural model of heterosexism as minority stress in the workplace. *Journal of Counseling Psychology, 46*(2), 218–232.

Watson, T. J. (2009). Narrative, life story and manager identity: A case study in autobiographical identity work. *Human relations, 62*(3), 425–452.

Weisberg, R. W. (2009). On "out-of-the-box" thinking in creativity. In A. B. Markman & K. L. Wood (Eds.), *Tools for innovation* (pp. 23–47). Oxford, England: Oxford University Press.

Westwood, R., & Low, D. R. (2003). The multicultural muse culture, creativity and innovation. *International Journal of Cross Cultural Management, 3*(2), 235–259.

White, S. G., & Hatcher, C. (1984). Couple complementarity and similarity: A review of the literature. *American Journal of Family Therapy, 12*(1), 15–25.

Wiersema, M. F., & Bantel, K. A. (1992). Top management team demography and corporate strategic change. *Academy of Management journal, 35*(1), 91–121.

Yoddumnern-Attig, B., Attig, G., & Boonchalaksi, W. (1991). Benefits and precautions in qualitative research. In B. Yoddumnern-Attig, G. Attig, & W. Boonchalaksi (Eds.), *A field manual on selected qualitative research methods* (p. 3). Thailand: Institute for Population and Social Research, Mahidol University.

Zhu, W. Y., & Yin, Q. (2016). The influence of TMT characteristics on technological innovation: Evidence from it public listed companies in China. In *Proceedings of the 6th International Asia Conference on Industrial Engineering and Management Innovation* (pp. 963–970). Palgrave Macmillan, UK: Atlantis Press.

6

What Does It Take? New Praxes of Cross-Cultural Competency for Global Virtual Teams as Innovative Work Structure

Norhayati Zakaria

Introduction

The digital era has led multinational corporations (MNCs) to experiment with varied forms of innovation, including new technology-based work structures. Information technology enables people to collaborate and communicate in virtual teams without the need to meet face-to-face. Yet, focusing only on technological changes as a competitive advantage is insufficient. Rather, a company must also prioritize its human capital as a primary value-added advantage. Despite the benefits of the "digital wave" that allows people to work anytime, anywhere and with

A shorter three-page version of this paper was published by Elsevier in 2013 in The Academic Executive Brief. Here, it has been significantly expanded and revised, to suit the theme of this edited book.

N. Zakaria (✉)
University of Wollongong in Dubai, UAE and Universiti Utara,
Kedah, Malaysia

© The Author(s) 2017
S. Kundu, S. Munjal (eds.), *Human Capital and Innovation*,
DOI 10.1057/978-1-137-56561-7_6

131

anyone—known as global virtual team (GVT), such novelty work structure has also heightened the need for employees who are culturally competent (Lockwood, 2015; Marcoccia, 2012). The radical changes that
have taken place in the work landscape have compelled MNCs to rethink
and re-strategize their approach to global human capital to better accommodate these technological changes; a significant part of this is through
innovative forms and praxes of cross-cultural competency.

At a global workplace, innovation entails people to alter the way they
usually operate. Renowned gurus of the innovation and strategic change
in organization, O'Reilly and Tushman (2011), simply assert that *innovation* is about execution as well as about getting it done. As such, innovation can be viewed from two different perspectives, which is either from
a result or outcome-orientation concept or from a process-orientation
concept. In this chapter, my premise of argument on innovation will
be based on the process-orientation concept. In specific, I conceptualize
innovation in the form of "a new mindset and creativity" in approaching
teamwork. It is crucial for MNCs to pay attention on ways to materialize
their innovative structure because innovative structure needs new and
creative ways of thinking, managing emotions, and molding behaviors
that lead to high performing GVTs.

For example, both team members and team leaders must be able to
handle culturally complex scenarios such as the following: working with
team members who are separated by a 12-hour time difference (e.g.,
Thailand and the USA) resulting in meetings being conducted at odd
hours, working with people with different attitudes toward deadlines
(urgent vs. laid-back), accommodating those with different structural
preferences (rigid vs. flexible rules and procedures) when engaging in
assigned tasks, or bringing together people who deal with conflicts in a
blunt and straightforward manner versus those who prefer a subtle and
polite approach. These are some significant and multifaceted cultural
challenges that can arise in the GVT novelty work structure.

In addition, the digital wave offers new platforms and opportunities
for MNCs to operate in a sharing economy. The sharing economy is a
new economic model that enables consumers to share, swap, trade, and
rent products and services via a digital platform; it is also known as collaborative consumption. MNCs can use this same concept by sharing

their global human capital, allowing them to collaborate using digital platforms. This novel work structure such as GVTs leads to several key concerns: How do MNCs recognize and recruit global talent capable of working in GVTs? What creative forms of cultural competency are desirable when people work in a GVT environment? How can we ensure they are both culturally savvy and technologically savvy, in order to become high performing teams? What are the new praxes necessary for GVTs to thrive in terms of practices, procedures, and processes?

In this chapter, I will discuss how the digital wave requires organizations to rethink and re-strategize their human capital competency and cultural praxes. I will define several key concepts, such as global virtual teams, culture and intercultural communication; all of these are important elements that bind together GVTs and new praxes of cross-cultural competency. I will introduce a new framework called the C.A.B. cross-cultural competency, which is compatible with the GVT work structure, and propose some innovative practices and processes for collaborating effectively in the context of a GVT. For example, I will emphasize how GVT members and leaders need to be creative in coming up with ways to replicate face-to-face situations in a virtual team, or strategies to ensure that (e.g.) low context people understand about the value of relationship, instead of just focusing on task orientation. In the next section, I will present managerial guidelines for human resources and management, and offer some culturally attuned guidelines for building new forms of specialized GVT competencies that integrate culture and technology. Finally, I provide few concluding remarks and suggest fruitful directions for future research.

Global Virtual Teams as Innovative Work Structures

Most people today are competent in the use of numerous technological tools that enable them to work effectively, but they may have little or no experience working with culturally diverse team members at a distance. Imagine this: a team of engineers from India needs to collaborate with a team in Germany to develop a new transportation hub in Saudi Arabia.

These teams need to complete their work within six months in order to lay out the plans and begin implementation. They will need to work with and trust other members with whom they have no historical background, manage different technological systems, navigate cultural differences in work practices and communication styles, overcome geographical distance and time differences, and so on.

MNCs introduced virtual work platforms as a way of staying competitive and agile by cutting costs related to travel and the expatriation/repatriation process. To fully exploit this virtual workspace, MNCs need to seek out and recruit global talent, employees who are competent not only in working with people of different cultural backgrounds, but also in working together at a distance—that is, virtually (Chang, Hung, & Hsieh, 2014). This work structure, which is increasingly common in MNCs, is called a global virtual team or GVT. GVTs consist of team members from different cultures, who work together from different geographical locations, using computer-mediated technologies to collaborate and communicate across disparate time zones in a non-collocated workspace (Chang et al., 2014; Jarvenpaa & Leidner, 1998; Zakaria, 2009). To excel in such an environment requires two kinds of competencies: cultural and technological. It is not easy for an organization to recruit people who have experience in working with a heterogeneous team in a virtual work setting.

GVTs have received a good deal of attention in the field of Information Systems (IS) in the past few decades, following the emergence of computer-mediated communication such as email, videoconferencing and instant messaging (Chen & Hung, 2010; David, Chand, Newell, & Resende-Santos, 2008; Sarker, Sarker, & Jana, 2010). Scholars in the fields of cross-cultural management and international management have extensively argued about the impact of culture on work practices, attitudes, and values (Brooks & Pitts, 2016; Dekker, Rutte, & Van den Berg, 2008; Froese, Peltokorpi, & Ko, 2012; Johnson, Lenartowitcz & Apud, 2006; Zakaria, 2006; Zhu, Bhat, & Nel, 2005), but all agree that cultural differences do exist between many Western and Eastern management practices and processes in face-to-face teams, including decision making, negotiation, leadership methods, and communication styles. However, cultural impacts in the context of GVTs are not fully understood, particularly in the area of management practices. Scholars further theorize that as globalization continues, the use of GVTs in multinational corporations will become more prevalent. Global talent must be recruited more vigorously as the demand rises for human capital with specific competencies tailored for the global market. As such, innovative practices and processes need to be incorporated in MNCs to ensure global talent recruited for GVT is a sustainable and competitive source of human capital.

Leveraging Culture for Innovation

According to O'Reilly and Tushman (2013), to win through innovation, organizations need to introduce organizational cultures that thrive on the concept called "ambidextrous organization." Such organizations uphold that organizational culture is the main engine that can initiate revolutionary change and continuous and discontinuous innovation. Organizations need to participate in ongoing changes to help promote high level of alignment and fit among several factors like people, strategy, structure, individual competencies, culture, and processes. In essence, a crucial question like "How can MNCs leverage on culture to create innovation and obtain competitive advantage?" demands an understanding of both the organization as well as the national culture.

Not only organizational culture matters in organizations, people also need to have the appropriate cross-cultural competency as manifested in individuals' acts and values. The key to understanding cross-cultural competency lies in the concept of culture itself. Over the last few decades, more than 160 definitions of culture have been developed by scholars in fields such as anthropology, cross-cultural management, and international business and management. Significant aspects of culture are that it is dynamic rather than static, is transferable from one generation to the next, and is learned, rather than inherited, by a society or group of people over time (Browaeys & Price, 2014). Hofstede (1984) defines culture as the mental programming of human beings, in that it shapes the way people think, feel, and act. Hall (1976), on the other hand, defines culture in terms of communicative behavior, where communication is culture and culture is communication.

According to Rogers (1979), cultural changes are not automatically accepted or adopted. First, people need to screen and select cultural changes. They evaluate cultural changes based on whether they are (1) better and more useful, (2) consistent with existing practices, (3) easily learned, (4) testable through trial and error, and (5) confer benefits recognized by all members of the society. Second, cultural borrowing is a reciprocal process. Those who receive the cultural change and those who instigate the change need to be equally accepting. It cannot be a one-way street. Third, the transference of culture may be incomplete, and the end result may differ from either of the original forms. People may eliminate some things and introduce new things. Leaders may model certain practices by making modifications as necessary to fit with their current context and culture, whether organizational or national. Fourth, cultural change is difficult because it is not easy to transfer patterns of behaviors, belief systems, and values. As Ferraro (2010) asserts, "some cultural practices are more easily diffused than others" (p. 33).

There is a strong interaction between organizational culture and national culture. In order to understand the effects of culture in an organization, both perspectives must be considered: the influence of national cultural values on development of individual and team behaviors, and the effects of organizational culture on the processes, practices, and values of those who inhabit the workplace.

Understanding Intercultural Communication

In intercultural communication, one has to manage their own communication styles with others and at the same time handle other people's communication styles (Hu & Fan, 2011). The way people communicate, both verbally and non-verbally, is highly influenced by their own cultural practice (Kealey, 2015, Lieberman & Gamst, 2015; Martin, 2015). A number of cultural dimensions have been developed to facilitate the understanding of cultural differences in communication, and one of the main dimensions is called "context" (Gudykunst et al., 1996; Hall, 1976; Hofstede, 1984; Wang, & Kulich, 2015). In his renowned book *Beyond Culture*, the intercultural communication theorist Edward Hall (1976) affirms that context is a process, an important aspect of communication that has as yet received insufficient explanation. He further states that "[t]his brings us to the point where it is possible to discuss context in relation to meaning, because what one pays attention to or does not attend to is largely a matter of context" (p. 90) (Hall, 1976). Context plays the role of a medium that carries the meaning of the message.

Although Hall defined—and I will discuss—context as having two extremes, high context and low context, it is useful to bear in mind that context is a continuum, and despite their cultural backgrounds people may fall anywhere along the continuum from high to low. As previously defined briefly, context can also explain why in some cultures messages are implied through non-verbal means while in others they are verbally written or spoken. In a "context culture" (high on the context spectrum) people depend largely on non-verbal cues conveyed by the other person's behavior or word choice to fully interpret messages. In a context culture, the words chosen are indirect, tactful, polite, and ambiguous. Conversely, in a "content culture" (low on the context spectrum), messages are interpreted directly from the exact words that are written or spoken. The words chosen are direct, succinct, and specific. Examples of high context cultures include Malaysia, India, China, Sweden, Thailand, and many more (the majority are Eastern countries), whereas low context cultures include the USA, the UK, Germany, Australia, and many Western European countries.

High context people value building a relationship before collaborating or working with another person. They feel that knowing others on a personal level will enhance their understanding and improve their interpretation of the messages they receive (Gudykunst et al., 1997). Non-verbal cues such as body language, tone of voice, facial expression, and gestures are important elements for effective intercultural communication with high context people. The information cues used by low context individuals, on the other hand, are very different. They do not place much importance on relationship-building; rather, they prefer to conduct business or engage in collaboration through formal agreements such as a written contract between two parties. During collaboration, they are strongly focused on the task to be achieved, and much less focused on relationships. In essence, the understanding of high vs low context for GVT can be explored in studies of between-the-team communications (Xiao & Huang, 2015).

Developing New Praxes for GVTs Using the C.A.B. Cross-Cultural Competency Framework

Cultural competencies are crucial for success in today's rapidly globalizing workplace, in which no dominant monoculture drives work values and business practices. In such an environment, teams and managers must be culturally competent to make the most of their human capital in order to maintain a competitive advantage. Yet oftentimes employees are hired without the necessary competencies to meet the demands of a complex culturally attuned work environment. The challenges of intercultural communication are often intensified in a GVT situation, since virtual collaboration requires the use of technology and not all people are comfortable using a communication medium with limited non-verbal cues, such as email. But computer-mediated technology—both synchronous tools like Skype, Instant Messaging, or Twitter, and asynchronous tools like email—are vital for companies operating in a global environment. Indeed, with the rise of the global market and the global information society, it is likely that GVT members will encounter more different cultures than ever before, now that there is no boundary to collaboration. How do MNCs move forward with GVTs in terms of human capital? What new kinds of processes or procedures need to be developed and deployed to take advantage of or add value to the current practices of virtual teamwork?

According to Chen and Starosta (1996), there are three aspects to the development of cultural competencies: cognitive, affective, and behavioral, which are abbreviated as C.A.B. in this paper. According to Zakaria (2013), these three areas can be used as a basis for developing a set of cross-cultural competencies:

1. *Cognitive Skills*—leaders need to educate and disseminate knowledge to their members regarding the cultural frames and values that may impede their effectiveness. Team members thus become more knowledgeable and informed about cultural conflicts and differences.
2. *Affective Skills*—leaders need to show compassion and be sensitive to the errors and misunderstandings that may arise based on cultural dif-

ferences among the team members. Tolerance, appreciation, and sensitivity among team members will enable everyone to operate more effectively across distance and cultural differences.

3. *Behavioral Skills*—leaders need to understand and model relevant congruent behaviors that complement their team members and are appropriate responses to cultural differences; this behavior can then be observed and replicated by team members.

Based on these three aspects, I introduce new praxes of cross-cultural competencies in the context of GVTs, built on a new framework: the C.A.B. cross-cultural competency for GVTs (Fig. 6.1). In the C.A.B. framework, cultural competency formation begins with information and knowledge about a culture at the cognitive level, which shapes one's mindset with the right amount of knowledge (quantity) as well as knowledge that is relevant and accurate (quality). Without both quantity and quality of cultural knowledge, GVT members will be at a loss, confused or frustrated by the behaviors of their colleagues. The key question at this level is to ensure that team members can answer the following: *What* is culture? *Who* is impacted by it and *how* in this new environment which limits face-to-face interactions? The goal at this first level is to achieve cultural awareness.

Once adequate cross-cultural training has been provided and appropriate cultural knowledge acquired, the next step is to create an emotional state in which members are appreciative of and empathize with the cultural complexities they encounter. Given information about a culture, a person will have a heightened sensitivity to and tolerance for differences in cultural values, attitudes, and beliefs. The key question is *why* do we need to understand culture? The goal is to inculcate cultural sensitivity. Once a person is sensitive to and appreciative of differences, they begin to demonstrate appropriate behaviors and take appropriate action to avoid any cultural misunderstandings or blunders.

The last phase is to identify and practice appropriate and effective culturally oriented behaviors. Blunders and miscommunication are costly when a team is engaged in an ad-hoc project that lasts only a few weeks or months. The key questions are: *How* can we better understand what needs to be done, *what* actions to take that are appropriate and relevant to the

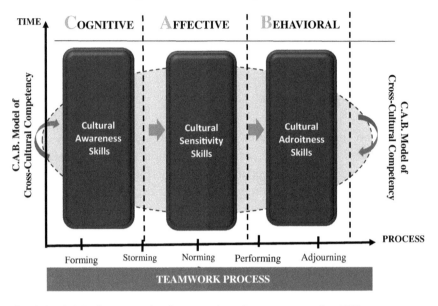

Fig. 6.1 C.A.B. framework of cross-cultural competency for GVT

people we are leading and managing, and *when* to behave in accordance with the cultural condition/situation? The goal of this stage is to develop cultural adroitness, where the appropriate behavior comes naturally and easily. As a result, by modeling appropriate behaviors, other people can learn. In turn, these individuals can model behaviors, educating others, thus new knowledge is created and awareness is increased.

Although the C.A.B. framework provides three aspects to consider and each aspect can be thought of as a phase to pass through, the phases are not simply a linear process with a starting point and an end point. The process does not always follow the sequential stages of cognitive, affective, and then behavioral, nor does it stop at the behavior stage. The process is iterative, and continues to feed each stage back until the culturally attuned behavior is habitual and natural, and true cross-cultural competence is reached. This is a time-consuming process, and a complex one to manage (Kim, 2015).

The order of the stages can also change—for example, one might begin with a behavior, then move to affective acknowledgement, and finally to cognitive knowledge. That is, a person could initially begin by mimicking the behavior of others without thinking much about it. For example, taking off one's shoes is a customary practice when entering an Asian home and thus a person may naturally take off his or her shoes as they step in the door. A person may be ignorant of the cultural nature of this practice and not formally educated in such procedures, yet follow this action simply out of respect. Afterward, he or she might ask, "Why do you take off your shoes?" The answer will educate them and provide them with cognitive information about how to behave appropriately next time they encounter a similar situation. Consequently, a person will learn to appreciate such behavior and be tolerant of the cultural custom of removing one's shoes, even though that practice is not a habit for Western cultures. At the end, with an open heart, this induces an affective reasoning process which will further shape and reinforce the person's logical thoughts at the cognitive level. Such is the cyclical nature of the cultural competence process as it moves from one stage to another, though it may begin at a different stage for a different person, contingent upon their existing level of cultural competency.

Given the abovementioned fundamentals of C.A.B framework, new procedures, practices, and processes (praxes) need to be developed in the context of GVTs. Taking off one's shoes is not relevant in the virtual work space, of course, but there are praxes inherent in a face-to-face work setting which are equally important in the virtual context. The challenge of developing cultural competency is intensified in the context of a virtual work setting because team members don't just need to get to know each other; they also need to engage in decision making, communication, negotiation, trust formation, teamwork, and so on effectively and efficiently. GVT members have fewer opportunities to observe behaviors than if they were face-to-face. The following section details the process of developing cross-cultural competency in its cognitive, affective, and behavioral aspects.

Creating Cultural Awareness and Innovative Thinking Skills

Based on the theory of mind (Hughes & Devine, 2015), the ability of a person to interpret another's actions is dependent on the person's mental state of a person and how they make sense of their own and others' behavior, filtered through the articulation of their beliefs and desires. Davidson (1984) further points out that cognitive ability also depends on linguistic ability, because language is the main medium by which humans express thoughts, desires, and intentions. These can be directly expressed in words like "I would like to have coffee in the café this evening with you." On the other hand, a person can also use language in an indirect manner to suggest or imply their intentions. For example: "How are you? So, what are you doing this evening? Do you think you might have time to go out? If so, maybe you'd like to have coffee?"

The first step in building cross-cultural competency is developing cultural awareness. This means acquiring knowledge about, or providing information to others about, the new culture. Organizations can provide different kinds of cross-cultural training, both general and culture-specific (e.g., a list of "do's and don'ts"), to educate GVT members on what to expect from their colleagues and how to avoid blunders, misinterpretations, and miscommunication. If organizations provide the relevant culturally related knowledge to GVT participants, members will have the right mindset and will be prepared at the cognitive level.

Prepared with the right intellectual information, people will begin to attune their cognitive thinking and to develop the right attitude and mind set. For teams to work together effectively, members need to be cognitively prepared at an early stage. Normally, in a face-to-face setting, members engage in a "forming" stage, during which they meet and get to know each other; this "warm-up" session helps build initial trust. Team members learn about each other through activities that bind them together such as orientations, introductory meetings, welcome parties, and/or briefings about the new project. However, for GVTs, the "forming" stage is different since team members don't have the opportunity to meet each other face-to-face. The "getting to know you" stage has to take place virtually and lacks any of the usual activities that are possible face-to-face. So, how do organizations create an environment conducive to people in a GVT getting to know each other? How can members be made to feel the presence and the excitement of others?' How do members develop initial trust when they are working with strangers?

To create awareness of the other cultures represented in the GVT and to enable members to get to know each other, GVT members need to undergo the same process during the "forming" stage as they would if they were physically collocated. At this stage, it is crucial for team members to understand what cultural backgrounds are present, who will be impacted by such diversity, and how. The forming stage normally begins with members introducing themselves, exchanging names, organization, position, experience, and so on. This is crucial in providing first impressions among the members and affects the extent to which a feeling of trust is generated, enabling people to continue to the next stage.

What is challenging for GVTs is that the team members are strangers and the only way for them to get to know each other is via email or some other form of computer-mediated communication. GVT members will need to exchange emails frequently to get the ball rolling. In addition, in the virtual environment, people cannot see one another's faces, so it is difficult or impossible to recognize non-verbal cues such as facial expressions, gestures, body movements and so on, which are necessary elements of communication in certain cultures (Marcoccia, 2012). To overcome this problem, organizations can encourage GVTs to conduct meetings online using Skype or videoconferencing; this will enable high context members to feel more comfortable since it is similar to a face-to-face setting. Organizations using GVTs need to provide the option of an environment that closely replicates face-to-face so that members have a strong foundation for building effective and cohesive teamwork.

Proposition 1 GVT members that are educated about culture and provided with training about culture become more aware, knowledgeable, and informed about cultural differences and potential conflicts.

Managerial Guidelines

- GVT members need to cultivate an open mindset and be receptive to and accepting of cultural differences.
- GVT members must also develop innovative and creative thinking skills with the given information, knowledge, and training in order to appreciate changes.
- GVT members must be open to trusting others on short acquaintance, so that all members of the group can reach a common ground and find an acceptable balance between task achievement and relationship-building.
- GVT members must educate one another regarding any cultural attitudes, viewpoints, and values that may impede the team's effectiveness.

Culturally Attuned Guidelines for Creating Innovative Strategies

- *Low context* GVT members need to take time during the early "getting to know each other" stage to create a sense of warmth toward high context members. They also need to engage in building relationships before jumping straight to the task, in order to build rapport with high context members who value relationships. They need to demonstrate that they care by creating a strong sense of belonging within the team.
- *High context* GVT members need to demonstrate that they have a strong knowledge of the task to be accomplished (i.e., "know your stuff!") They also need to establish strong credentials regarding what they can do and how they can perform at their best, as this is important for working effectively with low context members. Strive to prioritize task orientation over relationship-building, and stay focused on the job at hand.

Instilling Intercultural Sensitivity and Appreciation for Innovation and Changes

What is the effect of emotional state in building cross-cultural competencies in GVTs? The theory of mind as abovementioned also states that a person's mental state covers a range of elements, one of which is the person's emotional state that results in actions. In this section, we will explore the role of emotions in GVT behaviors. For example, at the intellectual cognitive level, a person can attempt to guess or interpret what is in the mind of another, that is, mind-reading. What about the use of intuition or "gut feelings" at the affective level? Intercultural sensitivity was defined as "an individual's ability to develop a positive emotion towards understanding and appreciating cultural differences that promotes appropriate and effective behavior in intercultural communication" (Chen & Starosta, 1997, p. 5). With the same kind of logic, intuition allows a person to use their affective judgment to feel or understand the feelings of others and to assess others' intentions and desires. To what extent is this type of emotion valuable in producing high performing GVTs? And what is the role of emotion in enhancing GVT performance?

According to Murphy, Hine, and Kiffin-Petersen (2014), there is a significant relationship between motivational systems and emotion in virtual work, just as there is in face-to-face work. They found that managers of virtual teams need to recognize the differences in motivational level that result from different emotional states, which consequently affect virtual performance. Some of the key emotions they identified are anger, anxiety, annoyance, nervousness, and distress. Cultural differences that create challenges in working with GVT members of diverse backgrounds can create these kinds of negative emotions. On the other hand, positive emotions such as joy, excitement, gratitude, hope, pride, inspiration, and love can create team cohesion, leading to better team performance.

At the affective level, a person needs to cultivate a high level of sensitivity when confronted with cultural frustrations. They must be considerate and appreciative of cultural differences; this will enable them to be composed, patient, and flexible when faced with cultural complexities. A culturally sensitive person will try to adjust to differences in others, and take measures to ensure that differences do not lead to conflict. At this level, a person will use his or her own intuition, wisdom, and values to identify the cultural synergies that are possible by working with others. Ultimately, they will develop the emotional intelligence that is necessary for understanding another culture.

When we think of emotion, we should also consider the concept of empathy. Empathy is defined as the ability to understand and share the feeling of others. Consider these two common maxims: *Do unto others as you would have others do unto you*, and *put yourself in the other person's shoes*. For example, suppose that a deadline is approaching and a team member will be unable to meet it because he is sick, and that this news was not communicated to you thousands of miles away? How do you put yourself in his shoes when you know that this missed deadline will result in delays in fulfilling a contract, and consequently will incur costly penalty fees? GVT members cannot empathize with one another if they don't have enough information, or if they are unaware of the situation that the other member is experiencing. How do you learn to be sensitive to others when others fail to communicate their intentions to you or to reach out at an affective level?

Many scholars in the cross-cultural management field argue that there is a greater need for emotional intelligence when people work in a multicultural workforce (Crowne, 2013). The development of emotional intelligence requires addressing two basic questions: What is the ability of a person to precisely evaluate the emotional state of himself and others? How do people use feelings to motivate, plan, and achieve their goals? Wong (2016) explored the role and significance of emotions when communicating intentions face-to-face in the context of international diplomatic negotiations and found that when people collaborate, they reveal their preferences, and when they compete, they misrepresent their intentions. In other words, collaboration results in greater honesty than competition. He further found that words and verbal expressions are not the only messages that diplomats pay attention to when negotiating; they also pay attention to emotional cues. For instance, the way people choose their words, the intonation used when speaking, the emotive gestures observed in hand and body movements—all of these cues can be vital in correctly evaluating a situation.

In the context of GVTs, organizations need to recognize that team members working in a non-collocated environment are less able, or have less opportunity, to assess non-verbal cues, which can pose a cultural challenge. For instance, in a high context culture people do not readily demonstrate their feelings unless they have a strong bond with the other person, and when they do express emotions, they may do so indirectly. On the other hand, people from a low context culture are willing to express their emotions directly and make clear how those feelings affect their actions. In a virtual environment, low context team members may experience difficulty interpreting the actions of a team member from a high context culture, while a high context team member might perceive the straightforward or blunt verbal statements made by a low context team member as hurtful or hostile. Hence, GVT members need to be equipped with the emotional intelligence to be able to accurately assess the intentions and desires of others within the limitations of whatever technological platform(s) the team is using to communicate. Members need to be sensitive to and observant of the situation at hand. This heightened awareness can come from several sources: concrete knowledge, past experiences, wisdom, values, beliefs.

Proposition 2 When cultural blunders occur, GVT members need to look carefully for non-verbal cues or behaviors in order to respond with the correct level of empathy, kindness, and compassion. Tolerance, appreciation, and sensitivity among team members will enable everyone to operate more effectively despite distance and cultural differences.

Managerial Guidelines

- GVT members need to cultivate a warm-hearted attitude, with a high tolerance for and appreciation of cultural diversity.
- GVT members need to nurture the many characteristics that enhance emotional honesty, such as empathy, consideration, kindness, warmth, affection, and sincerity; all of these aid in recognizing the true feelings of others.
- GVT members need to learn to accurately read the feelings of others by developing good intuition and gut feelings based on reflections of past experiences that have resulted in strong and lasting relationships.

Culturally Attuned Guidelines for Creating Innovative Strategies

During the "Forming" Stage

- *Low context* GVT members need to be sensitive to the way communication takes place in the early stages. *High context* members value relationships; their need for an emotional connection needs to be considered in terms of word choice and the manner in which verbal communications are delivered and presented. For example, team members could be encouraged to ask each other questions about their hometowns, or to share pictures of their families; such actions create a friendly environment conducive to emotional connection.
- GVT leaders should, if possible, employ technological platforms that allow *high context* members to observe the non-verbal cues necessary for them to interpret and understand the content of a communication (e.g., videoconferencing rather than text-based chat). Team members can use emoticons in their text communications to create a heightened awareness of their emotional state at the time of writing.

During the "Storming" or Crisis Stage

- If a crisis or conflict arises, *high context* GVT members need to clearly communicate their feelings. Messages, whether or verbal or written, need to be clearly delivered, explained, and justified to avoid any confusion. *Low context* people prefer to deal with problems in an open and transparent manner, thus in a GVT setting, the level of transparency needs to be high to reduce the chance of miscommunication. *High context* members should ask questions as needed for clarification to reduce misinterpretations among them. If there is a conflict, *high context* members appreciate it when the confrontation takes place in a private setting, one-on-one, or through intermediaries, rather than in the open via public criticism.
- *High context* members need to avoid using the "silence" strategy in a GVT environment, because it is likely to complicate the issue and cre-

ate unnecessary delays in solving a problem. In a face-to-face setting, silence can convey a message through the use of non-verbal cues, such as smiling, frowning, looking bored, or nodding in agreement. However, in a virtual setting, silence conveys no message at all; this leads to a "clueless" work environment for both parties and is not effective for solving problems.

- Both *low context and high context* GVT members need to be creative in their communication styles so as not to offend or irritate one another, and develop a cohesive collaboration. Creativity in virtual communication might include using an informal yet fun social media platform such as online chat to create a sense of relaxation, harmony, and belonging by replicating a face-to-face office gathering.

Modeling Culturally Appropriate Behaviors and Innovative Actions

When you first encounter a new culture in one of your team members, how do you act appropriately? How do you practice the old saying, "When in Rome, do as the Romans do?" At the affective level, a culturally sensitive person will naturally adopt and mimic the behavior of others, thereby acquiring culturally appropriate behaviors. What they see, they will try to emulate, repeating an action, process, or activity. A person who is culturally sensitive may also innovate by performing an action based not on copying others but on his or her own understanding and knowledge of the culture. Once an innovation is accepted by others in the culture, that new knowledge becomes part of the cognitive intellectual process for those who are at the first step of acquiring cultural awareness.

In the third phase, one's actions are culturally appropriate in response to a situation. In the context of GVTs, all participants need to acknowledge the cultural diversity that exists among the team members. According to Earley, Ang, and Tan (2006), cultural intelligence is a requirement for global teams: it provides a competitive advantage and strategic benefits for individuals and organizations. How do you define cultural intelligence (CQ)? Earley et al. define CQ as "a person's capability for successful adaptation to new cultural settings, that is, for unfamiliar settings attributable to cultural context" (p. 5), and propose three elements: cultural strategic thinking, motivations, and behavior. These three elements are associated with three questions:

- How and why do people do what they do here?
- Am I motivated to do something here?
- Am I doing the right thing?

All three of these questions are important for MNCs to answer as they create new processes, practices, and procedures for their GVTs. Since the work structure and space change the landscape of work itself, thus the praxes also need to be changed to accord with new behavioral dimensions. CQ suggests that certain aspects of culture need to be consciously considered to build a high performing GVT (Shirish, Boughzala, & Srivastave, 2015). Each team member needs to identify and recognize his or her own identity and individual culture in terms of self-image (personal identity) and role identity.

Markus and Kitayama (1991) in their work on cultural variations in self-concept highlight an interesting cultural distinction between East and West, based on the contradictory maxims of "The squeaky wheel gets the grease" and "The nail that sticks up will be hammered down." These two proverbs illustrate a cultural distinction in how the individual sees himself with respect to others: the first suggests that calling attention to oneself has positive results, while the second suggests that it has negative consequences. Hofstede (1984) described this as a cultural dimension in which individualistic acts are balanced against the collectivistic goals of a society. Several points are involved in discovering one's self-image from a cultural standpoint. One must first recognize what one is capable of doing, why one acts in certain ways and manners, why certain actions lead to others, how one's actions reflect the cultural values one subscribes to, and when is the right time to behave in a certain way. Self-image and self-identity are rooted in cultural beliefs, attitudes, and values. If I am unable to understand the cultural roots that influence my behavior, I am unlikely to be able to appreciate the cultural values of my GVT colleagues. Self-concept is comprised of experiences, traits, goals, and ideas;

in the context of the workplace, these inform us how work is to be conducted and managed. According to Earley et al. (2006):

[S]elf concept is regulated by culture as well as features of one's work. For example, people living in a high power-differentiated culture such as Thailand have a self-image that endorses respect for authority, deference to seniors, and so on. A Thai manager satisfies his self-motives by culturally acceptable methods, so he maintains high self-enhancement by being shown proper respect by people who are subordinates to him—that is, he will seek out situations that provide opportunities for recognition. (p. 153)

Turning from self-identity to role identity, GVT members need to understand how different roles give rise to different attitudes, values, and beliefs in different cultures and societies. A person's cultural values result in different interpretations of role identity. As suggested by Trompenaars and Hampden-Turner (2004) in their cultural dimension of achievement versus ascription, in an achievement-oriented culture people are valued or respected in the workplace based on their credentials, achievements, and qualifications. For instance, in a French company my PhD might be valued because French culture places a high value on expertise and formal education. An ascription-oriented culture, on the other hand, prioritizes a person's role identity—for example, I am the Marketing Manager and that role identity is respected because it equates to authority and power in the work place; it gives me a specific role identity that identifies and acknowledges my level of importance.

In a study by Groves, Feyerherm, and Gu (2014), they describe cases in which international negotiation failed due to a lack of cultural intelligence, resulting in a failure to communicate with people of diverse cultures, a lack of understanding of other cultures, and an inability to adapt and tolerate situations of cultural unfamiliarity. In a similar vein, a study by Shirish et al. (2015) found that culturally bound discontinuities in GVTs such as geography, organizational outlook, work practices, and attitudes toward technology could only be bridged by developing high CQ. In short, CQ is vital for GVTs since culture forms the core of team members' actions and strategic capabilities. GVTs need to be alert to any processes, procedures and practices that impede team cohesiveness and team effectiveness, and take steps to modify them as needed.

Proposition 3 GVT members need observe their own and others' behaviors, acquire knowledge about the cultural roots of that behavior, and cultivate open-mindedness toward cultural diversity. Team members need to accumulate solid cultural knowledge, emotional readiness, and appreciation in order to develop a high level of cultural intelligence (CQ).

Managerial Guidelines

- GVT members need to be receptive to cultural differences by responding to actions immediately and sincerely; do not delay responses or feedback because it may result in miscommunication.
- GVT members must be willing to adjust their responses and demonstrate culturally fit behaviors that are congruent with their thoughts and feelings when faced with a difficult situation. Team members should exercise restraint and not over-react in a conflict.
- GVT members need to acquire a cultural knowledge that is all-inclusive or holistic, rather than just a random set of isolated facts. Inaccurate information and shallow knowledge can distort one's behavioral choices and consequently produce cultural blunders. Effective cross-cultural training can provide this comprehensive foundation.

Culturally Attuned Guidelines for Creating Innovative Strategies

- *Low context* GVT members need to ensure that team charters and goals are defined through productive discussions in the early stages that involve all members of the team. Such inclusive measures taken at the "forming" stage will encourage the formation of trust among members, since teams that practice engagement and participation create an environment of collaboration. Low context GVT members should not treat the team's goals as purely individual responsibilities;

rather, they need to act as team players. For example, if they have completed their own assigned tasks, they can assist others, acting in a collectivistic manner.

- *Low context* GVT leaders need to ensure clear communication with high context team members. For example, use several different technological platforms including both synchronous and asynchronous. High context members usually appreciate being offered a variety of communication platforms because this demonstrates sensitivity to their communication preferences.
- *High context* members need to learn to actively engage during team discussions and brainstorming sessions and to risk offering creative and innovative ideas, either verbally or in writing. They need to get comfortable taking ownership of their ideas and expressing their thoughts and feelings openly. They cannot expect people to continuously provide guidelines and instructions, or read between the lines and correctly infer what they intended to propose. In a virtual environment, everything needs to be explicitly spelled out. Non-verbal cues are of limited use and relying on them can cause miscommunication. There should be no guessing games; teams should be built upon clear communication.
- *High context* members need to acknowledge that in a GVT environment, establishing rapport may have to take second place due to time constraints. It takes longer to develop relationships with strangers in virtual setting, and GVTs must often complete their work in a limited time frame. Instead of their usual relationship-orientation, they need to focus on task-oriented behaviors to earn the trust and acknowledgement from low context members. The ascription orientation that values "who I know or affiliated with" is less practical in GVTs than "what I can contribute"—the achievement orientation.

The preceding three sections discussed the three components of the C.A.B. cultural model—cognitive, affective, and behavioral—in order to explore the new praxes that need to be developed for GVTs. We also discussed the three kinds of intelligences required to build on innovative praxes: cognitive intelligence (IQ), emotional intelligence (EQ), and cultural intelligence (CQ). Each of these components and intelligences must be considered at each of the classic teamwork stages of forming, norming, storming, performing, and adjourning (Tuckman & Jensen, 1977), but tailored to a GVT context. The most critical stage is the first, forming, since it sets the tone and direction for the GVT's work. A second critical stage is storming, which is when teams are likely to encounter conflicts and crises. Cultural challenges will arise in all the stages, but mastering the different forms of intelligence is sure to enhance GVT performance.

Theoretical Implications for MNCs in Training and Educating GVTs

Traditionally, teams have been a group of people that meet regularly face-to-face to work on a common project or toward a common goal. But the past two decades have witnessed a dramatic shift in our understanding of the working of teams, with conventional team structures increasingly giving way to virtual teams. With the constant stream of technological innovations in communication, GVTs have become even more convenient, which has led to their becoming more common. In our increasingly global world, GVTs have also become popular not only for their ease of use, but also as an excellent tool to foster diversity, flexibility, and strong task-oriented focus, all of which are vital in meeting the demands of today's changing business world. GVTs are no longer simply an option; for many multinational corporations who employ GVTs as their innovative work structure, they are a necessity.

Employees are more valuable if they have obtained as much experience as possible; this makes them more competitive and, as a consequence, they are also more flexible when it comes to working in a new organizational structure such as a GVT. Multinational companies want new recruits who are equipped with the right levels of competencies, the right mindset, and experience with the right technologies. People who are potentially to be recruited need to have flexibility in their behaviors in order to acculturate to the new cultures when engaging in GVT (Van Oudenhoven & Benet-Martinez, 2015). Given this demand in the

Table 6.1 Five key considerations for training and educating GVT members

1. Ensure teams fully understand the teamwork cycle of forming, storming, norming, performing and adjourning, and that this cycle can be iterative rather than linear
2. Encourage team members to develop relationships and friendship so that those whose cultural backgrounds base their performance on trust will be able to quickly develop it
3. Practice leadership without a formal appointment—leadership attributes should not be practiced by only one person; every member needs to play a leadership role
4. Experiment with new and different management skills—use the team as a training ground to establish the arts of planning, coordinating, leading, controlling, and organizing while working at a distance
5. Use more than one type of CMC (Skype, Facebook, Instant messaging)—keep updated with new developments, especially Web 2.0 options such as Whatsapp or Twitter, to ensure members can be reached easily and cheaply

industry, the responsibility lies with both educational institutions and organizations to put in place the appropriate training and grooming for the talents of the future. Table 6.1 suggests several points to be considered when training and educating people to be effective GVT members.

In addition, Earley et al. (2006) suggest few directions for training and educating individuals, which could be applied in the context of GVTs to obtain efficiency and effectiveness in teamwork (see below in Table 6.2):

Table 6.2 Characteristics of cultural strategic thinking for GVT innovativeness

1. Open, alert, and sensitive to new cultures between members that exist within the teamwork
2. Able to draw distinction and to identify similarities between different cultures because GVTs need to work within a short period of time
3. Able to develop different strategies for acquiring knowledge relevant to adapting to different cultures and achieve high level of cognitive intelligence for developing cultural awareness skills as well as emotional intelligence for creating cultural sensitivity skills.
4. Able to engage in active and dynamic thinking in interacting with people from different cultures, able to plan, check, and learn from each encounter, and able to resolve cultural dilemmas or problem in the encounter—all useful to achieve GVT cohesiveness.

Conclusions and Future Research Directions

The continuing globalization of the workforce creates new challenges which require innovative cultural competencies capable of addressing the complexity present in multicultural situations such as GVTs. In this chapter, I have addressed the following questions: How do team members successfully work with people who are totally different in terms of work practices, values, and attitudes? What does it take to be an effective team in the digital era and in a global work context? These questions are highly relevant given today's borderless world, where GVTs are becoming the work structure of choice for corporations with global ambitions or commitments. The challenges are multiplied by culture, which can result in confrontations and complicated dynamics between team leaders and team members as well as within the team itself. The cultural challenges that may arise are exacerbated by differences in time and space as well as in working attitudes and styles.

MNCs need to assess the compatibility between the practices and patterns of collaborating using technology, and their employees' cultural values (Borges, Brezilon, Pino & Pomerol, 2007; Lin, Standing & Liu, 2008). The wisest strategy for MNCs is to educate at the individual, team, and organizational level to develop both technological and cultural competencies, and build a workforce that understands the unique needs of a team comprised of people from different cultural backgrounds working together at a distance.

Since the work environment is ever more complex in this digital age, MNCs need to reorganize and re-strategize at every level, from vision and mission, to organizational culture and values, to specific practices and procedures, so as to successfully deploy and manage GVTs. Cultural differences should not be a barrier to developing competent teams and global leaders because all individuals have the same aspiration, need, and talents to become innovative and competitive. To be successful and effective, GVTs need the guidance of leaders with a global outlook, who fully understand that different cultures have different ways of working in terms of cognition, emotion, and behaviors.

In terms of future research, several questions remain to be asked and answered: (1) How do organizations develop culturally competent global leaders capable of successfully dealing with virtual multicultural teams? (2) How do organizations encourage leaders to be open to the many idiosyncrasies of behavior, the turmoil of emotions, and the unpredictable patterns of thought that may arise from divergent culturally rooted behaviors? (3) Can team members learn to trust members of diverse cultural backgrounds in a virtual workspace on short acquaintance? (4) Can team members develop the ability to alter their behavior to accommodate to the variation of communicative behaviors that exist among the diverse cultural backgrounds?

References

Borges, M. R. S., Brezilon, P., Pino, J. A., & Pomerol, J. (2007). Dealing with the effects of context mismatch in group work. *Decision Support Systems, 43*(4), 1692–1706.

Brooks, C. F., & Pitts, M. J. (2016). Communication and identity management in a globally-connected classroom: An online international and intercultural learning experience. *Journal of International and Intercultural Communication, 9*(1), 52–68.

Browaeys, M.-J., & Price, R. (2014). *Understanding cross-cultural management.* New York: Prentice Hall.

Chang, H. H., Hung, C.-J., & Hsieh, H.-W. (2014). Virtual teams: Cultural adaptation, communication quality, and interpersonal trust. *Total Quality Management & Business Excellence, 25*(11/12), 1318–1335.

Chen, C. J., & Hung, S. W. (2010). To give or to receive? Factors influencing members' knowledge sharing and community promotion in professional virtual communities. *Information and Management, 47*(4), 226–236.

Chen, G. M., & Starosta, W. J. (1996). Intercultural communication competence: A synthesis In B. Burleson (Ed.), *Communication yearbook 19* (pp. 353–383). Thousand Oaks: Sage.

Chen, G. M., & Starosta, W. J. (1997). A review of the concept of intercultural sensitivity. *Human Communication, 1*, 1–16.

Crowne, K. A. (2013). Cultural exposure, emotional intelligence, and cultural intelligence: An exploratory study. *International Journal of Cross Cultural Management, 13*(1), 5–22.

Davidson, R. (1984). Affect, cognition and hemispheric specialization. In C. E. Izard, J. Kagan, & R. B. Zajonic (Eds.), *Emotions, cognition and behavior* (pp. 320–365). New York: Cambridge University Press.

David, G. C., Chand, D., Newell, S., & Resende-Santos, J. O. (2008). Integrated collaboration across distributed sites: The perils of process and the promise of practice. *Journal of Information Technology, 23*(1), 44–54.

Dekker, D. M., Rutte, C. G., & Van den Berg, P. T. (2008). Cultural differences in the perception of critical interaction behaviours in global virtual teams. *International Journal of Intercultural Relations, 32*(5), 441–452.

Earley, P. C., Ang, S., & Tan, J. (2006). *Developing cultural intelligence at work*. Stanford, CA: Stanford University Press.

Ferraro, G. P. (2010). *The cultural dimensions of international business* (6th ed.). Pearson. Upper Saddle River: New Jersey.

Froese, F. J., Peltokorpi, V., & Ko, K. A. (2012). The influence of intercultural communication on cross-cultural adjustment and work attitudes: Foreign workers in South Korea. *International Journal of Intercultural Relations, 36*(3), 331–342.

Groves, K. S., Feyerherm, A., & Gu, M. (2014). Cultural exposure, emotional intelligence, and cultural intelligence: An exploratory study. *International Journal of Cross Cultural Management, 13*(1), 5–22.

Gudykunst, W. B., Matsumoto, Y., Ting-Toomey, S., Nishida, T., Kim, K., & Heyman, S. (1996). The influence of cultural individualism-collectivism, self construals, and individual values on communication styles across cultures. *Human Communication Research, 22*(4), 510–543.

Hall, E. T. (1976). *Beyond culture*. Garden City, NJ: Anchor Books/Doubleday.

Hofstede, G. (1984). *Culture's consequences: International differences in work-related values*. Newbury Park: Sage.

Hu, Y., & Fan, W. (2011). An exploratory study on intercultural communication research contents and methods: A survey based on the international and domestic journal papers published from 2001 to 2005. *International Journal of Intercultural Relations, 35*(5), 554–566.

Hughes, C., & Devine, T. (2015). A social perspective on the theory of mind. In R. M. Lerner & M. E. Lamb (Eds.), Socio-emotional processes, *Handbook of child psychology* (7th ed., vol 3, pp. 564–609). Hoboken, NJ: John Wiley.

Jarvenpaa, S. L., & Leidner, D. E. (1998). Communication virtual trust teams in global virtual teams. *Journal of Computer-Mediated Communication, 10*(6), 791–815.

Johnson, J. P., Lenartowicz, T., & Apud, S. (2006). Cross-cultural competence in international business: Toward a definition and a model. *Journal of International Business Studies, 37*(4), 525–543.

Kealey, D. J. (2015). Some strengths and weaknesses of 25 years of Research on Intercultural Communication Competence: Personal Reflections. *International Journal of Intercultural Relations, 48*, 14–16.

Kim, Y. Y. (2015). Achieving synchrony: A foundational dimension of intercultural communication competence. *International Journal of Intercultural Relations, 48*, 27–37.

Lieberman, D. A., & Gamst, G. (2015). Intercultural communication competence revisited: Linking the intercultural and multicultural fields. *International Journal of Intercultural Relations, 48*, 17–19.

Lin, C., Standing, C., & Liu, Y. (2008). A model to develop effective virtual teams. *Decision Support Systems, 45*(4), 1031–1045.

Lockwood, J. (2015). Virtual team management: What is causing communication breakdown? *Language and Intercultural Communication, 15*(1), 125–140.

Marcoccia, M. (2012). The internet, intercultural communication and cultural variation. *Language and Intercultural Communication, 12*(4), 353–368.

Markus, H. R., & Kitayama, S. (1991). Culture and the self: Implications for cognition, emotion, and motivation. *Psychological Review, 98*(2), 224–253.

Martin, J. N. (2015). Revisiting intercultural communication competence: Where to go from here. *International Journal of Intercultural Relations, 48*, 6–8.

Murphy, S. A., Hine, M. J., & Kiffin-Petersen, S. (2014). The role of motivational systems and emotions in virtual work. *Communications of the IIMA, 14*(3), Article 6.

O'Reilly III, C. A., & Tushman, M. L. (2011). Organizational ambidexterity in action: How managers explore and exploit. *California Management Review, 53*(4), 5–21.

O'Reilly III, C. A., & Tushman, M. L. (2013). Organizational ambidexterity: Past, present, and future. *Academy of Management Perspectives, 27*, 324–338.

Rogers, E. (1979). New product adoption and diffusion. *Journal of Consumer Research* (March), 290–301, reprinted in B. Enis & K. Cox (Eds.) Marketing classics: A selection of influential articles, (5th ed., pp. 164–179). Boston, MA: Alllyn and Bacon.

Sarker, S., Sarker, S., & Jana, D. (2010). The impact of the nature of globally distributed work arrangement on work–life conflict and valence: The Indian

GSD professionals' perspective. *European Journal of Information Systems, 19*(2), 209–222.

Shirish, A., Boughzala, I., & Srivastava, S. C. (2015). Bridging cultural discontinuities in global virtual teams: Role of cultural intelligence. In "*Thirty Sixth International Conference on Information Systems*" (ICIS 2015), December 13–16, 2015, Fort Worth, TX.

Trompenaars, F., & Hampden Turner, C. (2004). *Managing people across cultures*. West Sussex: Capstone.

Tuckman, B. W., & Jensen, M. A. C. (1977). Stages of small group development revisited. *Group and Organizational Studies, 2*, 419–427.

Van Oudenhoven, J. P., & Benet-Martinez, V. (2015). In search of a cultural home: From acculturation to frame-switching and intercultural competencies. *International Journal of Intercultural Relations, 46*, 47–54.

Wang, Y. A., & Kulich, S. J. (2015). Does context count? Developing and assessing intercultural competence through an interview- and model-based domestic course design in China. *International Journal of Intercultural Relations, 48*, 38–57.

Wong, S. S. (2016). Emotions and the communication of intentions in face-to-face diplomacy. *European Journal of International Relations, 22*(1), 144–167.

Xiao, L., & Huang, D. (2015). Between-team communication in the intercultural context. *Information, Communication & Society*, 1–16.

Zakaria, N. (2006). *Culture matters? The impact of context on globally distributed Civil Society decision making processes during WSIS*. Syracuse University.

Zakaria, N. (2009). Using computer mediated communication as a tool to facilitate intercultural collaboration of global virtual teams. In M. Pagani (Ed.), *Encyclopedia of multimedia technology and networking* (pp. 1115–1123). New York: Information Science Reference.

Zakaria, N. (2013). Creating cross-culturally competent leaders for global virtual teams. *The Academic Executive Review, 3*(2), 17–18.

Zhu, Y., Bhat, R., & Nel, P. (2005). Building business relationships: A preliminary study of business execuitve views. *Cross Cultural Management, 12*(3), 63–84.

7

From Outsourcing to Best-Sourcing? The Global Search for Talent and Innovation

Srinivas Rao Pingali, Janet Rovenpor, and Grishma Shah

Introduction

Outsourcing has received a poor reputation in the media, general public, and political arena in the Western world. It has been criticized for domestic job losses and the exploitation of unskilled workers in developing countries. What most opponents do not realize, however, is that there are different types of outsourcing, some of which may involve corporate efforts to lower overhead costs by gaining access to low-waged labor while others entail the acquisition and retention of highly skilled and talented professionals who are valued for their ability to innovate. There is no one-size-fits-all approach and not all outsourcing is harmful. A KPMG survey, entitled, *Top Market Trends and Predictions for 2016 and Beyond*, revealed

S.R. Pingali
Quatrro Global Services, Atlanta, GA, USA

J. Rovenpor • G. Shah (✉)
Department of Management and Marketing, Manhattan College, New York, NY, USA

© The Author(s) 2017
S. Kundu, S. Munjal (eds.), *Human Capital and Innovation*,
DOI 10.1057/978-1-137-56561-7_7

that talent shortages and challenges were of the highest concern and had the largest negative impact on businesses. Global companies can create a competitive advantage in the market place by attracting the best people from all corners of the world. The "war for talent" has become "the new norm" (Brown, 2016).

During the last two decades, American firms have sourced talent for white-collar jobs from across the globe. While this was originally only for low-end business processes, the work now sourced from abroad is highly skilled and technical. For example, according to Google's corporate website (2016), Google has more than 10,000 employees in India and despite having no consumer presence in China, it still employs close to 1,000 engineers in Beijing and Shanghai. In fact, more than 55 % of Googlers are employed outside the USA, with a majority of them being in emerging or developing markets. Digging deeper, we find that many firms, including large banks, social media and technology companies, like Goldman Sachs, Facebook, and Microsoft, source a large chunk of their talent from abroad, often through third-party contractors. Apple Inc. compensates independent software programmers to develop iPhone apps; Forbes.com relies on its own journalists as well as external bloggers for its content; Bharti Airtel relies on IBM and Ericsson for critical mobile phone infrastructure services (Power, 2013).

Similarly, the search for outstanding athletes from around the globe is common in professional sports organizations—the NBA, FIFA, MLB, NHL, and MLS (Foster, O'Reilly, & Davila, 2016). On opening night of the 2015–2016 NBA season, player rosters featured 100 international players from 37 countries and territories (up from only 21 international players in 1990–91).[1] Gearing up for the 2014 World Cup in Brazil, the US men's soccer team recruited an increasing number of players from Germany who were fortunate enough to enjoy dual German–American citizenship (Sciaretta, 2011). It is the premise of this chapter that a new revolutionary form of outsourcing has been occurring. It is simply a prudent strategy in which a company seeks the best talent in whichever geographic area it can be found, often leading to innovative advantages.

---

[1] http://www.nba.com/2015/news/10/27/nba-rosters-feature-100-international-players/;   http://www.nba.com/2014/news/10/28/international-players-on-opening-day-rosters-2014-15/

In this chapter, we review the history of outsourcing, define commonly used terms such as "outsourcing" and "offshoring" and provide details on a new generation of outsourcing—i.e., the global search for talent or what we are calling "best-sourcing"—that has quietly evolved over the last 20 years. We discuss the various forces and trends that have the potential to encourage firms to intensify their outsourcing efforts for knowledge professionals (e.g., expanding opportunities in cloud computing). Via case studies, we illustrate the growing trend involving the outsourcing of high-end, value-creating, knowledge-based activities and argue that significant benefits in innovation can be achieved, leading to superior competitive advantage.

Global Business and Outsourcing: A Historical Context

Throughout history, advances in transportation and communication technology have led to tremendous developments for the global economy. For example, the steam engine and the printing press were pivotal to the industrial revolution and subsequently, what many consider the first significant wave of economic globalization (Osterhammel & Petersson, 2009). Since then, there have been ebbs, (i.e., World War I to World War II) and flows (World War II and onward) in global trade. Between the end of World War II to the early nineties, international business or trade was more or less limited to the "Triad" of North America, Western Europe, and Japan (Peng, 2013). The oil crisis of the 1970s forced multinationals to seek contractual arrangements via outsourcing to reduce costs (Buckley & Casson, 2014). The early nineties marked a continued revolution in global business.

The fall of the Berlin Wall followed by the breakup of the Soviet Union and the subsequent end of the Cold War opened up the world for capitalism. In the nineties, the World Bank (WB), International Monetary Fund (IMF), and the World Trade Organization (WTO), also known as the institutions of globalization, paved the road for institutional shifts toward economic liberalization around the globe. The neo-liberal policies pushed forth by the institutions of globalization led to a significant opening of borders through the reduction of trade barriers. Within a decade, global trade increased dramatically. More than one-quarter of the world's GDP now comes from emerging economies and of that more than 60 % comes from the BRIC (Brazil, Russia, India, China) economies. Undoubtedly, the liberalization polices of the nineties set the stage for unprecedented transformation throughout the world. The manifestation of these policies is conspicuous in international business. The global economy is no longer dominated by Triad economies (Peng, 2013). Indeed, we find that international business is truly global as trade and business are not one directional (i.e., Triad outward), but multidirectional and multilayered. No longer can we trace the origin of a product to one country. In unearthing the story of any product, we will find the story of globalization (Klein, 2009). As a result, we speak of global business as opposed to international business.

Along with institutional transitions across the globe, the revolution in Information and Communications Technology (ICT) has wholly altered modern business functions. While earlier advances in technology led to greater speeds in transportation and communications, real-time technology and communications are a new phenomenon. Friedman (2007) in his book, *The World is Flat: A Brief History of the 21st Century,* demonstrates how the information and communications revolution has created a flat world. Through ample examples, he illustrates how in a globalized world, firms do not operate on a vertical value chain, but a horizontal (or flat) value chain (Friedman, 2007). In a globally competitive environment, every firm must find which of its functions adds core value to the firm and which detracts from core value. In such a value chain analysis, a firm will discern that certain functions add tremendous value to the organization, while others are simply commoditized (Hashi & Buckley, 2009).

For example, in a vertical value chain, a car company would control everything from resource extraction (e.g., metal) to marketing, distribution, and service. However, in doing so, it is not necessarily adding value to the organization. A value chain analysis may demonstrate that making the tires in-house does not add value to the car company (in fact, it may detract from a value-adding core function) as the firm does not have the expertise in making tires. Hence, it is best to contract out or buy tires from a tire company. The tire company sets the benchmark for the tires as that is its core function, so it is best for the car company to "outsource" that function. In the same analysis, the car company may discern that it has superior expertise in fuel-efficient engines, so the firm retains that value-added activity in-house. On a simpler level, many firms recognize that certain business functions, such as book-keeping, payroll services, or healthcare administration do not add value to the core business, so the firm contracts out or "buys" these services from other firms.

Outsourcing has become one of three major step changes in the emergence of the "global factory" (Buckley, 2014). Buckley (2014) described how previously connected activities have become geographically separated via: (a) trade (the geographic separation of production and consumption), (b) foreign direct investment of multinational firms (the geographic separation of internal value-adding activities), and (c) offshoring (the geographic separation of specific tasks that can be reconnected via contractual agreements). In recent years, we have witnessed a tremendous increase in the types of activities outsourced.

In the last two decades, the words "outsourcing" and "offshoring" have become commonplace. However, the terms are used loosely without a clear understanding. In reality, as illustrated, the concept of outsourcing has existed in business for a long time. *Outsourcing* by definition is simply "turning over an organizational activity to an outside supplier that will perform it on behalf of the focal firm" or more concisely the act of contracting out an organizational activity or function to an outside firm (Peng, 2013). *Offshoring* is outsourcing to a foreign firm and *in-shoring* is contracting out to a domestic firm.

In the early nineties, when Nike made a conscious decision to shift all of its manufacturing to sub-contractors in Southeast Asia and own only the "brand," many criticized the move for a loss of American jobs. Nonetheless, the Nike Paradigm (as it is now described) is normal business strategy and Nike is considered a pioneer (Klein, 2009). It is common practice in the shoe and apparel industry to own just the brand and manufacture all of the products abroad via third party contractors. Nike simply recognized that what adds value to the organization is not how, where, or who makes the shoe, but more importantly, the brand value of the shoe. Nike understood very clearly that added value comes not from owning shoe factories, but sourcing from the most efficient suppliers of shoes (Klein, 2009). The offshoring of manufacturing from the USA and other industrialized countries in the last four decades elevated the USA to a service-based economy. The growth industries within these countries are service based (i.e., banking, insurance, healthcare, education), not manufacturing based.

The real-time ICT revolution of the new millennium pushed firms to re-evaluate their value-added activities even further. Functions that once were impossible to perform remotely can now be performed remotely (e.g., robotic surgery or teaching). Consequently, many business processes have been offshored in the last two decades. More recently, such outsourcing has been recognized not for its cost-cutting value, but for the vast amount of talent, knowledge, and innovation it brings to the firm. Inadvertently, many firms have found that knowledge processes can also be offshored. Often, the question becomes not where we can find the cheapest labor to perform mundane business functions, but more realistically, how can we source talent globally to increase knowledge and innovation.

Many firms are recognizing the value of sourcing talent from abroad and redesigning their business strategies accordingly so that the processes sought abroad become an integral part of the firm and its competitive advantage. In fact, we would argue that criticisms against "outsourcing" and "offshoring" are losing their bite when contextualized within the day-to-day operations of many firms, particularly service and tech firms and in fact what we are witnessing is a revolution in how such business is done in a globalized world, much like we witnessed in manufacturing in the nineties. As noted by Power (2013), "Companies are increasingly using outside specialists to do their work. Driven by the ever-lower costs of global communication and online collaboration tools, Henry Ford's vertically integrated organization is yielding to Procter & Gamble's network of external innovators."

Below, we highlight research studies and surveys attesting to how business process outsourcing has evolved from simple, routine functions to knowledge and talent sourcing and what many have cheerfully begun to refer to as "best-sourcing."

Best-Sourcing and the Global Search for Talent

Graen and Grace (2015, p. 5) recently asserted that "Because of the ubiquity of the Internet, a wide variety of new markets have emerged and companies with the best talent have become the new 'Wall Street stars'." While their work focuses on what companies should be doing to address the needs of millennials who seek greater flexibility at work and seek better work/life balance than their parents, other researchers are studying how companies are looking beyond national boundaries and racing to attract talent from abroad (Lewin, Massini, & Peeters, 2009). Empirical data document the growing phenomena of strategic outsourcing and offshoring and their impact on innovation:

- In 2005–2006, 26 % of offshore implementation involved product development, suggesting that firms were seeking innovation (Lewin et al., 2009). More often than not, these product development functions consisted of engineering, R&D, and product design (Manning, Massini, & Lewin, 2008).
- A 2010 Bain & Company study of 2,000 companies over 10 years found that the motivation for outsourcing extended beyond the desire to cut costs. 85 % of companies that benefited from a sustainable growth in profits used outsourcing to bring in global talent, penetrate new emerging markets before competitors, introduce new innovative products before their competitors, and disrupt conventional business models (Heric & Singh, 2010).
- In a study of 1,355 firms in 10 Eastern European and Central Asian economies, Boermans and Roelfsema (2015) found that outsourcing was associated with product innovation whereas exporting and FDI were related to patenting and spending on R&D.

Lewin et al. (2009) noted an interesting convergence of trends in the US labor market which has created the demand for global talent. A steady decline in the number of Americans graduating from US colleges with Master and PhD degrees in science and engineering, combined with the government's decision to return to pre-1998 quotas for H1B visas, at a time when GDP was growing, created a shortage of needed skills, especially for the science and technology industries. In addition, graduates seemed to have been drawn to lucrative careers in the banking and consulting industries (Manning et al., 2008). This conclusion was confirmed by a 2011 survey finding that "Most American companies say a shortage of skilled domestic employees—not cost cutting—is the primary reason why they move some job functions overseas" (as described in "Shortage of Skilled," 2011). Companies had no choice but to outsource advanced work to professionals in other countries. Among the benefits of such offshoring is improved flexibility with the potential for better service quality and better processes (Lewin, 2012). It also enhances a firm's competitive advantage by giving it access to cross-border knowledge flows and foreign knowledge sources (Jensen & Pedersen, 2011).

Outsourcing and offshoring are likely to continue. Human cloud platforms are making it easier for firms to tap into a vast labor pool of online, skilled professionals. The top four most common work activities that involve such platforms are all high end: content generation, sales and marketing, design and optimization, and research and development (Kaganer, Carmel, Hirscheim, & Olsen, 2013). On the other hand, a rising concern for firms is the protection of patents, trademarks, designs, business processes, and software. As noted by Wiederhold, Gupta, and Neuhold (2010), "… with every outsourced job, intellectual property is transferred as well." We expect to see firms become more and more sophisticated in the types of contracts signed and increased monitoring and enforcement of laws by international organizations such as the EU. Musteen and Ahsan (2013) suggest that the difficulty of enforcing contracts in many emerging economies coerces firms into building tighter and more trusting relationships, which leads to better information exchange, relational capabilities, and trust, developing the foundation of innovation.

Cappelli (2011) described two additional risks associated with outsourcing: reliability and responsiveness. Reliability refers to the timely arrival of raw materials and supplies, the age and condition of equipment, and employee performance. If components promised by outsourced suppliers are not delivered expeditiously with a predetermined level of quality, the manufacturing process will shut down; if the equipment being used by the outsourced supplier fails, delays will occur; if workers are dissatisfied or not skilled, they may go out on strike or detract from the quality of the final product or service. Responsiveness requires the firm to have the capability to meet successfully a sudden increase in demand or a change in the requirements of the product or service. It is difficult to redirect the activities of independent workers because terms of engagement have been agreed upon in advance via the contract. Companies are advised to develop contingency strategies and mitigation strategies to handle the two risks. One option is to use shorter term contracts with well-designed incentives (Su, Levina, & Ross, 2016). Contractor, Kumar, Kundu, and Pedersen (2010) suggest that "fine-slicing and organizational and geographical dispersion come at a cost in terms of increased complexity and coordination. At some point in time the increased management and coordination costs might exceed the benefits" (Contractor et al., 2010, p. 1425). Consequently, to retain an optimal level of benefits from best-sourcing for knowledge-based activities, firms need to develop superior management coordination, collaboration capabilities, and embed a culture of innovation.

Moreover, it is important to develop appropriate human resource management policies to maintain the job satisfaction and productivity of professionals who often times interact with others remotely in virtual global teams. In their study of business process outsourcing firms in the Philippines, Presbitero, Roxas, and Chadee (2016) found that HRM policies made a positive contribution to employee retention when there was a fit between employee values and organizational values. This suggests that in the recruitment process, HR specialists should screen job candidates with such survey instruments as the Allport-Vernon-Lindzey *Study of Values* (SOV) to ensure alignment of individual values with organizational values (Kopelman, Rovenpor, & Guan, 2003). Wickramsinghe (2015) found that talent engagement and job-related training positively affected the quality of service in offshore outsourcing firms in Sri Lanka. It is recommended, therefore, to match employee talent to the level of task difficulty and to provide training and development opportunities.

Lacity, Willcocks, and Rottman (2008) noted that interesting work was key to reducing turnover among Indian professionals:

These Indians were eager to develop new software for clients, to learn new skill sets, to work on emerging technologies, and to manage other people. They complained about performing monotonous maintenance on a client's existing applications and merely coding and testing programs from pre-defined specifications—the bulk of what many Western clients send off-shore. (Lacity et al., 2008, p. 22)

The job characteristic model of Hackman and Oldham (1976), consequently, can be used to ensure that workers are using different skills, work on complete projects from beginning to end, receive positive and negative feedback as a gauge to their performance, have some choices regarding how to complete their tasks, and are informed about the positive impact that their work has on clients. Regarding incentives for innovation, a survey conducted by Lacity and Willcocks (2014) found that clients and suppliers of outsourced services reported that mandatory productivity targets, innovation days, and gainsharing at the project-level, were most effective. The recent trend toward the offshoring of high-end, knowledge-based activities, such as innovation and strategic flexibility, requires that firms consider how cultural differences can affect interpersonal relationships and communication between partners (Clampit, Kedia, Fabian, & Gafney, 2015). As is often the case, managers of offshoring projects need to find the right balance between cultural differences and cultural complementarities. Clampit et al. (2015) argued that cultural differences can cause conflict and miscommunication and require training and new procedures but it can also foster creativity; cultural complementarities can contribute to offshoring satisfaction. The key is to match the culture to the specific offshoring stage.

Given the opportunities and challenges associated with outsourcing and offshoring, it is important to study best practices. Below, we consider in detail, best-sourcing in: (a) The Scientific Technical and Medical (STM) Content Industry and (b) The Pharmaceutical Research Industry. The outsourcing of content development and delivery has been a popular choice for organizations interested in reducing costs, improving speed to market, and reducing staff workloads since 2006 (Klingshirn & Wiseniewski, 2006). Individuals today, including physicians, academicians, lawyers, and students, rely on high quality content in the form of articles, reports, surveys, books, and empirical studies to inform them about cutting edge advances in their fields of interest. Inspired innovation is made possible through the dissemination of knowledge, but few content users really understand how the industry works. The STM Content Industry is part of a larger content information industry that delivers critical information to scientists, chemists, and engineers. It is chosen for additional analysis because outsourcing opportunities have made the industry more international, more inter-disciplinary and more collaborative. The Pharmaceutical Research Industry, especially in reference to the outsourcing of clinical trials, was chosen because of its importance to the health and well-being of individuals from around the world. A recent report by the Association of Clinical Research Organizations (Temkar, 2015) concluded that outsourced clinical trials are completed on average 30 % faster than when performed by sponsoring companies or in-house, resulting in an average time savings of 4–5 months (which can be critical for patients in need of urgent treatments).

Moreover, both sectors are excellent examples of industries that were in turmoil and had to reinvent themselves through innovation and change. A significant part of the innovation was delivered through a best-sourcing strategy that involved engaging global resources that contributed to knowledge and skills rather than focusing purely on lower cost resources and labor arbitrage. At the same time, best-sourcing helped both these industries to lower costs and release valuable assets to be refocused on technology, R&D, and innovation. These industries represent some of the highest end of best-sourcing work being performed through global resources. Both these industries also provide good illustrations in which firms built an eco-system of specialized partners where each partner brought best-in-class talent and technologies to certain part of their value chain. This helped companies distribute the cost of innovation. Each partner along the value chain was constantly innovating and this collectively helped the companies evolve and remain differentiated.

Access to the case studies was available from Quatrro Global Services, a global services company offering business and knowledge processing services to organizations seeking higher operational effectiveness, greater flexibility, and lower operating costs, headquartered in Gurgaon, India.

Fig. 7.1   Key stakeholders in STM industry

Best-Sourcing in the Scientific Technical and Medical Content Industry

Industry Background

The Scientific Technical and Medical (STM) content industry is a small but highly complex component of the larger content/information industry. According to the *Outsell Report of 2013*, STM accounted for $31 billion and approximately 4 % of the $712 billion content/information industry. The industry consists of two kinds of players—(1) Publishers who source and own content directly from authors and are known for depth and quality of content and (2) Aggregators who source content from various sources including publishers, free sources, industry feeds, etc., and are known more for scope of content. For example, Elsevier, Wiley, Springer, and Wolters Kluwer are some of the larger STM publishers and Proquest and EBSCO are some of the larger aggregators. The STM content industry continues to grow at ~4–5 %, but is undergoing tremendous structural changes.

Evolving Industry Structure

The STM content industry has three key stakeholders as noted in Fig. 7.1[2]—authors or content creators; the content information providers and the consumers who could be researchers, corporations, universities, and so on.

---

[2] All figures in this chapter were either created by the authors based on information provided by *Quatrro Global Services* or obtained directly from the Company's archives. The authors have full permission to publish the content.

Historically, the content value chain has been very linear and all stakeholders were located in the developed markets. Most of the authors, creating original content were located in universities, research facilities and corporations in North America or Western Europe. Publishers were also located in the same geographies along with consumers of the content. However, over the last decade, the structure of the industry has changed. More and more research is being generated in regions outside the traditional geographies. China, which ranked 9th in terms of original research documents produced in 1995, has moved to the 2nd place in 2013, India has moved to 6th rank from 12th. Newer countries such as South Korea, Brazil, Iran, Turkey, and Malaysia have also moved up significantly in the rankings (SJR, 2016).

Similarly, consumption of content is also transforming. Emerging economies have significantly increased their share of information consumption. Increased research, movement of key industries like pharmaceuticals and technology to these markets, and faster growth in local economies, have led to this increased appetite for content.

In addition to regional changes, other factors are also contributing to turbulence in this industry. Increased availability of free content is driving down price points at which data are being consumed. A dramatic increase in volume of content has also made search and relevance very critical for content providers to maintain market share. All this has led to increased investments in newer technologies and content platforms, driving up costs.

Innovating through Best-Sourcing

The structural changes in the markets have forced content providers to reexamine their marketing and delivery strategies. To remain competitive and keep their products current to market demands, they needed to innovate and evolve rapidly. However, due to shrinking margins, content providers lacked the technology or the resources to make revolutionary changes. This included:

1. Expand content sources to non-traditional markets
2. Evolve strategies to compete with free content
3. Dramatically reduce costs to cater to newer markets
4. Technology innovation to enhance discoverability of content

For content providers, survival was not about making evolutionary changes or reducing costs. It was more about building a completely new value chain and business model. The challenge for companies in the content industry was that they had been largely stable for decades and innovation and change were not part of their culture. However, over the last few years, a few of the more progressive companies have made huge strides in reinventing themselves to be the publishers of the future.

Globalization of content requires content to be collected from highly fragmented sources such as patent offices, universities, and local research institutes, at country and regional levels. Since this is a very localized process and requires local knowledge, content providers could not handle it on their own. The more successful providers created a network of collaboration partners in each region to assist in the data collection process. The role of these partners is to identify content sources, create business relationships to ensure steady flow of content, and manage local relationships. Quality and reach of collaboration of partners not only helped overcome the challenges of dealing with distributed content sources but also in differentiation through increased coverage of content.

The other challenge that emerged out of the globalization of content creation is the number of languages involved. Content providers traditionally dealt with English and a few European languages for a majority of their requirements. However, in the new scenario they had to deal with content in more than 20 languages that all needed to be translated to English. Translation of scientific documents is a specialized task and needs to be handled in-country by teams that understand both the content as well as language. Once again, this forced content providers to outsource language translation to country-specific partners. Some content providers, who did not want to deal with these complexities, outsourced their translation requirements to one provider who in turn had a network of in-country translators. The need to handle a multitude of languages also brought about investment in translation tools that automated a significant part of the process.

Simultaneously, content publishers needed to reduce their costs dramatically to compete with free content and also meet the demands of new customers in emerging economies who were not willing to pay the same prices as the traditional customers for content.

Curating content, before it is published, is a complex process with a number of steps and sub-steps. Content providers had to find a solution that reduced costs but at the same time maintained the quality of output. After experimenting with a few models, the more successful providers arrived at what is referred to as a "best-sourcing" model. To create this model, providers "de-coupled" the entire process into multiple groups of sub-processes, based on the complexity of work and skill set required. As illustrated in Fig. 7.2, some publishers grouped the sub-processes into three categories. Category 1 consisted of simple tasks that were repetitive, human-intensive and did not require much knowledge of the domain (e.g., typesetting). Category 2 involved tasks that were more complex,

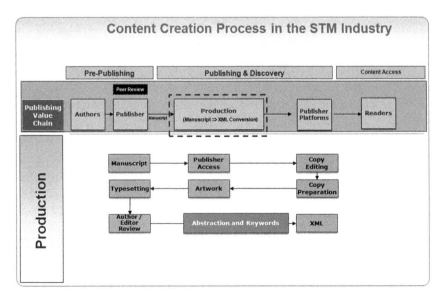

Fig. 7.2 Content creation process in the STM industry

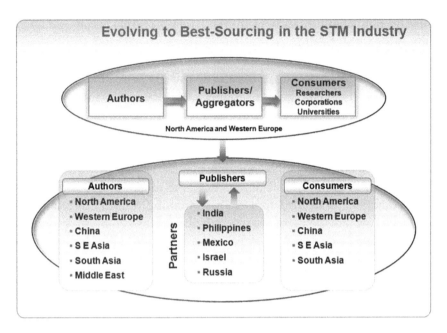

Fig. 7.3 Evolving to best-sourcing in the STM industry

needed some domain knowledge and could be automated to some extent (e.g., abstraction). Category 3 contained tasks that required extensive knowledge of the domain (e.g., editing). Once processes were disaggregated, content providers outsourced the tasks to the best location and partner that suited the task and at the same time provided the lowest cost solution. As shown in Fig. 7.3, Category 1 activities were outsourced to partners in smaller cities in India/Mexico/Philippines (where costs were far lower). Category 2 activities were primarily outsourced to larger cities in India and Philippines while Category 3 activities were retained in North America. A process that was once being handled out of a central office in New York City, was now being managed out of 3 global locations, coordinated with the help of workflow and collaboration tools.

While cost reduction is a clear benefit of this strategy, innovation and improvement in quality were equally important. The STM industry requires expert talent in various fields including Chemistry, Physics,

Engineering, Medicine, and Pharmaceuticals. By best-sourcing the process, content providers now have access to large pools of highly qualified technical resources across the globe. This allows them to increase the volume of content being processed at much better quality levels. This became even more critical as publishers needed to move to digital platforms and large quantities of historical content had to be converted from paper to digital formats. In an attempt to differentiate themselves, best-sourcing partners invested significantly to create a number of new tools and technologies that helped automate processes and increase quality and productivity of their output. For example, emerging markets, like India and China, are increasingly becoming consumers of content. "The demand for scientific and technical materials in any particular market is linked directly to the level of research and development spending. The commitment to R&D is long established in the U.S. and Europe. Now R&D spending is on the rise in places like China and India, so publishers have increased their presence in those markets" (Simba, 2009). However, the business models required to succeed in these markets have to be different from those in the traditional markets both in terms of overall costs and subscription models. Best-sourcing helped lower overall costs of content production and allowed content companies to provide pricing models more suited to these markets. Similarly, as content creation gets more international, collaborative and inter-disciplinary content providers need to differentiate by providing technology and platforms that support these changing needs. To tackle the challenges of discoverability, content providers need to move away from simple indexing to complex taxonomy and ontologies based classification. Once again providers were forced to look beyond their traditional geographies to find technology solutions in countries like Israel and Russia and then back this up with human curation in countries like India.

Providers also best-sourced a significant part of these investments to their global partners, thus reducing their need to make the investments internally. The providers were willing to make these investments as it helped them to differentiate against their competitors. Also by defraying the investment costs across multiple clients and engagements, the partners could offer these technology solutions at much lower costs to the content providers. From a content provider's perspective, this gave them instant access to best-in-class technologies and helped them to be nimble as newer technologies emerged. Best-sourcing helped content providers to become more cost effective, flexible, and expand their global reach. In a decade, the more successful content providers transformed themselves by "best-sourcing" their processes, technology, and innovation. As each partner was constantly progressing and innovating not only to be efficient, but to meet market demands, an eco-system of innovation without any significant investments from content providers was evolving. Concisely, the process of best-sourcing generated layers of innovative solutions from multiple partners.

Best-Sourcing in the Pharmaceutical Research Industry

Industry Background

The cost of developing prescription drugs has been steadily increasing over the last decade. According to a report published by the Tufts Center for the Study of Drug Development (CSDD), the cost of developing a prescription drug, that gains market approval, is $2.6 billion. This is a 145 % increase, correcting for inflation, over the estimate the center made in 2003 and includes an average $1.43 billion in out-of-pocket expenses (DiMasi, Grabowski, & Hansen, 2016). More than 60 % of the "out of pocket" costs of drug discovery are in the clinical trial phase, given that only 1 in 10 drugs that reach the clinical trial process receive approval. The high cost of drug discovery is driven by the time and cost of drug trials, increased regulatory requirements for drug approvals, and lower proportion of drugs getting approved at the end of the process. The typical lifecycle of a drug discovery process is illustrated in Fig. 7.4.

A clinical trial is a systematic study of new drugs in human subjects to generate data for discovering and verifying the efficacy and safety of a new drug. Clinical trials are highly regulated processes and can take place over a period of 5–10 years. The trials are spread across three phases prior to FDA approval with each phase having an increased patient sample size. The fourth phase is post launch and is to monitor safety of the drug on an ongoing basis.

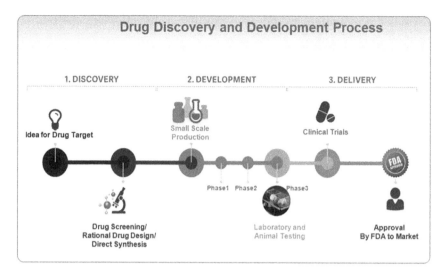

Fig. 7.4 Drug discovery and development process

Evolution of Outsourcing to Best-Sourcing in the Clinical Trial Process

Increased cost of launching prescription drugs directly impacts the cost of the final product. Rising healthcare costs in the USA have been a big concern for many years and cost of drugs is one of the key contributors to this rise. A typical drug receives a patent for 20 years, which includes the time for clinical trials. The longer the clinical trial period, the less the time for a pharmaceutical company to market the drug and recover its costs, directly impacting the launch price of the product. Pharmaceutical companies have therefore been seeking solutions to reduce the timelines for clinical trials in addition to reducing costs as both these are critical to reducing the overall price of the end product.

Most pharmaceutical companies test multiple products at the same time. This requires managing a huge infrastructure of people, processes, and technologies. As different products are at different stages of trial at any point of time, managing capacity of trial infrastructure at optimum levels becomes a challenge. When a key product is undergoing trials, there is a requirement to grow the infrastructure and when the trial for that product is completed, capacity is underutilized, until the next big product comes into the trial pipeline. The waxing and waning of trial infrastructure puts additional stress on the costs of trials.

To manage the above issues, pharmaceutical companies were forced to seek innovative solutions including outsourcing and offshoring. Outsourcing initially began with specialized companies that are referred to as Clinical Research Organizations (CROs) in the industry. The companies realized that outsourcing will help them in multiple ways:

1. Reduce the need to build and manage huge infrastructure.
2. Manage peaks and troughs.
3. Manage projects involving multiple trials.
4. Manage global trials (many products required trials to be conducted across the globe).
5. Distribute trials by phase and product type to specialists in that area (over a period of time, CROs became specialists in handling trials for certain disease types or geographic regions).

Traditionally, CROs were all US based and managed trials from the USA. However, as trials became complex and the need to crunch timelines became more and more critical, pharmaceutical companies realized that they needed to infuse technology and advanced data analytics models into the process. There was also a requirement for a lower cost workforce with a background in medicine and life sciences to monitor and process the enormous amount of data that was generated during a trial. This resulted in the second wave of outsourced partners, global Information Technology (IT) and Business Process Management (BPM) companies.

Today, clinical trials are a highly outsourced process with multiple partners spread across various geographies, with each partner handling a certain aspect of the trial process. The basis for division of work or "de-couplability" is based on the skills required, technology, proximity to clinical sites, and so on. An exploratory multiple case study from the pharmaceutical supply chain provides guidelines on how to best select and evaluate partners (Zhang, Pawar, Shah, & Mehta 2013). Outsourcing partners need to demonstrate their dynamic capabilities (e.g., project deliverables

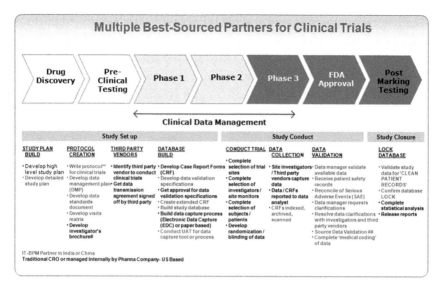

Fig. 7.5 Multiple best-sourced partners for clinical trials

and accuracy of costs), positions (e.g., financial assets and number of scientists), and paths (past experiences). A sample best-sourcing process for clinical trials is shown in Fig. 7.5.

The immediate benefits of a best-sourcing model are to leverage the skills and strengths of each of the partners. For example:

Partner	Skills/strengths
CROs	Manage onsite trial process
	Project management
	Data collection
IT Partner	Technology and tools
	Workflow management
	Advance database management tools
Business Process Management (BPM) Partner	Analytics
	Data management
	Provide lower cost workforce qualified in medicine/biology/life sciences/chemistry, etc. to analyze and report clinical data

The best-sourcing model has not only reduced the timelines for the trial process but has led to an overall reduction of costs to the extent of 10–15

%. However, across the board, there is a recognition that larger benefit of this distributed model is that it is allowing innovation to enter an industry that has been averse to change due to perceived risk. From a centrally controlled R&D function, pharmaceutical companies are moving to a best-sourced model with each partner in the eco-system bringing best practices and innovation in their specific areas of expertise. Some examples include:

- Optimized use of clinical data: Clinical trial data collection is a highly regulated process. Traditionally, pharmaceutical companies used the data only in the context of a single trial. With the advanced data management capabilities that IT and BPM partners bring to the eco-system, pharmaceutical companies now have the ability to look at these data across multiple trials, thus increasing the quality of decision making while reducing costs due to the reuse of data.
- Incorporation of wearable devices into the trial process: Data collection in the clinical trial process has always required a patient to walk into a hospital or doctors' office. With the incorporation of wearable devices, activity trackers, and mobile devices, the data collection process has the ability to rapidly evolve. For the first time, companies such as Google and Apple are becoming part of the clinical trial eco-system.
- Data Management: Best-sourcing partners are bringing advanced analytics to identify potential patient safety and operational performance issues in a pre-emptive manner, further mitigating risk during clinical trials.
- Pharmaceutical companies are now in the process of extending this model to the biology and chemistry side of drug discovery process, the phase that precedes trials and accounts for the remaining 40 % of the drug development process.

Pereira and Malik (2015) in their book, *Human Capital in the Indian IT/ BPO Industry*, note that while there is a stream of literature that points to cost reduction as a driver of offshoring, recent and more nuanced analyses point to a host of other drivers and outcomes. "The Process and product innovation of emerging businesses is often based on their ability to integrate, develop and reconfigure their internal capabilities and external competencies in order to address the changing environmental conditions and needs of their customers (Musteen & Ahsan, 2013, p. 426)." As described in the above case studies, many of the outcomes (i.e., STM disaggregation and distribution, data use for multiple trials, moving upstream to chemistry and biology, wearable devices tracking patient data) would not have come to fruition at such a rapid rate, nor would they have penetrated such markets without leveraging the benefits of best-sourcing (Pereira & Malik, 2015). Undoubtedly, speed to market and the offshoring of ancillary activities free up a firm's core resources leading to greater flexibility and innovation for the focal firm. However, here we also witness how partner firms leverage skills and resources in innovative ways to address the client needs, which in turn revolutionizes the whole industry.

Building a Culture of Innovation in Best-Sourcing Companies

Musteen and Ahsan (2013) suggest that quality and dynamism of intellectual capital will influence the degree to which offshoring will lead to innovation. They suggest that innovation is derived from leveraging intellectual capital, which consists of three interdependent components: human, social, and organizational. Human refers to individual skills and competences, social refers to the ability to employ those skills through relationship building and/or networking, and organizational refers to a firm's embedded routines, structures, and culture. Inarguably, while best-sourcing is important, innovation will lag unless the dynamics of human, social, and organizational capital are nurtured to foster innovation. Consequently, a firm's ability to not only source the best talent, but its ability to institutionalize a culture of innovation becomes critical (Musteen & Ahsan, 2013).

MacCormack, Forbath, Brooks, and Kalaher (2007) conclude that innovation should not be an assumed outcome of global sourcing, but a competitive advantage that results through collaboration. Such collaboration capabilities require the active engagement of people, processes, platforms, and programs and a mind set in which global offshore firms are understood to be collaborative partners and not cost-reduction centers (MacCormack et al., 2007). In alignment with Musteen and Ahsan (2013), MacCormack et al. (2007) suggest that a key strategy in developing collaborative capabilities that results in innovation is the development of not only people, but of their relational capabilities, meaning a significant investment in social capital. Moreover, absorptive capabilities by all partnering firms must be viewed as open, two-way channels and not as centrally controlled R & D moving in one direction. In this regard, Quatrro Global Services is a top-ranked business process-outsourcing and knowledge process-outsourcing supplier with over 21 years of experience. It has developed a set of proprietary tools and platforms to ensure value through innovation to clients. It provides advice on how to build a culture of innovation and how to develop successful HRM practices and policies. Consequently, best-sourcing partners in the two industries considered in this chapter have created a culture of innovation. This is driven primarily by a need to differentiate from their competitors and push from their clients, the pharmaceutical companies/publishers.

The workforce in best-sourcing companies, especially in emerging economies such as China, India, and Philippines, is very young and innovation needs to be institutionalized. Most companies have put a formal structure in place and it spans the entire lifecycle of an employee from hiring to ongoing management. Companies have also linked this to performance management and growth.

A typical innovation and quality framework is depicted in Fig. 7.6. Six Sigma and Lean are the basis for structural improvements while Kaizen is used for smaller but continuous improvements. The structure also spans all aspects of service delivery including people management, process and technology. Training on quality methodologies is provided to all employees and used as a motivator for retention. Best-sourcing companies are also aggressively getting external validation of their structure by getting themselves certified by global agencies like International Organization for Standardization (ISO) and Customer Experience Management (COPC).

The culture of innovation is also supported by comprehensive people practices as noted in Fig. 7.7.

These practices span recruitment and attracting the best talent, onboarding of new employees, retention through compensation, rewards linked to performance, ongoing training and education and growth

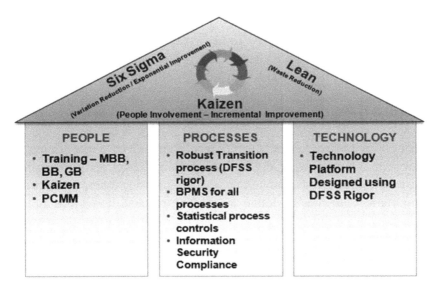

Fig. 7.6 Practices from global standards (COPC, DPA, PCMM, ISO, SSAE16)

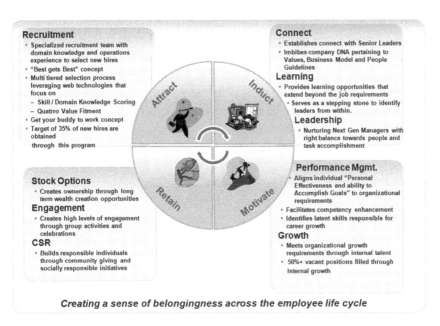

Fig. 7.7 People practices to build a culture of excellence

within an organization. Best-sourcing companies are continuously innovating and finding newer ways to keep employees motivated so they in turn can add value to their clients.

Future Trends and Challenges

Economic globalization and the ICT revolution provide fertile ground for new forms of outsourcing and offshoring. In this chapter, we highlighted the progression of outsourcing to best-sourcing using examples from two important industries. In doing so, we demonstrated how innovation is generated when industries maximize the utility of technology and essentially operate in a virtual environment by seeking the best global talent and resources regardless of national borders. We also show how increased complexity in these industries has been met by more innovative tools, policies, and strategies developed by best-sourcing firms. Simultaneously, we emphasized that outsourcing is not new. It has existed for more than a century and in this sense, the future will be no different. New forms of technology will continue to be disruptively innovative leading to significant strategy and market shifts (Christensen, Raynor, & McDonald, 2015). Quite possibly, the once-distant phenomenon in science fiction novels is closer than we imagine. The recent proliferation of cloud-based technologies will further boost "virtualization" of firms. The progression of the corporation from a national to a multinational entity will evolve to the next generation, possibly into a seamless web of best-sourced people and processes around the globe bound together by a common vision and mission and managed through collaborative tools leading to a plethora of innovations. The virtual corporation will have an amoeba-like structure that is constantly changing to meet current needs and assimilate best practices wherever they are located across the globe (i.e., such trends are already evident in innovations such as Bitcoin).

Nonetheless, this utopia of sourcing will not be without significant challenges. As noted by Woodard and Sherman (2015), much of the offshoring literature has focused on macro-level issues (e.g., why firms decide to offshore and why some ventures succeed while others fail), without considering the impact of exporting jobs on the attitudes and behaviors of the individuals who are performing the work. Specially designed HRM policies and practices need to be developed to keep workers motivated and engaged. The dearth of information on effective performance management systems for outsourcing work is especially noticeable in developing countries, such as Poland (Buchelt, 2015). Poland is one of the fastest growing economies in the EU and is ranked 9th for top countries in the world for outsourcing (Buchelt, 2015). Lajili (2015) has developed a conceptual framework, which suggests that HR policies intended to build and invest in human assets differ according to governance designs—that is, hierarchy (or firm governance), contract-based arrangements (or outsourcing/offshoring) and market-based (or arms' length) employment contracts. In a similar approach, Andersen (2015) hypothesized that successful implementation of: (a) "tactical offshore outsourcing" requires skill capability, inter-organizational communication, cross-cultural competencies and inter-organizational leadership; (b) "strategic offshore outsourcing" must be supported by knowledge management, human resource development support for innovation, and change management; (c) "transformational offshore outsourcing" is suitable for such HR practices as knowledge sharing and organizational development.

It also is important to recognize that the borderless virtual corporation is in fact grounded in a world bound by the national boundaries and regulations. Indeed, many thoughtful and novel regulatory changes are required to manage an evolving virtual corporation. Current regulations around cross-border immigration, finance, data privacy, intellectual property rights along with individual and employee rights need to be continually examined and re-examined. For example, while private firms are accustomed to best-sourcing, governments, often the most inefficient entities in many societies, struggle with outsourcing processes. In the past, the USA postal service outsourced some activities and now it has an arrangement with Staples (a private firm) to handle mail (FSRN, 2016). What's next? Social Security? Healthcare? Defense? For many, the question remains, exactly, where do you draw the line? What should be outsourced or in our case "best-sourced" next? Services traditionally provided by government? What are the implications and how will unions respond? Will employees be paid well? How will companies balance efficiency needs with quality and care for employee wellbeing? Rightly so, many governments struggle with the need to balance efficiency and employee wellbeing. The struggle between technological determinism and economic globalization on one side and individual, human and sovereign rights on the other will continue to be hotly contested. The pull of a borderless virtual corporation will incessantly push against societies bound by borders and undoubtedly, there will be a storm (or two) before the quiet.

References

Anderson, V. (2015). International HRD and offshore outsourcing: A conceptual review and research agenda. *Human Resource Development Review, 14*(3), 259–278.

Boermans, M. A., & Roelfsema, H. (2015). The effects of internationalization on innovation: Firm-level evidence for transition economies. *Open Economies Review, 26*(2), 333–350.

Brown, D. J. (2016, February). *Top global market trends and predictions for 2016 and beyond.* KPMG International. http://www.kpmg-institutes.com/institutes/shared-services-outsourcing-institute/articles/2016/02/sourcing-advisory-global-pulse-report-4q15.html

Buchelt, B. (2015). Performance management in polish companies internationalizing their market activities. *The International Journal of Human Resource Management, 26*(15), 1965–1982.

Buckley, P. J. (2014). International integration and coordination in the global factory. In P. J. Buckley (Ed.), *The multinational enterprise and the emergence of the global factory* (pp. 3–20). London: Palgrave Macmillan.

Buckley, P. J., & Casson, M. (2014). Marketing and the multinational: Extending internalisation theory. In P. J. Buckley (Ed.), *The multinational enterprise and the emergence of the global factory* (pp. 20–51). London: Palgrave Macmillan.

Cappelli, P. (2011). HR sourcing decisions and risk management. *Organizational Dynamics, 40*(4), 310–316.

Christensen, C. M., Raynor, M. E., & McDonald, R. (2015, December 1). *What is disruptive innovation?* Retrieved April 6, 2016, from https://hbr.org/2015/12/what-is-disruptive-innovation

Clampit, J., Kedia, B., Fabian, F., & Gaffney, N. (2015). Offshoring satisfaction: The role of partnership credibility and cultural complementarity. *Journal of World Business, 50*(1), 79–93.

Contractor, F. J., Kumar, V., Kundu, S. K., & Pedersen, T. (2010). Reconceptualizing the firm in a world of outsourcing and offshoring: The organizational and geographical relocation of high-value company functions. *Journal of Management Studies, 47*(8), 1417–1433.

DiMasi, J. A., Grabowski, H. G., & Hansen, R. A. (2016). Innovation in the pharmaceutical industry: New estimates of R&D costs. *Journal of Health Economics, 47*, 20–33.

Foster, G., O'Reilly, N., & Davila, A. (2016). *Sports Business Management.* NY: Routledge.

Friedman, T. L. (2007). *The world is flat: A brief history of the twenty-first century.* New York: Picador USA.

FSRN. (2016, April 30). *U.S. postal service workers protest outsourcing to big-box Staples—FSRN.* Retrieved April 6, 2016, from http://fsrn.org/2014/04/u-s-postal-service-workers-protest-outsourcing-to-big-box-staples/

Google Corporate Website—Google. (2016). Retrieved May 4, 2016, from https://www.google.com/about/company/

Graen, G., & Grace, M. (2015). New talent strategy: Attract, process, education, empower, engage and retain the best. SHRM-SIOP Science of HR White Paper Series. https://www.shrm.org/Research/Documents/SHRM-SIOP%20New%20Talent%20Strategy.pdf

Hackman, J. R., & Oldham, G. R. (1976). Motivation through the design of work: Test of a theory. *Organizational Behavior and Human Performance, 16*(2), 250–279.

Hashi, N., & Buckley, P. (2009). A global system view of firm boundaries. *Globalization and the Global Factory.* Edward Elgar Pub. Retrieved from https://www.e-elgar.com/shop/globalization-and-the-global-factory?_website=uk_warehouse

Heric, M., & Singh, B. (2010). Outsourcing can do much more that just cut costs. *Forbes,* 15 June. http://www.forbes.com/2010/06/15/outsourcing-capability-sourcing-leadership-managing-bain.html

Jensen, P. D. Ø., & Pedersen, T. (2011). The economic geography of offshoring: The fit between activities and local context. *Journal of Management Studies, 48*(2), 352–372.

Kaganer, E., Carmel, E., Hirscheim, R., & Olsen, T. (2013). Managing the human cloud. *MIT Sloan Management Review, 54*(2), 23–32.

Klein, N. (2009). *No logo: 10th Anniversary edition with a new introduction by the author* (10 Anniversary ed.). New York: Picador.

Klingshirn, R. G., & Wisniewski, B. (2006). Solving the offshoring dilemma. *T + D, 60*(6), 49–52.

Kopelman, R. E., Rovenpor, J. L., & Guan, M. (2003). The "study of values": Construction of the fourth edition. *Journal of Vocational Behavior, 62*(2), 203–220.

Lacity, M., & Willcocks, L. (2014). Business process outsourcing and dynamic innovation. *Strategic Outsourcing: An International Journal, 7*(1), 66–92.

Lacity, M. C., Willcocks, L. P., & Rottman, J. W. (2008). Global outsourcing of back office services: Lessons, trends, and enduring challenges. *Strategic Outsourcing: An International Journal, 1*(1), 13–34.

Lajili, K. (2015). Embedding human capital into governance design: A conceptual framework. *Journal of Management & Governance, 19*(4), 741–762.

Lewin, A. (2012, February 12). *Survey: Organizational flexibility as a new benefit of global outsourcing.* News release, Duke's Offshoring Research Network. http://www.fuqua.duke.edu/news_events/news-releases/offshoring-jan2012/#.VuytU85zqFI

Lewin, A.Y., Massini, S., & Carin, P. (2009). Why are companies offshoring innovation? The emerging global race for talent. *Journal of International Business Studies, 40*, 901–925.

MacCormack, A. D., Forbath, T., Brooks, P., & Kalaher, P. (2007). *Innovation through global collaboration: A new source of competitive advantage.* Division of Research, Harvard Business School.

Manning, S., Massini, S., & Lewin, A. Y.. (2008). A dynamic perspective on next-generation offshoring: The global sourcing of science and engineering talent. *Academy of Management Perspectives, 22*(3), 35–54. Retrieved from http://www.jstor.org/stable/27747462

Musteen, M., & Ahsan, M. (2013). Beyond cost: The role of intellectual capital in offshoring and innovation in young firms. *Entrepreneurship Theory and Practice, 37*(2), 421–434.

Osterhammel, J., & Petersson, N. P. (2009). *Globalization: A short history.* (D. Geyer, trans.). Princeton University Press. Outsell Report, 2013. Outsellinc.com

Peng, M. W. (2013). *Global business* (3rd ed.). Eagan, MN: South-Western College Publishing.

Pereira, V., & Malik, A. (2015). *Human capital in the Indian IT/BPO industry* (2015 edition). Houndmills, Basingstoke; Hampshire; New York, NY: Palgrave Macmillan.

Power, B. (2013, February 7). Keeping work organized when your team is fragmented. *Harvard Business Review.* https://hbr.org/2013/02/keeping-work-organized-when-your-team-is-fragmented

Presbitero, A., Roxas, B., & Chadee, D. (2016). Looking beyond HRM practices in enhancing employee retention in BPOs: Focus on employee-organisation value fit. *The International Journal of Human Resource Management, 27*(6), 635–652.

Sciaretta, B. (2011). Tutored in Germany, playing for the US. *The New York Times*, 11 November. http://www.nytimes.com/2011/11/11/sports/soccer/in-global-search-for-talent-us-soccer-team-trends-german.html?_r=0

Shortage of Skilled Workers is Primary Reason for Offshoring Jobs. (2011, January 19). News release, Duke's offshoring research network. http://www.fuqua.duke.edu/news_events/newsreleases/offshoring_jan_2011/#.VusvgRIrJUM

Simba. (2009). *Global STM Publishing 2008–2009 : Market Research Report.* Simba Information. Retrieved from http://www.simbainformation.com/Global-STM-Publishing-1609434/

SJR. (2016). *SJR—International Science Ranking.* Retrieved April 12, 2016, from http://www.scimagojr.com/countryrank.php?area=0&category=0&region=all&year=2014&order=it&min=0&min_type=it

Su, N., Levina, N., & Ross, J. W. (2016). The long-tail strategy of IT outsourcing. *MIT Sloan Management Review, 57*(2), 81–89.

Temkar, P. (2015). Clinical operations generation next... the age of technology and outsourcing. *Perspectives in Clinical Research, 6*(4), 175–178.

Wickramasinghe, V. (2015). Effects of human resource development practices on service quality of services offshore outsourcing firms. *The International Journal of Quality & Reliability Management, 32*(7), 703–717.

Wiederhold, G., Gupta, A., & Neuhod, E. (2010). Offshoring and transfer of intellectual property. *Resources Management Journal, 23*(1), 74–93.

Woodard, M. S., & Sherman, K. E. (2015). Toward a more complete understanding of offshoring: Bringing employees into the conversation. *The International Journal of Human Resource Management, 26*(16), 2019.

Zhang, M., Pawar, K. S., Shah, J., & Mehta, P. (2013). Evaluating outsourcing partners' capability: A case study from the pharmaceutical supply chain. *Journal of Manufacturing Technology Management, 24*(8), 1080–1101.

8

Chinese Innovation Performance Development and Evolving Forms of Global Talent Flow

Paula Makkonen

Introduction

Individuals have greater freedom to choose where to study, work, and live than ever before. Therefore, the mobility of people across geographic and cultural boundaries has fundamental implications for globalisation (Shenkar, 2004). No wonder human capital has been described as central not only to the growth of a country's economy but also to its competitiveness in the knowledge-based global economy (Daugeliene & Marcinkeviciene, 2015). This is because global talent flow (see Carr, Inkson, & Thorn, 2005) helps transfer technologies and knowledge across borders (Daugeliene & Marcinkeviciene, 2015). An increased level of mobility is hence an important manifestation of the internationalisation of professions and professional labour markets as well as the development of innovation performance in individual nations (Carr et al., 2005; Søberg,

P. Makkonen (✉)
Department of Management, University of Vaasa, Vaasa, Finland

© The Author(s) 2017
S. Kundu, S. Munjal (eds.), *Human Capital and Innovation*,
DOI 10.1057/978-1-137-56561-7_8

2010). Consequently, labour-based migration is 'likely to continue to be important in the future, because of continuing strong pressures for global integration, capitalism's demand for certain type of labour, and people's desire to migrate in order to improve their life-chances' (King, 2012, p. 26).

Innovation performance refers to a nation's capability to create new innovations (Søberg, 2010). Innovations are said to require a recognised need, financial resources, relevant technology but especially human capital, in the form of competent people (Engelberger, 1982). Human capital, which incorporates talented individuals and their capacity to transfer their knowledge, skills, and abilities are hence said to be the most important elements demonstrating a country's ability to compete in the global market (Daugeliene & Marcinkeviciene, 2015).

China is one of the world's most rapidly developing markets (Morrison, 2014) and has announced its intention to transform itself into an innovative society by 2020, and to be a world leader in science and technology by 2050 (Abrami, Kirby, & McFarlan, 2014). One scheme facilitating this target is a recent 'Made in China 2025' programme, which according to Chinese Premier Li Keqian aims to 'seek innovation-driven development, apply smart technologies, strengthen foundations, pursue green development and redouble our efforts upgrade China from a manufacturer of quantity to one of quality.' This target is driven, like in many other emerging countries by central government policies including interventions, regulations, execution of controlled integration, generous funding for public companies (Reslinger, 2013) as well as incentives for attracting western-educated talent, both foreign and Chinese origin to return (Zweig, 2006). Commentators, however, report challenges to this aspiration. Chinese culture is based on a natural preference for knowledge exploitation—an activity that favours making use of knowledge over creating new knowledge (Baark, 2007), a cultural feature that will make it difficult to meet the growth aspirations announced. Different forms of global talent flow—brain gain (Saxenian, 2005), brain drain (Baruch, Budhwar, & Khatri, 2007; Beine, Docquier, & Rapoport, 2008; Docquier & Rapoport, 2012), and reverse brain drain, sometimes referred as brain circulation (Saxenian, 2005; Daugeliene & Marcinkeviciene, 2009)—could therefore be expected to contribute to this ambitious plan. However, little is known of how China might move from imitation to innovation (see Yip & McKern, 2014) or how different forms of global talent flow appear from the perspective of innovation performance development in China.

This study is hence focused on answering the question: *How do different forms of global talent flow (brain drain, brain gain, and reverse brain drain) appear in the different phases of China's innovation performance development and why.* By answering this question, this study contributes to the talent mobility and innovation literatures. This is done by illustrating the innovation performance development of China and explaining the impacts and appearance of different kinds of global talent flow (see also King, 2012 for labour-related migration) during each innovation process development phase. Global talent flow, for example immigration and repatriation of self-initiated expatriates (SIEs), has been theoretically explained by using push and pull factors as well as intervening obstacles (Lee, 1966) or shocks (Tharenou & Caulfield, 2010). Also in this study, these factors are used to facilitate answering the research question. Pull factors are attributes that increase global talent flow and enhance China's innovation capability, whereas push factors are the ones that decrease it. This understanding is relevant not only for other emerging markets aiming to develop their innovation performance, but also for organisations focused on investing in and transferring their core technologies to emerging economies.

The study starts with a review of the literature on the different modes of global talent flow and of China as a context for studying innovation performance development, and modes of global talent flow. After the presentation of the methods, findings, and the discussion section, the study addresses its practical implications and limitations, and finally offers suggestions for further research.

Literature Review

Modes of Global Talent Flow

Global talent flow (see Carr et al., 2005) is the phenomenon of individuals with a high level of skills, qualifications, and competence moving across borders. Daugeliene (2007) has discussed global talent flow with reference to highly skilled individuals who are able to convert knowledge, intellect, wisdom, and ideas into tangible innovative products or services. As a result, global talent flow has been said to be a vital process for nations and for the world's economic development (Daugeliene & Marcinkeviciene, 2015).

Literature recognises three forms of talent flow, which are not only interconnected but could also be expected to have implications for the innovation performance development of an individual nation or organisation. The best known form of global talent flow is the *brain drain,* which often has a negative connotation. It is a phenomenon in which educated talent moves for professional/economical purposes from the country of origin (Baruch et al., 2007; Beine et al., 2008). Brain drain has largely been discussed with reference to educated individuals from developing countries moving to the benefit of developed countries, most notably from Asia to North America and Europe (e.g. No & Walsh, 2010). However, in the era of global economies does the phenomenon of brain drain concern the developed countries alike. Brain drain occupies not only students, but there are also other mobile employee groups, which are involved. One, which is increasing in importance, is SIEs. SIEs with a difference to organisation sent expatriates (OEs), whose mobility is inter-organisational (Andresen, Bergdolt, Margenfeld, & Dickmann, 2014), 'self-initiate their international relocation, with the intentions of regular employment and temporary stay' (Cerdin & Selmer, 2014, p. 1293). In the literature, these two employee groups differ from immigrants, who are often referred as individuals from ethnic minorities who have moved to developed countries for economical or humanitarian reasons (Al Ariss & Syed, 2011; Andresen et al., 2014).

The second form of global talent flow is *reverse brain drain,* also known as *brain circulation* (Saxenian, 2005; Daugeliene & Marcinkeviciene, 2009; Sabharwal & Varma, 2012). Reverse brain drain refers to the migration (repatriation) of highly skilled people, who in line with the conceptual development of Daugeliene and Marcinkeviciene (2015), could be defined as individuals who have studied and/or worked in a foreign country, but return to work in (and therefore benefit) their country of origin. Such labour force mobility brings new patterns of immigration and emigration as it involves the temporary two-way movement of a skilled labour force between their home and host countries (Chen, 2008).

Migration literature has considered repatriation both as a movement of failure and success (King, 2012). Returnees are pulled to their home countries by career and economic opportunities as well as by the national identity or the family concerns, but they may also be pushed away by severe difficulties related to cultural assimilation upon repatriation (Tharenou & Seet, 2014). For instance, in China many returnees seem to be reluctant to stay permanently, but instead prefer part-time or visiting posts, or stay for a while before leaving permanently. In addition, the quality of the returnees may not meet the expectations of home country employers (Zeithammer & Kellogg, 2013). From expatriate perspective, which is typically focused on temporary stay, global mobility often targets at positive career outcomes upon repatriation. However, opposite experiences are not uncommon (Begley, Collings, & Scullion, 2008; Doherty & Dickmann, 2009; Makkonen, 2015a). As a result, individuals may choose not to repatriate (Tharenou & Caulfield, 2010), but to more permanently contribute to the third recognised form of global talent flow, the *brain gain* (e.g. Saxenian, 2005; Tung & Lazarova, 2006). Brain gain refers to positive outcomes of brain drain for the beneficiary nation. Although these three forms are well defined in the literature, prior studies do not explain how and why different forms of global talent flow predominate in different phases of the innovation performance development of a country.

China as Context for Studying Innovation Performance Development and Modes of Global Talent Flow

China has been among the world's fastest growing economies for the last 30 years (World Bank, 2013; OECD, 2013, pp. 9–11) during which time it has been a major attractor of foreign investment (Yifei, Von Zedtwitz, & Simon, 2007). It is also said to be the world's largest manufacturer (United Nations, 2015). In 1990, only 3 % of the global production output by value was manufactured in China. Today, the value is approximately 25 %. For example, 80 % of air-conditioners, 70 %

of mobile phones, and 60 % of shoes are manufactured in China (The Economist, 2015). Much of this progress has been attributed to advanced western technology transfers and the spillover effects of foreign investments in China (Sun & Du, 2010). It could therefore be argued that foreign investments and knowledge transfer in particular have played a major role in developing the innovation performance of China.

Since the late 1970s, the Chinese government actively encouraged talented Chinese to study abroad with the goal of ensuring they contributed to China's innovation performance development upon their repatriation (Zweig, 2006). Although many have returned, the ratio has not been quite as high as expected (Zweig & Changgui, 2013). As a result, China has taken measures to attract both Chinese and foreign talent in the form of launching special incentive programmes, which it is hoped to contribute to meeting the demand for high-level expertise in the key sectors of China's socio-economic development. An example would be the Talent1000 programme, which according to its official targets aims to 'recruit non-ethnic Chinese experts who are under 65 years of age, and in principle, have his/her doctorate granted by overseas educational institutions and are able to work in China for three consecutive years with at least nine months for each.' These individuals are expected to be 'strategic scientists, leading experts in science and technology, or internationalised innovative teams capable of achieving critical technological breakthroughs, advancing the high-tech industries and promoting new disciplines' (Zweig, Fung, & Han, 2008; http://1000plan.safea.gov.cn/).

With the power of China's state-led industrial system model, which is typical of many emerging Asian countries (Reslinger, 2013), the Chinese government has also been determined to use significant public funds and political power to reduce the importance of imported western technologies on certain strategic sectors. The government has also taken action to increase both the quantity and quality of home-grown innovation in China (Abrami et al., 2014). A practical means of contributing to innovation performance is exemplified by China's proactive approach in establishing Chinese R&D centres in the west (see also Gammeltoft, 2006). China has also been active in acquiring western high-tech companies with access to western knowledge portfolios and senior local talent, which has often proved reluctant to move to China owing to the cultural challenges involved (Harryson & Søberg, 2009; Abrami et al., 2014, Osawa & Mozur, 2014).

Despite these efforts, scholars suggest China might well potentially be at a crossroads in terms of its economical and technological development. Although many Chinese companies, such as Lenovo, Coolpad, Xiaomi, and Oneplus in the telecoms and consumer electronics field, or Alibaba and Baidu for internet-related services and products are able to challenge global market leaders and set trends, China is still considered a context in which local R&D is diligently pursued but breakthroughs remain rare (Osawa & Mozur, 2014). Although both economical and technological development of China are well documented, little is known of how China's innovation performance development is affected the different forms of global talent flow.

Methods

This qualitative study is focused on enhancing our understanding of certain under-researched phenomena. It does so by adopting a non-linear, non-positivistic abductive approach of *systematic combining* (Dubois & Gadde, 2002). Systematic combining is a process where 'theoretical framework, empirical fieldwork, and case analysis evolve simultaneously' (Dubois & Gadde, 2002 p. 554). This approach scrutinises a particular phenomenon rather than increasing the number of cases while considering the richness of the research context (Dyer & Wilkings, 1991). Interviews were chosen as the best means of collecting data, because they offer a suitable and efficient way to obtain highly personalised data with a good return rate (David & Sutton, 2004, p. 214).

The informant selection of this study followed the spirit of a non-linear abductive research approach and the recommendations of Halinen and Törnroos (2005). Accordingly, the informants were chosen by way of a purposive sampling strategy (Saunders, 2012). Consequently, only Western informants with personal work experience in the fields of innovation or business development, or in R&D functions in China were interviewed. Their hands-on experience from a variety of industries and organisations operating in China, as well as their exemplifying national, organisational, or individual aspects of the phenomenon increase the validity of the findings (Yin, 2014) and provide multiple sources of evidence (Lincoln & Guba, 1985). The informants were located and approached via *LinkedIn* and through personal contacts. These informant selection strategies also provided a source for further snowballing. As a result, 55 informants were interviewed in two waves either via Skype, or in person in China between 2013 and 2015. The first round in late 2013 and early 2014 was focused on the experiences of western professionals with either personal managerial or operative responsibility with western MNCs in China in Guangdong province, Beijing, and Shanghai. The second round took place in late 2015 and was focused on individuals with either consultancy or governmental experience in China from the R&D and innovation development perspectives. The interview selection process was intended to provide rich subjective and contextual insights into the topic from multiple perspectives (Prasad & Prasad, 2002), and deliver enough material to achieve data saturation (Saunders, 2012).

All informants were informed of the purpose of the research and offered an opportunity to withdraw from the interview at any point or decline to answer any uncomfortable questions. All informants were also guaranteed anonymity and that their contribution would be anonymous, as recommended in the literature (Saunders, Lewis, & Thornhill, 2009). These terms encouraged informants to participate and enhanced their willingness to share their experiences. Therefore, and due to the sensitive nature of themes emerging from the data, this study does not reveal the names of companies or detailed information on the informants. All informants were invited to choose the interview spot and time that would foster a relaxed atmosphere for the interviews. Consequently, all face-to-face interviews were conducted in relaxed and comfortable surroundings such as cafés, restaurants, private homes, or hotel lobbies in China (Saunders et al., 2009). Following the suggestion in the literature, a language equality approach was adopted for those informants who used the same mother tongue as the author. For the other non-native English speakers, the mutual disadvantage approach was applied by using English as the interview language (Marschan-Piekkari & Reis, 2004). Further background information on the informants is presented in Table 8.1 below.

Table 8.1 Background information on the informants

Gender	Female	Male	In total
No of informants	8	47	55

Length of professional experience in China	>5 years	5–10 years	10< years	In total
No of informants	30	13	12	55

Type of position	General mgmt	HR	R&D	Legal	Governmental position	In total
No of informants	12	13	10	4	6	55

Field of industry	Government	Consumer electronics	Machinery	Metallurgy	Plastics	Automation	Consultancy	Software	In total
No of informants	6	14	6	4	7	6	6	6	55

Informants were given broad themes to reflect upon and were invited to relate their experiences of and observations on China. Themes were related to the development of China and how different forms of global talent flow contribute to that phenomenon. Discussion topics included: the technological and economic development of China, so as to identify the innovation development performance phases; the identification and development of the different types of talent pool available in China, so as to bolster understanding of the various forms of global talent flow; and other factors that contribute to each phase and why. In addition, the informants were canvassed for their opinions on the role of Westerners and western organisations in China. These themes were selected to provide a detailed understanding of the research question from multiple perspectives. This approach led to a substantial amount of iterative questioning and probing as new issues emerged, or as consequence of information gathered in previous interviews (Saunders et al., 2009). All interviews were recorded with the permission of the informants and transcribed verbatim.

Initially, the transcriptions of the interview content and the accompanying notes were read several times. All the findings related to the research question were then coded and arranged on a timeline in accordance with the interpretative content analysis approach (Yin, 2014; Mayring, 2004. The next step was to identify those findings related to the different phases of the development of innovation performance. This stage involved the identification of the product, service, and manufacturing types present in China. There followed an assessment of how different types of global talent flow appeared in each identified innovation performance development phase and why. These assessment steps followed the idea of Lee's (1966) pull and push factors as well as intervening obstacles, which must be overcome during the evolution of each phase in China. Pull factors in this study refer to factors that enhance global talent flow for the favour of China's innovation performance development, whereas push factors have the opposite effect. The non-linear research approach meant the assessment of data took place in parallel with the data collection, and the assessment stage featured a considerable amount of iteration. Below, all the findings of the current research are illustrated by direct quotations as suggested in the qualitative research literature (Saunders, 2012). Each presented quote illustrates typical reflections emerging from the data.

Findings

The findings emerging from the data suggest three innovation performance development phases that have occurred in China to date. In the current research, these phases are arranged and explained as the eras of copy and imitation; of evolution; and of revolution.

The Era of Copying and Imitation

The first chronologically identified phase was an era of copying and imitation. According to the findings, the era of copying and imitation represents an innovation performance development phase observed in China during which two different forms of global talent flow were present from the Chinese perspective: brain gain and government facilitated purposive brain drain.

This era represents a phase starting in the 1990s that formed a platform for the following innovation development phases of China. This foundation was laid on the massive knowledge and technology transfer from the west to China. Western MNCs, for example in the telecom and electronics industry sectors, took a strategic approach to move manufacturing to China while looking for cheaper labour costs and access to expanding Chinese consumer markets. This brain gain facilitated by western MNCs not only involved process and product development transfer, but also significant western input into the training of local employees. The following interview excerpt recalls a typical business start-up situation of a western MNC in China.

> It was in the late 1990s. I was called and asked if I'd like to go to China to start our factory there. It was interesting but challenging. At that time, it was really difficult to find competent local staff. All the technology came from (the western) HQ and we urgently needed to transfer the processes

and to train the locals in order to meet the capacity that was needed. (Former operative manager of western MNC)

The challenges described by the informants during the phase related not only to a lack of competent local staff, but also to the difficulty of managing the attrition among the MNC's trained local personnel. This brain gain of local staff often resulted as severe intellectual property rights (IPR) problems such as imitated western products appearing in local markets, and that scenario prompted the naming of the first identified innovation performance development phase. The following excerpt illustrates the challenges related to these phenomena.

There was also a real challenge with the local staff, who would just steal the product and take it to the next house or simply leave the company with all the knowledge. They [Chinese] would just copy it, without even knowing what it was for, without having all the features of the product. Soon you would find localised variants [imitations] of those products in accordance to their local taste and needs. They have always been very good and fast at copying and manufacturing, once they figured out what and how to do that. (Former production manager of western MNC)

During this era, the respondents reported the brain gain aspect became more organised and legitimate. In the 2000s, there were approximately 600 western R&D centres in China and by 2010 that number had more than doubled (Abrami et al., 2014). By the start of this century, the Chinese government was also focused on attracting western MNCs to form joint ventures with local organisations. Quite often however, those joint ventures were reported to have been unsuccessful, but proved to be effective sources of brain gain for the benefit of the Chinese organisations.

Many companies have been attracted to come here to form joint ventures. However, Westerners have always, in my opinion, been too wide-eyed with that. Over time they'd change the rules, the composition and ownership of joint ventures would be turned around. There were often several local companies formed based on the same imported technology, some companies were even forced to hand over their whole patent portfolio for the benefit for the joint venture. You can just imagine how that story ended up.

> Eventually the joint ventures would often dry out, everything gone: the IPR, the customers… (A current western government official)

From the brain drain perspective, this era represents a phase during which atypical, but purposive forms of brain drain occurred. In contrast to the traditional format of brain drain in emerging economies, the local Chinese government was particularly active in sending talent to be educated abroad. This purposive brain drain was eventually expected to contribute to the development of Chinese innovation performance in the form of reverse brain drain.

> There was a lot of Chinese talent moving abroad, they still are. Particularly the local government was sending them out to the Americas, Australia and Europe, the most talented. (Former HR manager of western MNC)

As a whole, from the pull perspective, the era of copy and imitation proved to be an effective means of transferring knowledge and technology from the western organisations to China regardless of push factors and intervening obstacles related to local culture, IPR challenges, local staff attrition, and immature legal system of China, which have caused considerations over the knowledge and technology transfer operations to China. Despite the government-sponsored brain drain, the volume of brain gain pulled by governmental actions has proved the policy successful. This innovation development phase significantly improved the capabilities of local organisations and paved the way for the following era of evolution.

The Era of Evolution

The second chronologically identified phase was the era of evolution. This phase represents how the current innovation development phase in China is seen by western informants. During this phase, China has taken an even more pragmatic and determined approach to its innovation performance development. This phase emphasises both brain gain and reverse brain drain. During this phase, Chinese companies and products have come to be seen as trend setters and challengers to the western market leaders. Examples include Lenovo, Xiaomi, and OnePlus in the consumer electronics business segment, or internet-based service providers such as Baidu and Alibaba. Such strategies involve also attracting Western executives and specialists to contribute to success of local organisations. For example Hugo Barra, a former product spokesman of Google's Android division joined Xiaomi in 2013. This hire has been referred as one of the most significant moves for the current success of Xiaomi. Since the release of its first smart phone in 2011, Xiaomi has become one of the largest smart phone manufacturers. There is more and more western talent, both SIEs and OEs hired by the local organisations, which seek knowledge transfer, technological advancement, and means for entering international markets.

> I used to be in charge of this specific product line, that's what I had done for the past 15 years. They hired me because of that knowledge, and that's what they got. (Repatriated western self-initiated expatriate employed by a local Chinese organisation)

However, the current innovations and pipeline products are still based on existing (western) technology platforms.

> They (the Chinese) are very good at launching products based on western innovations into markets. Their products also compete very well, but are much more cost efficient than the western ones. Sometimes the quality of their products may not exceed or totally achieve the level of western alternatives, but who cares, in pricing they are invincible. That quality versus efficiency is difficult to compete against. They have also become very nationalistic in the product choices. Western products are no longer their first choice. They can make products that better suit their local needs and taste. (A current Western government technology officer placed to China)

This quote illustrated the efficiency of approaches where China takes advantage of the outcomes of brain gain received from the west. As a result, adaptation of existing western technologies has become a new standard and highly lucrative practice. At the same time, reverse *brain drain* stemming from returning western-educated Chinese is increasing as a result of improving living standards and career opportunities in China. This new talent pool provides human capital, which is needed both by the Chinese and western MNCs alike. For example, the strategic focus of western MNCs on rapidly changing local Chinese markets requires local competencies and market understanding, which western expatriates typically lack. Individuals with both Chinese and western understanding can thus be assets contributing to meeting that need.

> Nowadays it is easier to find competent locals. There are Hai Gui's (returning Chinese) coming back from the States and Europe with western business experience. As a result, the number of expatriates in China (in MNCs) is dramatically decreasing. It is also due to changing consumer behaviour of the locals. MNCs must also have locals in the management, who understand how the local market works. (A current operative manager of western MNC)

Reverse brain drain, which is expected to contribute to China developing a competitive edge, is not only based on the self-directed repatriation of Chinese immigrants. The Chinese government is actively encouraging reverse brain drain in the form of incentivising the returning Chinese, and brain gain in the form of encouraging foreign talent to live and work in China. As an example, the Chinese government has allocated substantial funds both for Chinese and foreign talent, both professional and academics, willing to live and work in China. This talent pool is expected to contribute to the innovation performance of China, leverage the competitive advantage of Chinese universities and organisations, and to smooth access for Chinese companies to western markets.

> Despite their competitive edge, Chinese organisations still need Westerners—for the sake of internationalisation. They do realise it's worth buying the competencies they need. One good example is the 1000talent programme, which is not only focused on attracting the Chinese, but also the Westerners. They get very good benefits if they get accepted to the programme. (A Western freelance HR professional operating in China)

It is not brain gain and reverse brain drain alone that have contributed to the current innovation performance level of China. According to the findings, China has efficiently taken advantage of its huge internal market potential and volumes, but is still in urgent need of more advanced technology. The country still has very practical needs in the fields of clean technology, energy, and transportation for instance, and that those needs are recognised by the Chinese state is evident in the drive for efficient knowledge and technology exploitation encapsulated in the government's current five-year plan.

> The Chinese are very pragmatic nowadays and their need for technology transfer is defined in their five-year plan, after which the plan is efficiently executed. There is a clear change in that. Only a few years ago their (Chinese government technology officers') doors were always open (for all national representatives and organisations), but today they make us compete harshly against each other and they'd choose carefully only the partners who will bring the most benefit. Often they do not need us anymore, but we do need them. (A current governmental technology officer placed to China)

In the above referenced phase of evolution, China's institutional structure and growing internal market as pull factors means China has been able to exploit the economies of scale inherent in the country and benefit from the brain gain spurred by the employment opportunities offered by both local organisations and western MNCs to achieve a certain level of innovation capability. However, there seems to be increasing amounts of push factors alike, which seem to be connected to China's interest to regulate the type and amount of foreign talent, but also control the business activities of foreign MNCs operating in China. The findings also offer evidence of China's systematic attempts to transform its traditional brain drain into reverse brain drain, and China has certainly succeeded in upgrading its innovative status and progress towards the next crucial innovation development phase, the era of revolution.

The Era of Revolution

The era of revolution is the third chronologically identified innovation performance development phase in China. The era of revolution can be distinguished from the era of evolution in so far as revolution encompasses a capability to initiate innovation that is not based on existing technology platforms.

Regardless of efforts made during the phase of evolution to reduce China's dependence on western technology platforms and the recognition of an urgent need to resolve the acute challenges in the fields of energy and clean technology for example, China has not yet entered the era of revolution. Although China as a context is rapidly changing, there are still challenges perceived to be connected to Chinese culture, and the way people are managed and educated. These contextual attributes of China reduce individuals' contribution and willingness to challenge the existing solutions and outperform.

> One bottle-neck used to be the Chinese education system. Today many universities in China are however very highly ranked. But because of the local culture, how people and organisations are managed, the people are not used to question the present without fear of losing face. If you fail, there are always new people that can replace you. (Current HR director of MNC)

The data illustrate a strong optimism over the future capabilities of local talent and shed light on how China is about to progress to the next innovation performance phase. Examples include taking advantage of digitalisation, but also emphasise the importance of active technology and innovation scouting, and the establishment and acquisition of R&D centres and technology companies abroad.

> We are about to witness huge innovation leaps coming from China, by the Chinese, particularly if they will succeed with the aim of digitalisation and robotics. China has an opportunity to achieve the era of revolution during the next decade or so, but just not yet. They do realise that they still need the innovation seeds, the technology platforms, coming from outside. That's why they are doing huge amounts of innovation scouting: establishing RD centres and purchasing companies abroad. (Current technology officer of MNC)

The Chinese are also perceived to have other competitive advantages that are difficult to compete against, and which foster progress towards the following phase. Those advantages include economies of scale resulting from enormous internal demand, and moreover, the political will to allocate public funds to deliver such an aim. Nevertheless, the recent economic developments in China have caused some concern over its capability to tackle a potential middle-income trap. The following excerpt sheds light on these concerns, but also on the anticipated strengths of China.

> They (Chinese) are just superior in process innovation and achieving cost efficient ways of doing things. That is their competitive advantage, which comes from the huge volumes, the fact of having financing and the political will, and is thus impossible (for the Western organisations) to compete against. That's why so many Western companies are leaving the country. But they'd still need to avoid the middle-income trap, if they wish to become a true innovation leader. I believe that digitalisation will help them to avoid such a trap. The only thing that can get in the way is global economics, if the bubble bursts and they won't have the capital to achieve what they have planned, that is the only thing. (Current Western governmental officer placed in China)

An interesting question is how the different forms of global talent flow might manifest themselves during the era of revolution. The literature currently suggests China will aim for talent self-sufficiency and an advanced level of inborn innovation performance. Recent reports confirm tightening restrictions for foreign companies over certain business segments as well as restrictions for growth, setting up operations, obtaining licences, but more over for foreign talent management. For example European MNCs report increasing difficulties in obtaining visas and work permits for their home country employees needed in China (European Chamber, 2016). The findings of the current research support that supposition, as it reveals an emphasis on the reverse brain drain aspect of the returning Chinese and the utilisation of inborn talent. However, despite diligent attempts to attract and retain returning western-educated Chinese, both returnees and locally educated Chinese may subsequently emigrate permanently due to environmental issues or personal challenges connected to the Chinese culture.

> There will be a lot of Chinese talent returning to China, only if they will be able to tackle their environmental issues. However, there are also many of returnees who will re-immigrate because of these cultural issues, those who

have learned to work in the west. But one thing that is for sure: China does not lack talent. The Chinese are hardworking and talented, more determined to perform than the Westerners. With this amount of people, the number of highly intelligent individuals is huge. I am sure that in the future we will be fighting for the Chinese talent. (Current R&D officer of MNC)

As a summary, regardless of China's efforts to benefit from brain gain and reverse brain drain, and to progress innovation performance development, there are still several push factors and intervening obstacles that hinder country's ability to enter the era of revolution. Much of this is related to issues of trust and national protectionism. However, China is expected to reach that phase within a decade with the aid of its enormous inborn talent pool and by reaping the benefits from the innovation seeds it has been sowing.

Discussion

Global talent flow is said to help to transfer technologies and knowledge across borders (Daugeliene & Marcinkeviciene, 2015) and contribute to the innovation performance of the receiving country (Søberg, 2010). The current study sheds light on the development of the innovation performance of China and how emerging countries might acquire new knowledge and learn new ways of being innovative (Kuznetsov & Sabel, 2006). To do so it posed the research questions: *How do different forms of global talent flow (brain drain, brain gain, and reverse brain drain) appear in different phases of China's innovation performance development and why.* The research questions were addressed by assessing different types of innovation performance development phases, as well as the appearance of three different modes of global talent flow in China.

Developed economies have often been blamed for talent deployment of emerging economies. Even if the accusations are well founded, the current study offers other kinds of plausible interpretations and alternative viewpoints of the brain drain and brain gain phenomena. In contrast to mainstream literature, the current study illustrates how the issues of global talent flow are not challenging for emerging countries alone, but are a challenge for organisations and countries from the developed world too.

In discussing these themes, this qualitative study makes key contributions to two bodies of literature. First, the current research contributes to the small volume of innovation literature on China and to our current understanding of the development of the innovation performance phases observed in China. Yip and McKern (2014) posed the question of how China was moving from imitation to innovation without apparent distinctions between the innovation phases. The current study offers a more refined assessment of the innovation phases of China and provides explanations for such transitions. Second, the current research contributes to the global talent mobility literature by illustrating and explaining the involvement of different modes of global talent flow at each phase.

The current study identified three distinctive innovation performance development phases in China: the eras of copy and imitation; of evolution; and of revolution. Each of these phases emphasises different forms of global talent flow. Emerging economies are typically reported to suffer from the effects of brain drain of locally educated talent (Beine et al., 2008). However, in the case of China, the situation seems unconventional. In contrast to the suggestions of the mainstream global talent flow literature examining emerging markets, China does not seem to have suffered from the effects of brain drain. Instead, Chinese brain drain has been a strategy facilitated at governmental level and one highly very deliberately encouraging reverse brain drain. Hence, this study meets the recommendation of Baark (2007) and sheds light on how innovation performance development in China is being built on the foundation of the technological exploitation of western innovations and of western knowledge.

The assessment of different innovation phases of China revealed how as Engelberger (1982) suggested, the capability to innovate is related to need, the amount of capital, relevant technology, and availability of talent. Regarding the third identified and forthcoming era, the *era of revolution*, China has announced its intention to become an innovative society by 2020 and a world leader in science and technology by 2050 (Abrami et al., 2014). The findings of this study permit us to assess whether the aspiration is a realistic one, and reveal how much is related to and expected of China being able to reap the benefits of the innovation seeds it sowed. Other pull factors that facilitate this aim are related to the need for such innovations, high volumes of local talent, and moreover to political will, and access to public capital. This political announcement does however reflect the current challenges China is facing. Although China does possess the features of an innovative society that can be expected to contribute to transformation (Abrami et al., 2014), the findings highlight the push factors that hinder its efforts of advancing to the next innovation phase of revolution.

The findings of this study complement the available literature in offering multiple explanations for such push factors and intervening obstacles (e.g. Baark, 2007). Examples include governmental policies that aim at attracting chosen talent and technologies, but on the other hand increase restrictions for the movements of foreign capital and labour force. Those explanations relate also to China's political systems as well as its cultural and institutional context, for example, local organisations being managed and students educated based on hierarchical and paternal management structures and practices (Baark, 2007; Yip & McKern, 2014; Søberg & Han, 2014), or perhaps the emphasis on groups rather than individuals. Challenges also include the tradition of controlling the distribution of information and knowledge among the population (Spencer, 2001; Baark, 2007), and also those related to the transition from central planning to a market economy (Liu & White, 2001). Moreover, the findings confirm how aspects of innovation that are collaborative, but which demand trust have been neglected in China (Søberg & Han, 2014), something confirmed by the findings of this study. For example, although recent reports indicate improvements (European Chamber, 2016), has the Chinese government been accused of failing to protect IPR (Abrami et al., 2014). Many western organisations with substantial R&D investments in China have already left the country, not only due to financial considerations, but also as a result of technology and knowledge exploitation. It might perhaps be reasonable to argue that in order to achieve the next phase, there should be what Daugeliene and Marcinkeviciene (2009, p. 50) described as 'changes not only (related to) economic cooperation, but also the mindset of societies and management principles.' Despite efforts to enhance IPR legislation, China is still a place where trust is vital but cannot be taken for granted due to the shortcomings of its legal system (Jansson, Johanson, & Ramström, 2007). The goal of talent self-sufficiency and an advanced level of inborn innovation performance may seem like an ambitious, but achievable target; however, many significant innovations are based on long-term collaborative cooperation between nations based on trust, not on exploitation.

Practical Implications, Limitations, and Further Research Potential

The findings of this study have practical implications. The findings illustrate how each of three modes of global talent flow contributes to innovation performance development. They also shed light on how China, as an example of an emerging economy, has been able to benefit from the different forms of global talent flow by applying a systematic approach over a relatively short period and by utilising knowledge and technology exploitation. Although China has never suffered from the traditional form of brain drain (migration of educated talent), it has actively implemented political measures to boost brain gain and reverse brain drain. This understanding is significant for the policymakers of countries who would like to follow the example of China, as well as that of Japan on stable political will and long-term planning (see Nonaka & Takeuchi, 1995). An understanding of the positive aspects of brain drain could provide practical tools for other emerging economies struggling with the negative aspects of global talent flow. The findings similarly highlight a need for cross-border cooperation on innovations among smaller countries, in order to compete against those with a wealth of talent and bountiful financial resources.

The findings of this study also allowed us to assess the development aspects of the innovation performance of China and offer some explanations for the rapid transformation of a single nation. These observations provide practical examples for policymakers of the benefits of long-term planning and political will. The study also sheds light on the cultural hurdles one country can face on its way towards the era of revolution.

This aspect suggests scholars might need to re-evaluate the managerial and pedagogical practices employed in their countries.

The current research also has practical implications for MNCs considering business opportunities and joint ventures in emerging countries. The findings highlight how, in line with the suggestions of Oorschot, Solli-Sæther, and Karlsen (2014), such organisations might face difficult trade-offs involved in collaborating with local organisations. Any collaboration involving technology and knowledge sharing could trigger knowledge leakage and espionage resulting in systematic knowledge and innovation exploitation by the local organisation. The risk appears to be particularly high in emerging markets with limited IPR protection legislation, as literature suggests (van Oorschot et al., 2014).

From the HRM perspective, literature of global talent flow has mostly focused on the expatriation, adaptation, and repatriation of organisation sent expatriates, which presents challenges both for the individuals and for the organisations (Nery-Kjerfve & McLean, 2012). However, there is little empirical evidence on how organisations could take advantage of the reverse brain drain of SIEs (Suutari & Brewster, 2000), for example. The mobility of such individuals might provide an alternative source of staffing with accordant substantial opportunities for contextual knowledge transfer. Studies over the career trajectories of SIEs in China (see e.g. Makkonen, 2015, 2016) indicate that the group could also provide a talent pool for local organisations looking for knowledge and skills in short supply locally.

The limitations of this study include that it focused on the different modes of global talent flow and how those appear during the different innovation phases in China from the western perspective. This monodimensional (focus on western perceptions and experiences) approach to research questions and findings is hence subjective, value-based and context-related, and thus offers only one aspect of the reality. Further empirical research on the topic in other contexts and perspectives would be welcome. Such empirical research could offer a more comprehensive understanding of the different forms of global talent flow and how those appear and why. For example, the perceptions of locals in China or in other emerging countries would no doubt offer a more complete picture of the issue and provide avenues for further research. Subjective experiences are also subject to biased opinions and therefore the findings cannot be generalised as such.

These subjective Western perceptions and interpretations of the outcomes of global talent flow phenomena do however signal potential reluctance for the future cooperative innovation performance development opportunities and could hence prevent or seriously hinder opportunities to achieve the ambitious innovation performance targets of China. This understanding together with existing literature provides some alternative explanations for the delayed appearance of an innovation revolution in China. Further empirical studies focused on that particular aspect would be welcome.

References

Abrami, R. M., Kirby, W. C., & McFarlan, F. W. (2014). Why China can't innovate. *Harvard Business Review, 92*(3), 107–111.

Al Ariss, A., & Syed, J. (2011). Capital mobilization of skilled migrants: A relational perspective. *British Journal of Management, 22*, 286–304.

Andresen, M., Bergdolt, F., Margenfeld, J., & Dickmann, M. (2014). Addressing international mobility confusion—Developing definitions and differentiations for self-initiated and assigned expatriates as well as migrants. *International Journal of Human Resource Management, 25*(16), 2295–2318.

Baark, E. (2007). Knowledge and innovation in China: Historical legacies and emerging institutions. *Asia Pacific Business Review, 13*(3), 337–356.

Baruch, Y., Budhwar, P. S., & Khatri, N. (2007). Brain drain: Inclination to stay abroad after studies. *Journal of World Business, 42*(1), 99–112.

Begley, A., Collings, D. G., & Scullion, H. (2008). The cross-cultural adjustment experiences of self-initiated repatriates to the Republic of Ireland labour market. *Employee Relations, 30*, 264–282.

Beine, M., Docquier, F., & Rapoport, H. (2008). Brain drain and human capital formation in developing countries: Winners and losers. *The Economic Journal, 118*(528), 631–652.

Carr, S. C., Inkson, K., & Thorn, K. (2005). From global careers to talent flow: Reinterpreting 'brain drain'. *Journal of World Business, 40*(4), 386–398.

Cerdin, J.-L., & Selmer, J. (2014). Who is a self-initiated expatriate? Towards conceptual clarity of a common notion. *The International Journal of Human Resource Management, 25*(9), 1281–1301.

Chen, Y. C. (2008). The limits of brain circulation: Chinese returnees and technological development in Beijing. *Pacific Affairs, 81*(2), 195–215.

Daugeliene, R. (2007). The position of knowledge workers in knowledge-based economy: Migration aspect. *European Integration Studies, 1*, 103–112.

Daugeliene, R., & Marcinkeviciene, R. (2009). Brain circulation: Theoretical considerations. *Inzinerine Ekonomika-Engineering Economics, 3*, 49–57.

Daugeliene, R., & Marcinkeviciene, R. (2015). Brain circulation: Theoretical considerations. *Engineering Economics, 63*(4).

David, M., & Sutton, C. D. (2004). *Social research the basics*. London: SAGE Publications.

Docquier, F., & Rapoport, H. (2012). Globalization, brain drain, and development. *Journal of Economic Literature, 50*(3), 681–730.

Doherty, N., & Dickmann, M. (2009). Exposing the symbolic capital of international assignments. *International Journal of Human Resource Management, 20*, 301–320.

Dubois, A., & Gadde, L.-E. (2002). Systematic combining: An abductive approach to case research. *Journal of Business Research, 55*, 553–560.

Dyer, W. G., & Wilkins, A. L. (1991). Better stories, not better constructs, to generate better theory: A rejoinder to Eisenhardt. *Academy of Management Review, 16*(3), 613–619

Economist. (2015). Made in China. 14 March.

Engelberger, J. F. (1982). Robotics in practice: Future capabilities. *Electronic Service and Technology Magazine*.

European Chamber. (2016). European business in China: Position paper 2015/2016. *European Union Chamber of Commerce in China*.

Gammeltoft, P. (2006). Internationalisation of R&D: Trends, drivers and managerial challenges. *International Journal of Technology and Globalisation, 2*(1), 177–199.

Halinen, A., & Törnroos, J. Å. (2005). Using case methods in the study of contemporary business networks. *Journal of Business Research, 58*(9), 1285–1297.

Harryson, S. J., & Søberg, P. V. (2009). How transfer of R&D to emerging markets nurtures global innovation performance. *International Journal of Technology and Globalisation, 4*(4), 367–391.

Jansson, H., Johanson, M., & Ramström, J. (2007). Institutions and business networks: A comparative analysis of the Chinese, Russian, and West European markets. *Industrial Marketing Management, 36*(7), 955–967.

King, R. (2012). *Theories and typologies of migration: An overview and a primer*. Willy Brandt Series of Working Papers in International Migration and Ethnic

Relations 3/12. Malmö Institute for Studies of Migration, Diversity and Welfare (MIM) Malmö University.

Kuznetsov, Y., & Sabel, C. (2006). International migration of talent, diaspora networks, and development: Overview of main issues. In Kuznetsov. Y (Ed.). *Diaspora networks and the international migration of skills: How countries can draw on their talent abroad*, Washington DC: The World Bank, 3–20.

Lee, E. S. (1966). A theory of migration. *Demography, 3*(1), 47–57.

Lincoln, Y. S., & Guba, E. G. (1985). *Naturalistic inquiry.* Newbury Park, CA: Sage Publications.

Liu, X., & White, S. (2001). Comparing innovation systems: A framework and application to China's transitional context. *Research Policy, 30*(7), 1091–1114.

Makkonen, P. (2015). Perceived employability development of western self-initiated expatriates in local organisations in China. *The Journal of Global Mobility, 3*(4), 350–377.

Makkonen, P. (2016). Career self-management behaviour of western self-initiated expatriates in local organizations in China. *The International Journal of Human Resource Management, 27*(11), 1135–1157.

Marschan-Piekkari, R., & Reis, C. (2004). Language and languages in cross-cultural interviewing. In R. Marschan-Piekkari & C. Welch (Eds.), *Handbook of qualitative research methods for international business* (pp. 224–243). Cheltenham: Edward Elgar.

Mayring, P. (2004). Qualitative content analysis. In U. Flick, E. von Kardorff, & I. Steinke (Eds.), *A companion to qualitative research* (pp. 266–269). Thousand Oaks, CA: SAGE.

Morrison, W. M. (2014). *China's economic rise: History, trends, challenges and implications for the United States.* Washington, DC: Congressional Research Service.

Nery-Kjerfve, T., & McLean, G. N. (2012). Repatriation of expatriate employees, knowledge transfer, and organizational learning: What do we know? *European Journal of Training and Development, 36*(6), 614–629.

No, Y., & Walsh, J. P. (2010). The importance of foreign-born talent for US innovation. *Nature Biotechnology, 28*(3), 289–291.

Nonaka, I., & Takeuchi, H. (1995). *The knowledge-creating company: How Japanese companies create the dynamics of innovation.* Oxford: Oxford university press.

OECD. (2013). Global trends 2030: Alternative worlds. *FDI in figures report 2012.* National Intelligence Council.

Osawa, J., & Mozur, P. (2014, January 16). The rise of China's innovation machine. *The Wall Street Journal, 35.* Online: http://www.wsj.com/news/articles/SB10001424052702303819704579320544231396168

Prasad, A., & Prasad, P. (2002). The coming of age of interpretive organizational research. *Organizational Research Methods, 5*(1), 4–11.

Reslinger, C. (2013). Is there an Asian model of technological emergence? *Socio-Economic Review, 11*(2), 371–408.

Sabharwal, M., & Varma, R. (2012, June). *Why one leaves? Return migration of academic scientists and engineers from the United States to India.* 9th IZA Annual Migration Meeting, Bonn, Germany.

Saunders, M. N. K. (2012). Choosing research participants. In G. Symon & C. Cassell (Eds.), *The practice of qualitative organizational research: Core methods and current challenges* (pp. 37–55). London: Sage.

Saunders, M. N. K., Lewis, P., & Thornhill, A. (2009). *Research methods for business students* (5th ed.). Harlow and Prentice Hall: Financial Times.

Saxenian, A. (2005). From brain drain to brain circulation: Transnational communities and regional upgrading in India and China. *Studies in comparative international development, 40*(2), 35–61.

Shenkar, O. (2004). One more time: International business in a global economy. *Journal of International Business Studies, 35*(2), 161–171.

Søberg, P. V. (2010). Industrial influences on R&D transfer to China. *Chinese Management Studies, 4*(4), 322–338.

Søberg, P. V., & Han, Y. (2014). Institutional influences on R&D collaboration in China. *International Business: Research, Teaching and Practice, 8*(1), 1–16.

Spencer, J. W. (2001). How relevant is university-based scientific research to private high-technology firms? A United States–Japan comparison. *Academy of Management Journal, 44*(2), 432–440.

Sun, Y., & Du, D. (2010). Determinants of industrial innovation in China: Evidence from its recent economic census. *Technovation, 30*(9-10), 540–550.

Suutari, V., & Brewster, C. (2000). Making their own way: International experience through self-initiated foreign assignments. *Journal of World Business, 35*(4), 417–436.

Tharenou, P., & Caulfield, N. (2010). Will I stay or will I go? Explaining expatriation by self-initiated expatriates. *Academy of Management Journal, 53*(5), 1009–1028.

Tharenou, P., & Seet, P. S. (2014). China's reverse brain drain: Regaining and retaining talent. *International Studies of Management & Organization, 44*(2), 55–74.

Tung, R. L., & Lazarova, M. (2006). Brain drain versus brain gain: An exploratory study of ex-host country nationals in Central and East Europe. *The International Journal of Human Resource Management, 17*(11), 1853–1872.

United Nations. (2015). *World Statistic Pocketbook*. United Nations Statistics Division. Retrieved from data.un.org

van Oorschot, K., Solli-Sæther, H., & Karlsen J.T. (2014). Sharing knowledge or not? Innovation and imitation in shipbuilding projects in China. *Academy of Management Proceedings, 2014*(1), 17388.

World Bank. (2013). *China 2030*. Retrieved from http://www-wds.worldbank.org

Yifei, S., Von Zedtwitz, M., & Simon, D. F. (2007). Globalization of R&D and China: An introduction. *Asia Pacific Business Review, 13*(3), 311–319.

Yin, R. K. (2014). *Case study research* (5th ed.). Thousand Oaks, CA: SAGE.

Yip, G., & McKern, B. (2014). Innovation in emerging markets—The case of China. *International Journal of Emerging Markets, 9*(1), 2–10.

Zeithammer, R., & Kellogg, R. P. (2013). The hesitant hai gui: Return-migration preferences of US-educated Chinese scientists and engineers. *Journal of Marketing Research, 50*(5), 644–663.

Zweig, D. (2006). Competing for talent: China's strategies to reverse the brain drain. *International Labour Review, 145*(1-2), 65–89.

Zweig, D., & Changgui, C. (2013). *China's brain drain to uni sta*. London: Routledge.

Zweig, D., Fung, C. S., & Han, D. (2008). Redefining the brain drain China's 'diaspora option'. *Science Technology & Society, 13*(1), 1–33.

9

Theorising Human Capital Formation for Innovation in India's Global Information Technology Sector

Ashish Malik and Vijay Pereira

Introduction

In recent years, many Anglo-Saxon countries, enterprises, and policy-makers have attempted to address issues of competition and globalisation through appropriate interventions in their training systems. At a national level, investment in training has enhanced international competitiveness and minimised the risk of unemployment (ABS, 1994; OECD, 1994). At a policy level, much of the debate in the last two decades has focussed on the role of training in improving the competitiveness of firms (Malik & Rowley, 2015a; NTITSD, 1998; Pereira & Malik, 2015; Stevens & Walsh, 1991). However, research suggests that improvements at a national level can only occur in the context of improving training

A. Malik (✉)
Newcastle Business School, Newcastle, NSW, Australia

V. Pereira
University of Wollongong, Dubai, UAE
University of Portsmouth, Portsmouth, UK

© The Author(s) 2017
S. Kundu, S. Munjal (eds.), *Human Capital and Innovation*,
DOI 10.1057/978-1-137-56561-7_9

provision at a firm level (Cappelli, 1995; Porter, Schwab, Sala-I-Martin, & Lopez-Claros, 2004).

Further, innovation is seen as a source of sustained competitive advantage in hyper-competitive environments (Damanpour & Schneider, 2006). Recent research suggests an increasing number of firms in emerging markets are focusing on innovation and differentiation as a key strategy for achieving sustained competitive advantage (Govindrajan & Trimble, 2012; Kumar & Puranam, 2012). While the body of research on organisational level understandings of building innovative capacity is well established (Prajogo & Ahmed, 2006; Smith, Courvisanos, Tuck, & McEachern, 2012), there exists a limited understanding of the micro- (individual) level foundations of the role of cognitive and non-cognitive abilities of individuals in building innovative capacity. Investment in training and fostering a learning culture (Foss & Larsen, 2003; Mark & Akhtar, 2003) has been noted to be key stimuli for building a firm's innovative capacity. More recently, academics have link learning in organisations with their ability to innovate as well as develop their innovation capability (Akbar & Tzokas, 2013; Alegre & Chiva, 2008; García-Morales, Lloréns-Montes, & Verdú-Jover, 2007). Further, as Zeytinoglu and Gordon (2009) note through employer-funded training, firms can develop increased levels of innovation capability as they often engage in sharing their new knowledge and provide feedback to the employees. Such an approach is typical of firms who are committed to learning (Jeon & Kim, 2012).

In this conceptual chapter, using Dubin's (1978) hypothetico-deductive approach to theory-building, we attempt to model the various macro-, micro-, and meso-level influences on human capital formation and innovation in the context of India's high-technology information technology (IT), business process outsourcing (BPO), and IT product development (ITPRD) firms. The rest of this conceptual, theory-building chapter is organised as follows. First, we begin with a brief review of human capital formation in the firms in general, considering the factors that trigger and stabilise skill formation, with a specific focus on the Indian IT industry. Second, we provide a brief overview of the research context for setting the boundaries to which this theorisation is applicable. Next, we elaborate on Dubin's (1978) hypothetico-deductive approach to theory-building that a researcher–theorist must embrace before proposing their theorisation. It is in this major piece of review and theorisation that we identify the key units of our theory and propose our theoretical framework of theorising human capital formation for innovation in India's IT sector. In the subsequent sections, we outline the laws of interactions between the various units of theory and present a conclusion with directions for researcher–theorists to empirically test our theory.

Modelling Enterprise Training and Skills Formation: Organisational Level Attempts

In the last decade, the field of HRD has witnessed an intense debate on issues ranging from its definition, purpose, to theory-building attempts (McLean, 1998; Swanson, 1999, 2001), and has been confronted with challenges such as globalisation, managing diversity, moving away from an *inward-looking* approach to an *outward-looking* approach, serving the needs of a wider community of stakeholders (Malik & Rowley, 2015a; Pereira & Malik, 2015; Pereira & Budhwar, 2015), and minimising the disconnect between HRD theory and practice to ensure its future (Bing, Kehrhahn, & Short, 2003; Chermack, Lynham, & Ruona, 2003). Increased levels of globalisation, outsourcing, and innovation necessitate investment in human capital in general and enterprise training in particular (Malik & Rowley, 2015a; Pereira & Malik, 2015a). For instance, recent studies on the Indian IT industry, which is truly a born-global industry, have noted increased levels of investment in training for dealing with operational demands (Malik, 2009; Malik & Nilakant, 2011), as well as strategic issues such as investing in organisational learning, quality management, and market-sensing capabilities (Malik, Sinha & Blumenfeld, 2012; Malik & Blumenfeld, 2012) for managing an inward- and outward-looking approach.

To understand how this may work at a firm level, numerous attempts have been made to model the factors that influence the provision of enterprise training and the role of human resource development in firms undergoing rapid change (Blumenfeld & Malik, 2007; OECD/CERI, 1986, 1988; Sparrow & Pettigrew, 1985; Finegold & Soscike,

1988; Hayton et al., 1996; Smith & Hayton, 1999; Ridoutt, Dutneall, Hummel, & Smith, 2002; Smith, Oczkowksi, Noble, & Macklin, 2002; Pereira, Malik, & Sharma, 2015). The main thrust of these studies is that the *nature* and *extent* of enterprise training is largely dependent on three elements: training drivers, environmental factors, and mediating factors, although a number of other factors are also proposed in the literature pertinent to enterprise training.

However, with regard to developing countries like India, limited research has been undertaken in the field of HRD, and particularly there is little theoretical basis for understanding factors that influence enterprise training. Researchers from India (Yadapadithaya, 1999; Rao & Abraham, 1986; Malik, 2013b; Pereira & Malik, 2015) have looked at the emerging trends and drivers of skill and human capital formation in the manufacturing and services sector in a pre- and post-national liberalisation era. While previous attempts to theorise human capital formation have focussed on the manufacturing and services sector, but to a lesser extent on the high-technology sectors such as the information technology (IT) sector, there is even sparse research that focuses on linking human capital formation and innovation. In the main, most literature on the IT sector of India is concentrated more on the low-value-added segment of the IT industry, such as inbound and outbound call centres and customer service centres (Taylor & Bain, 2004), and only limited efforts have been made to undertake research on the linkages between human capital management practices, including training and development and knowledge integration capabilities and achieving a range innovation outcomes (Malik, 2013a; Malik & Nilakant, 2015). Much of the research broadly focuses on three main strands. The first dominant strand of literature focuses on the organisation of work within a Taylorist paradigm, usually focusing on issues related to monotonous work, and excessive monitoring and control (Taylor & Bain, 2001). The second strand of literature focuses on employee voice, resistance, and other forms of coping mechanisms (van den Broek, 2002). The third strand focuses on the unitary and a strategic human resource management approach and focuses on issues dealing with labour turnover, employee commitment, service quality, staff training, managing stress, and so on in these organisations (Carton, Jerrard, Shah, & Gannon, 2004; Hutchinson et al., 2001; Pereira & Scott, 2014; Pereira & Fontinha, 2014).

Further, attempts to theorise factors influencing enterprise training mostly consider an organisational perspective, serving a narrow group of stakeholders. None of the studies have adopted an *outward-looking* approach analysing the influence of an organisation's customer-orientation approach on enterprise training (Bing et al., 2003; Chermack et al., 2003). Further, extant literature on enterprise training does not examine the influence of geographical and temporal dimension of training and its relationship with an organisation's product or service life cycle development on enterprise training. This present chapter attempts to bridge the above noted gaps in theory-building in enterprise training in the context of India's IT sector. The following section provides a brief overview of the Indian IT sector.

India's IT Industry

For more than a decade now, India's IT sector has witnessed steady growth in revenues and employment. The sector can be classified under three broad categories: IT hardware manufacturing (ITHM), IT software services (ITSS), and IT-enabled services (ITeS), which also includes BPO services. As noted above, literature is concentrated more on the ITeS/BPO sector, namely the call centres, and limited research has been undertaken on other sectors that make up the IT sector of India.

The greatest area of growth in the context of the Indian economy is with regard to the BPO industry, which was worth $ 100 billion in 2013, and predicted plan to grow to $ 300 billion by 2020 (Economic Times, 2013). In 2012, it was estimated to have contributed 7.5 % to India's GDP and was directly employing close to 2.2 million people (NASSCOM, 2012; Laleman, Pereira, & Malik, 2015). Further, in 2012, the overall Indian IT/BPO aggregate revenues exceeded USD 100 billion, with exports in 2014 expected to cross USD 84–87 billion (NASSCOM, 2014).

Further, as improvements at a national level can be achieved by making appropriate investments in training at a firm level (Cappelli, 1995; Porter et al., 2004; Pereira & Malik, 2015), it is important for policymakers and businesses to understand the interrelationships that exist between various explanatory factors and how they influence the nature and extent of human capital formation and innovation, especially in the light of recent policy-level national HRD interventions by the Government of India for its IT sector.

Using existing frameworks from the literature on enterprise training (Hayton et al., 1996; Smith & Hayton, 1999; Ridoutt et al., 2002; Smith et al., 2002; Pereira & Malik, 2015) and Dubin's (1978) theory-building method, this chapter will attempt to theorise the factors that influence the provision of enterprise training typical to enterprises in the IT sector of India.

Methodology

As noted in the preceding section, numerous factors have been proposed in the literature that might influence the provision of training in an organisation. Long, Ryan, Bourke, and Hopkins (1999, as cited in Ridoutt et al., 2002) developed a taxonomy of factors affecting the provision of enterprise training, highlighting three main categories: worker characteristics, enterprise characteristics, and socio-political and economic environment characteristics. This chapter will consider some of the units in a general model of enterprise training (Hayton et al., 1996) and some additional factors that have not been considered in previous attempts to theorise enterprise training. To this end, Hayton et al.'s model is modified to suit the Indian cultural context, and additional units of theory that are important to innovation.

A combination of empirical-analytic and interpretive methodology will be followed, but for the purposes of this chapter, Dubin's (1978) approach to theory building is presented. To this end, this chapter presents the relationships and interrelationships between various units of theory and their impact on the *nature* and *extent* of training provision in organisations in the Indian IT sector.

Applied disciplines, like HRD, require theory that has some practical value (Swanson, 1999). *Theory* is described as 'a coherent description, explanation, and representation of observed or experienced phenomenon' (Gioia & Pitre, 1990, p. 587). Theory building is the ongoing process of producing, confirming, applying, and adapting theory. Dubin (1978) advocates a theory-to-research strategy and quantitative hypothetico-deductive approach to applied theory building. Dubin (1978) advanced a two-staged and eight-stepped model for theory-to-research cycle. The hypothetico-deductive approach to the construction of knowledge informs the second part of his model, which develops a strategy for theory development and verification. Elaboration of first four steps will complete the theory development part of the theory-building method specified by Dubin (1978). These steps are: (i) identifying the units of the theory; (ii) establishing the laws of interaction; (iii) determining the boundaries of the theory; and (iv) specifying the system states. Elaboration of the second stage of Dubin's theory-building method is beyond the scope of this chapter, but to offer a complete understanding of this approach, a brief description of the second stage is provided below. The second stage also comprises four steps, which forms the research operation side of the theory-to-research cycle. These are: (v) specifying the propositions of the theory; (vi) identification of empirical indicators of the theory; (vii) construction of hypotheses; and (viii) development and implementation of a research plan to test the theory. Completion of the two stages outlined above will result in an empirically tested theory of enterprise training for the IT sector of India. The following section describes the first stage of Dubin's (1978) hypothetico-deductive approach to theory building, and as a result a conceptual model for enterprise training for India's IT sector is presented.

Theory Building and Quantitative Research

A conceptual model for a theory of human capital formation for innovation in India's IT sector is shown in Fig. 9.1. This theory modifies and extends the existing theories advanced in the literature on enterprise training and skill formation for innovation, and provides a much needed framework for understanding the phenomenon in operation within the IT sector of India.

Identifying the units of the theory: Units of analysis constitute the concepts or the things that a researcher is trying to make sense of; they are mainly informed by literature and the personal experiences of

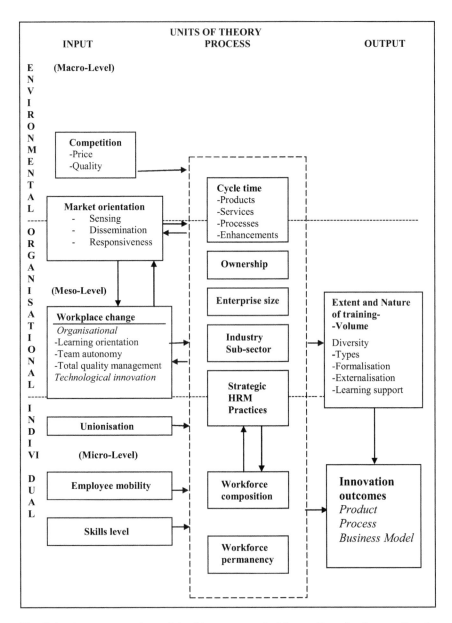

Fig. 9.1 A conceptual model of human capital formation for innovation in India's information technology sector

the researcher. By translating these concepts into units of analysis, the researcher–theorist attempts to make sense of the phenomenon through the interactions that occur between these variables (Dubin, 1978). The choice of units of theory for this research project is mainly informed by extant literature on theorising enterprise training (Hayton et al., 1996; Smith et al., 2002; Ridoutt et al., 2002). Each unit of theory is shown in a box in Fig. 9.1. The units of the theory are discussed in a reverse order from output units to process to input units.

Output Units

Volume of training: This unit of the theory is defined as the percentage of employees trained and the percentage of payroll spent on training in the last 12 months. Although there are other specifications such as average person-hours or person-days of training per annum, the above two measures are the most commonly cited metrics in the literature pertinent to measuring volume of enterprise training (Hayton et al., 1996; Smith et al., 2002; Ridoutt et al., 2002). Scholars studying the Indian IT/BPO industry employed hours per week as a commonly used measure to capture the extent of employer-funded training provided by firms (Malik, 2009; Malik & Nilakant, 2011; Malik, 2015a, 2015b; Pereira & Malik, 2015).

Training diversity: This unit of the theory is defined as the different types of training activities that the organisation is engaged in. Researchers have captured diversity of training arrangements by including training activities that cover all forms of formal and informal skill formation activity relevant to the operation of the enterprise (Hayton et al., 1996; Ridoutt et al., 2002). It includes all formal and informal training, on-site and off-site education, and development and learning initiatives provided by the organisation. Research on the Indian IT/BPO industry found that IT and BPO firms and ITPRD firms provided a range of formal and informal approaches to training (Malik, 2009; Malik & Nilakant, 2011; Pereira & Malik, 2015). There were distinctive differences between IT services and product development firms, wherein the former group of firms, especially large firms, employed extensive use of formal and structured approaches to training. In the case of IT product development firms, small and large, a significant difference was noted in that these firms relied more on informal and incidental approaches to training provision.

Externalisation: This unit of the theory is defined as the extent to which different training activities are sourced from external providers such as apprenticeship schemes, traineeships, formal and informal educational institutions such as universities and private training establishments, industry associations, and includes training opportunities to attend other worksites, availability of training by other institutions (Hayton et al., 1996; Smith et al., 2002; Ridoutt et al., 2002). Large firms in the Indian IT industry relied more on internal mechanisms and often established large training infrastructures to deal with the relevant skills shortage that was created by the educational system—as most of the graduates are not industry ready and had to go to finishing schools in the form of corporate universities set up by some of the larger IT majors (Malik, 2009; Malik, 2015a, 2015b). In the case of smaller firms, they often relied on poaching the trained and experienced resources from the larger firms as they were unable to invest in a training infrastructure.

Types: This unit of theory is defined as the extent to which the organisation offers different types of training. Measuring the organisation's focus on behavioural and generic skills versus technical and domain specific skills specifies this unit. Extant literature suggests that organisations are moving away from technical training to generic and behavioural training (Osterman, 1995; Ridoutt et al., 2002; Smith et al., 2002; Yadapadithaya, 1999). In the main, the evidence suggests that larger firms, who had invested in a training infrastructure, often offered a variety of training to different levels of employees in the workforce. They even mandated a minimum number of hours per annum dedicated to ongoing skills development for career development as well as meeting the dynamic needs of their client portfolio (Malik, 2015a, 2015b).

Formalisation: This unit of the theory is defined as the presence of a training infrastructure in an organisation, and activities such as formal induction programmes; conducting a formal training needs analysis; structured job rotation; design and development of in-house training and development programmes; evaluation of training provided; number of training/HRD or human resource management personnel responsible for the training function(s); whether organisation is a registered training provider; existence of a written training plan; and specialist training facilities (Hayton et al., 1996; Smith et al., 2002; Ridoutt et al., 2002). Research on the Indian IT industry suggested larger firms, the presence of quality management frameworks, and client specifications drove significant levels of formalisation of training.

Learning support: This unit of the theory is defined as the level of support provided for education and training of employees. Support can be in the form of: course fees for training at outside venues, and allowing paid time off to attend these courses and/or programmes at a university or a college of education; availability of in-house training programmes; and opportunities for employees to attend other worksites.

Innovation outcomes: According to Alegre and Chiva (2008), innovation can be described as an approach that focuses on development of new ways to solve current and future problems. Often times, such an approach is a result of the interactions between individual- or group-level problem-solving, using existing or new knowledge or its combinations to achieve innovative outcomes (García-Morales et al., 2007). Innovation can be viewed on a continuum of continuous and discontinuous change (Morris, 2013). Commonly noted forms of innovation associated with continuous change are incremental, process, managerial, and synthetic innovations, whereas discontinuous change is often associated with radical and game-changing innovations such as new product development and business model innovation (Amit & Zott, 2012; Chesbrough, 2007, 2010). For example, in the context of the Indian IT industry, there is evidence of both forms of innovation as the industry matures and puts more demand from its clients for seeking better ways of organising (Malik, 2013a, 2015a). At a macro-level, the Indian IT industry has demonstrated resilience through innovations in its business models (Malik & Rowley, 2015), for example, from a cost-arbitrage, body shopping business model through a client-driven model to one which is driven by disruptive technologies such as the SMAC (Social Media, Mobility Devices, Analytics and Big data and Cloud Computing) stack of innovation (Malik & Rowley, 2015).

Process Units

Process units of the theory relate to the environmental units of the theory and the complex interaction these have with the organisational system units and input units to influence the output units.

Nature of competition: For the purposes of this study, competition is defined in terms of its *intensity* (from high to low) on the basis of price or quality. Numerous authors have identified the influence of competition on the provision of enterprise training (Ergas & Wright, 1995; Hayton et al., 1996).

Enterprise size: This unit of theory is defined as the number of employees in an enterprise. Extant literature suggests a strong relationship between enterprise size and the *nature* and *extent* of training provision (Hayton et al., 1996; Ridoutt et al., 2002). The relationship between enterprise size and training activity is not linear, that is, small enterprises do little training and large enterprises do more training. Rather, the training activity is context specific and is expressed in different ways in each organisational situation. For example, an individual worksite, which is part of a larger organisation, may have differing training demands than the organisation as a whole (Hayton et al., 1996). In other cases, it is argued that small- to medium-sized enterprises are disadvantaged through this measure, as they do not have an internal person dedicated for training activities, but still provide informal learning in numerous innovative ways (NECA, 1998, as cited in Ridoutt et al., 2002). Research on the Indian IT industry found size to be a major explanatory factor of volume, diversity, and formalisation of training (Malik, 2009; Malik & Nilakant, 2011; Malik, 2015a, 2015b).

Industry group: This unit of theory is defined as per the industry sub-group as specified by NASSCOM and follows the following classification: IT software services; ITeS/BPO services; and IT hardware manufacturing. Industry group/type has been regarded as an important explanatory factor in explaining the *nature* of enterprise training, rather than its *extent,* as each industry group organises its training requirements in unique ways (Ridoutt et al., 2002; Smith et al., 2002). Industry sub-sector was noted as a key factor in the Indian IT industry in explaining the nature and extent of skill formation and training. For example, BPOs typically investment in more volume and diversity of training, relative to IT services and product development firms. Furthermore, the frequency of ongoing training was much higher in BPO relative to IT technology firms (Malik, 2009, 2015a, 2015b).

Ownership: This unit of theory defines the ownership profile of the organisation as per the following ownership categories: public limited, private limited, government owned, multinational corporations, and Indian joint-venture multinational corporations. Ownership of enterprises also has an effect on the level of enterprise training. Yadapadithaya (1999) found that ownership patterns significantly influences an organisation's perception towards competition. This is likely to have an effect on its response towards workplace change, and consequently, on enterprise training. There was little differentiation noted by way of ownership as an explanatory factor in the provision of training in Indian IT industry (Malik, 2009, 2015a, 2015b).

Strategic HRM practices: This unit of theory is defined as organisations with a strategic approach to its HRM practices (Fombrun, Tichy, & Devanna, 1984; Kane, Abraham, & Crawford, 1994). To this end, the presence of a strategic approach to HRM will be analysed by considering the following aspects of SHRM: importance of *skills* in the recruitment process, measuring *HR performance*, the use of *competencies, transferability of skills to* other organisations, and the *level of skills* in the organisation. Wright and McMahan (1992) argue that human resources can improve the performance of an enterprise by developing those skills and attributes that cannot be easily imitated by its rivals, thus giving the firm a source of sustained competitive advantage. The nature and extent of SHRM practices had a profound impact on the skills formation and training decisions of IT, BPO, and ITPRD firms in India.

Permanency of workforce: Unit of workforce permanency is defined as the percentage of permanent full-time, part-time, casual, and contract employees in an organisation. Extant literature suggests that workforce permanency encourages a higher investment in training (Groot, 1997). Ridoutt et al. (2002) found that workforce permanence to be significantly and positively related to a number of training activities, such as training diversity, external reliance, formalisation, learning support, and individualisation. However, there was no relationship observed between workforce permanency and the volume of training. In terms of casual and part-time workers, research from OECD countries (OECD, 1999) suggests that these employees receive less training than their full-time and permanent counterparts.

Workforce composition: This unit of theory is defined as the percentage of an organisation's employees in three occupational groups, namely strategic/managerial group, operational/technical group, and administrative/support group. Hayton et al. (1996) termed this variable as 'occupational structure' to measure the proportional difference between professional/managerial and other occupations and found this variable was related to the volume of training and the engagement of training reform agenda. Hayton et al. (1996) also found a significant relationship between occupational structure and reliance on external training sources and individualisation of training decision-making.

Employee mobility: This unit of theory is defined as the percentage of employees who have left the organisation in the last 12 months. Extant literature suggests that the IT sector is characterised by high employee mobility rates and is faced with issues related to retention and career development (Carton et al., 2004; Taylor & Bain, 2004).

Input Units

Workplace change: This unit of theory is defined as the *extent* and *type* of *organisational change* and *technological innovations* that an organisation has gone through in the last two years. *Technological innovation* relates to changes in work processes, technology, and introduction of new products, services, and processes (Groot, 1997; Rogers, 1999). *Organisational change* relates to changes in the structure of jobs and includes organisational changes such as introduction of team processes and other new management practices such as learning orientation and TQM (Hayton et al., 1996; Ridoutt et al., 2002; Smith et al., 2002). As these organisation changes are on a continuum, they will be analysed separately. To this end, three main types of organisation change, as represented with the adoption of new management practices are considered, as these are common to, and are an integral part of, the Indian IT sector. These are *total quality management, learning orientation,* and *team working.* All three have been established in the extant literature as critical orientations and approaches for fostering innovation outcomes in the context of the Indian IT industry (Malik, 2013a).

Total quality management: TQM unit is defined as the presence of a quality management philosophy that focuses on *customer satisfaction, continuous improvement,* and *treating the organisation as a total system* (Dean & Snell, 1991). The presence of a TQM philosophy in an organisation not only requires data collection and analysis skills, but it also requires those involved in the programme to develop behavioural skills in the areas of communication and teamwork, and specifically customer service skills for those in service industries (Smith & Hayton, 1999). In a similar vein, Osterman (1995) and Smith et al. (2002) suggest that TQM has been the catalyst for firms to move away from technical training to behavioural training. Commitment to quality has increased significantly in Indian enterprises also, especially in the IT sector of India, where a number of organisations have adopted various quality accreditation standards such as ISO 9000, SEI-CMM (Software Engineering Institute's Capability Maturity Model), PCMM (People Capability Maturity Model), Six Sigma certification, etc., and most of these standards require support of an organisation's human resources management and training and development practices (NASSCOM, 2005). Studies on the Indian IT industry confirm that quality management systems develop a firms learning and market orientations, which are critical orientations for supporting innovative activities in these firms (Malik et al., 2012; Malik & Blumenfeld, 2012; Pereira & Malik, 2015)

Learning orientation: This unit of theory is defined in terms of three set of organisational values that are associated with an organisation's tendency to learn. These values are: commitment to learning, open-mindedness, and developing a shared vision to influence a firm's ability to create and use knowledge (Sinkula, Baker, & Noordeweir, 1997). Learning orientation influences the degree to which an organisation is satisfied with its theory in use and, hence, the degree to which proactive learning occurs as well as the degree to which a firm engages in open-mindedness and thus innovation (Senge, 1990; Sinkula et al., 1997). Malik et al. (2012)

noted the presence of learning orientation as a critical in shaping training provision in the Indian BPO sector.

Team working: This unit of theory is defined as the extent to which teams exercise autonomy in decision-making. One of the key elements that underwrite an approach to TQM or a learning organisation orientation is the emphasis on teamwork. Banker, Field, Schroeder, and Sinha (1996) identified six variants of modern team working. Team autonomy can be viewed as a continuum from low to high team autonomy. These variants include: traditional workgroups, quality circles, high-performance work teams, semi-autonomous workgroups, self-managing work teams, and self-designing teams. Quality-based team designs were noted to create the needs for soft skills and sharing of existing knowledge among technical and cross-functional teams in the Indian IT industry (Malik et al., 2012; Pereira & Malik, 2015).

Market orientation: This unit of theory is defined as an organisation's ability to sense, disseminate, and respond to market turbulence and customers' specifications or needs for various products, services, or processes (Kohli, Jaworski, & Kumar, 1993). Kohli et al. (1993) developed a measure for market orientation MARKOR, and defined market orientation as 'the organizationwide generation of market intelligence pertaining to current and future needs of customers, dissemination of information horizontally and vertically within the organization, and the organizationwide action or responsiveness to market intelligence' (p. 467). Most firms in the Indian IT industry adopt a market-driven approach rather than a market-driving approach, a trend that has led to new ways of thinking and looking at alternate forms of learning and knowledge (Malik & Blumenfeld, 2012; Malik et al., 2012; Malik, 2013a).

Establishing the Laws of Interaction

Laws of interaction explain the relationship that exists between various units of a theory and not the conceptual dimensions of a unit of a theory (Lynham, 2002). As outlined by Dubin (1978), there are three types of laws of interaction: categorical, sequential, and determinant. Categorical laws suggest that the values of a unit are associated with another unit, direction or order of association is not important here, which is determined by the sequential law of interaction. Expressions such as *preceded by* or *succeeded by* typify this type of law of interaction. Dubin (1978) suggests laws of interaction do not necessarily indicate causality, as the laws of interaction, *per se,* are not measured; only the units in a relationship are. Considering the scope of this chapter, a summary of specific interactions between various units of the theory is presented.

Competition and industry sub-sector. Industry sub-sector is likely to influence the unit of nature of competition. Nature of competition varies on the basis of price and quality for all the three sectors of the Indian IT industry. ITSS is more likely to compete on the basis of quality than on price. High levels of skill sets are a characteristic of the ITSS sector. Competition based on quality of products and services is likely to increase investment in training, whereas competition based on price increases the likelihood of decreased training effort (Ergas & Wright, 1995).

Market orientation, total quality management systems, and workplace change: Market orientation is interrelated with the units of workplace change, especially learning orientation and technological innovation. Organisations with high learning orientation are likely to question the existing knowledge they hold and maintain open-mindedness towards new ideas or any knowledge produced by market orientation through adaptive and generative learning processes. They may even challenge the market-orientated behaviours that firms have in any situation. It is possible that a strong market orientation could result in adaptive learning (Slater & Narver, 1995) but not in generative learning except in case of a strong learning orientation (Senge, 1990; Sinkula et al., 1997). In other words, high learning orientation is likely to enhance the market-orientated behaviours as a strong learning orientation constantly challenges its assumptions. In terms of adaptability for a new product or service, it is likely that strong market orientation will result in faster product development irrespective of its learning orientation, but strong learning orientation may not necessarily result in new product development as it relies on a range of additional information sources, including market intelligence processing to make informed decisions. To this end, firms with low learning orientation and high market orientation are likely to focus on product, service, and process enhancements than new products and innovations (Malik, 2013a). More recently, Malik et al. (2012) and Malik and Blumenfeld (2012) noted that in the context of Indian IT and BPO firms, their quality management systems have a positive impact on its market and learning orientations as well as skill formation and training practices.

Unionisation and SHRM practices: Unionisation has an influence on the units of human resource practices. Studies in Australia have shown that the presence of unions in organisations has a positive influence on enterprise training and adopting a pluralistic approach to HRM (Smith et al., 2002; Teicher & Grauze, 1996). Recent developments suggest that unionisation is likely to influence SHRM practices of high-technology sectors such as the IT sector (Verma, 2004; UNI-APRO, 2004).

Employee mobility and SHRM practices: Mobility of workforce has an influence on the unit of strategic HRM practices. Higher employee mobility is likely to result in low investments in training (Malik, 2009; Pereira & Malik, 2015). However, high levels of employee mobility in the Indian IT organisations influence high levels of investment in generic and firm-specific skills training, recruitment, remuneration and career development, and a strategic approach to HR practices.

Employee skill levels and SHRM practices: Employee skill levels influence the units of strategic HR practices. It may sound a bit paradoxical, but higher levels of employee skills are likely to have a positive influence on its HR practices such as training, remuneration and career development, especially if employee mobility is high. Further, considering the resource-based view, specific skills sets of firm can be the source of an organisation's sustained competitive advantage and engagement with innovation at the workplace (Malik, 2013; Mark & Akhtar, 2003). To ensure the organisation can sustain its competitive advantage, it invests in a range of strategic HR activities, including skills that can't be imitated by its rivals (Pereira & Malik, 2015; Wright & McMahan, 1992).

Employee permanency and SHRM practice: Employee permanency is interrelated with the units of SHRM practices. Workforce flexibility is often noted as an organisation's strategic HR response to manage competition and improve productivity. High levels of workforce permanency in an organisation are likely to influence levels of SHRM practices. Low levels of workforce permanency, or high rate of casualisation in an organisation is likely to result in lower levels of SHRM practices (Malik, 2009; Malik & Nilakant, 2011).

Employee mobility and industry sub-sector: Industry sub-sector influences the unit of employee mobility. The IT sector of India is broadly classified into three sub-sectors: ITSS, ITeS/BPO, and ITHM. Employees in ITeS/BPO sector are more likely to have higher employee mobility than those in the ITSS and ITHM sectors, in the same order.

Workplace change and SHRM practices: Organisational change can influence the units of SHRM practices. Organisation changes such as high levels of technological innovation and organisational change influences higher levels of SHRM practices (Pereira & Malik, 2015).

Industry sector and workplace change: Industry sub-sector influences the nature and extent of workplace change, as different types of workplace changes and technological innovations may be occurring at any given stage of an industry's life cycle. For example, only few business processes have high levels of maturity in the ITeS/BPO sector, and a lot of other new business processes are being continuously added as the industry grows. To summarise, the following laws of interaction are evident:

Law 1: Units of industry sub-sector, competition, market orientation, total quality management, workplace change, unionisation, skills levels, workforce mobility, cycle time, enterprise size, SHRM practices, workforce permanency, and composition are required for the outputs of the nature and extent of enterprise training and innovation outcomes.

Law 2: Units of market orientation are interrelated with the units of workplace change, innovation, and temporal and geographical dimension of training.

Law 3: Units of quality management and market orientation influence learning orientation units; and high levels of learning orientation and market orientation units influence temporal and geographical dimension units.

Law 4: Units of workplace change, unionisation, employee mobility, skill levels, and workforce permanency influence units of SHRM practices.

Law 5: Unit of industry sub-sector influences units of competition, work-place change, and employee mobility.

Law 6: Unit of SHRM practice influences units of workforce perma-nency, skills formation, and innovation outcomes.

Determining the Boundaries of the Theory

Boundary of theory is limited to a domain that the theorist is interested in, and it is this theoretical domain that will set the limit and distinguish it from other aspects of the real world that are not addressed. Dubin (1978) suggested two broad boundaries: an open and a closed boundary; an open system is one that interacts with the wider system and the environment under which it operates. Boundaries should be made through the logic of the researcher–theorist. The first boundary of 'A Theory of Human Capital formation for innovation in the Information Technology (IT) Sector of India' is first defined as a distinction between all organisational activity for enterprises and HRD and innovation activities in an IT enter-prise environment. Although the theory has been specifically modified and refined for the IT sector, but as prior research suggests (Ridoutt et al., 2002), it may be modified further to suit non-IT organisations' environ-ments. IT sector has been defined as comprising of three sub-sectors: ITSS, ITeS/BPO, and ITHM (NASSCOM, 2004), though it is likely to change as industry evolves through its development stages. As HRD activities are related to all types of organisational activities, this is an open boundary. The second boundary of this theory exists within the domain of HRD activities in IT enterprises. This theory applies to human capital formation within the broader domain of HRD. Human capital forma-tion here is 'considered to include all forms of skills formation activity relevant to the operation of the enterprise and includes formal and infor-mal training, and on-site and off-site education and training' (Hayton et al., 1996 as quoted in Ridoutt et al., 2002, p. 27), whereas innovation includes: product process and business model innovation outcomes in the context of the Indian IT industry (Malik, 2013a; Malik & Rowley, 2015). The units of theory fit within the sub-domain of enterprise train-ing, which falls within the broader domain of HRD; hence, this is also an open boundary. The boundaries of the model are depicted in Fig. 9.2, where HRD activities in IT enterprises and enterprise training in the Indian IT sector are shown as dotted oval lines. The identification and clarification of boundaries of the theory logically lead us to the last step of the first part of Dubin's (1978) theory-building approach, that is, specifying the system states of the theory.

Specifying the System States

All the units of the theory should have some values that are preserved over a period of time, irrespective of the length of time (Dubin, 1978). Researcher–theorists should consider the following criteria while identifying the system states of the theory: inclusiveness, persistence, and distinctiveness. Persistence refers to a meaningful period of time in the system state under which the theory holds true. Finally, distinctiveness refers to the distinctive and measurable values of each unit of the theory in a given system state (Dubin, 1978). In the author's opinion, as this chapter is written at a time when the Indian IT sector is witnessing high growth rates, the theory should explain such as system state. However, it is likely that some units of the theory will change when the industry stabilises, and/or enters a recessionary phase. To this end, it is likely

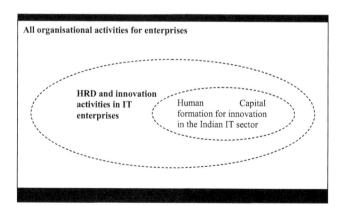

Fig. 9.2 Boundaries of a theory of enterprise training for the information technology sector of India

that the interactions and direction of some units of the theory will also change. This concludes the first part of Dubin's (1978) theory-to-research approach to quantitative theory building. The second part consists of four steps, which constitutes: specifying the propositions for the theory; identifying empirical indicators for the key units of the theory; constructing hypotheses for testing the theory; and developing an action plan for researcher–theorists to test the theory, is beyond the scope of this chapter, but through our existing programme of research, we have found significant support for these relationships (Malik, 2009, 2013a, 2013b; Malik et al., 2012; Malik & Nilakant, 2015; Malik & Rowley, 2015a, b; Pereira & Malik, 2015).

Conclusion

It is evident from the above discussion, the laws of interactions between different units of theory and its impact on the *nature* and *extent* of enterprise training. For practitioners, the model is a step towards understanding the complex interactions that take place in the context of India's IT sector, and for researcher–theorists, it serves as the basis for engaging in the next step of theory testing. Also, as noted above, triangulation of methodology should further strengthen the rigour and relevance of the model. It is also likely that the above model and its units will change in meaning and direction as the industry goes through its development stages. To this end, researchers will need to modify and enhance the relevance of the model. Once the eight steps of Dubin's (1978) two-staged model are completed, IT practitioners will have a better understanding of the units that influence provision of training and the *nature* and *extent* of training that is undertaken in different sub-sectors that make up the IT sector of India. This study will also reveal the extent to which organisations are relying of internal versus external training provision, and as a result, this will have some policy implications for addressing any gaps in the training and education sector of India.

References

Akbar, H., & Tzokas, N. (2013). An exploration of new product development's front-end knowledge conceptualization process in discontinuous innovations. *British Journal of Management, 24*(2), 245–263. doi:10.1111/j.1467-8551.2011.00801.x.

Alegre, J., & Chiva, R. (2008). Assessing the impact of organizational learning capability on product innovation performance: An empirical test. *Technovation, 28*(6), 315–326.

Amit, R., & Zott, C. (2012). Creating value through Business Model innovation. *MIT Sloan Management Review, 53*(3), 40–49. doi:10.1016/j.technovation.2007.09.003

Australian Bureau of Statistics. (1994). *Employer training expenditure, July–September 1993*. Canberra: AGPS.

Banker, R., Field, J., Schroeder, R., & Sinha, K. (1996). Impact of work teams on manufacturing performance: A longitudinal field study. *Academy of Management Journal, 39*(4), 867–890.

Bing, J. W., Kehrhahn, M., & Short, D. C. (2003). Challenges to the field of human resources development. *Advances in Developing Human Resources, 5*(3), 342–351.

Blumenfeld, S., & Malik, A. (2007). Through the out door: Drivers of training supported by New Zealand organisations. *New Zealand Journal of Employment Relations, 32*(1), 17–27.

Cappelli, P. (1995). Rethinking employment. *British Journal of Industrial Relations, 33*(4), 515–530.

Carton, P., Jerrard, M., Shah, K., & Gannon, M. (2004, August). *A practitioner's perspective of best practice call centre training: Matching the business cycle to training programme*. Paper presented at the 2nd National Call Centre Conference. Monash University, Gippsland.

Chermack, T. J., Lynham, S. A., & Ruona, W. E. A. (2003). Critical uncertainties confronting human resource development. *Advances in Developing Human Resources., 5*(3), 257–271.

Chesbrough, H. (2007). Business model innovation: It's not just about technology anymore. *Strategy & Leadership, 35*(6), 12–17. doi:10.1108/10878570710833714.

Chesbrough, H. (2010). Business model innovation: Opportunities and barriers. *Long Range Planning, 43*(2–3), 354–363. doi:10.1016/j.lrp.2009.07.010

Damanpour, F., & Schneider, M. (2006). Phases of the adoption of innovation in organizations: Effects of environment, organization, and top managers. *British Journal of Management, 17*, 215–236.

Dean Jr., J. W., & Snell, S. A. (1991). Integrated manufacturing and job design: Moderating effects of organisational inertia. *Academy of Management Journal, 34*(4), 776–804.

Dubin, R. (1978). *Theory building*. New York: New Free Press.

Economic Times. (2013). Online edition. Retrieved October 1, 2013, from.

Ergas, H. & Wright, M. (1995). Internationalisation, firm conduct and productivity. In P. Lowe & R. Dwyer (Eds.), *International integration of the Australian economy*. Sydney: RBI.

Finegold, D., & Soskice, D. (1988). The failure of British training: Analysis and prescriptions. *Oxford Review of Economic Policy, 4*, 21–53.

Fombrun, C. J., Tichy, N. M., & Devanna, M. A. (1984). *Strategic human resource management*. New York: Wiley.

Foss, N., & Larsen, K. (2003). New human resource management practices, complementarities and the impact on innovation performance. *Cambridge Journal of Economics, 27*, 243–263.

García-Morales, V. J., Lloréns-Montes, F. J., & Verdú-Jover, A. J. (2007). Influence of personal mastery on organizational performance through organizational learning and innovation in large firms and SMEs. *Technovation, 27*(9), 547–568. doi:10.1016/j.technovation.2007.02.013

Gioia, D. A., & Pitre, E. (1990). Multiparadigm perspectives in theory building. *Academy of Management Review, 15*(4), 584–602.

Govindarajan, V., & Trimble, C. (2012). Reverse innovation: A global growth strategy that could pre-empt disruption at home. *Strategy & Leadership, 40*(5), 5–11.

Groot, W. (1997). *Enterprise related training: A survey*. Melbourne: ACER, Monash University.

Hayton, G., McIntyre, J., Smart, R., McDonald, R., Noble, C., Smith, A., et al. (1996). *Final report: Enterprise training in Australia*. Melbourne: Office of Training and Further Education.

Hutchinson, S., Purcell, J., & Kinnie, N. (2001). Evolving high commitment management and the experience of the RAC call centre. *Human Resources Management Journal, 10*(1), 63–78.

Jeon, K. S., & Kim, K.-N. (2012). How do organizational and task factors influence informal learning in the workplace? *Human Resource Development International, 15*(2), 209–226.

Kane, R., Abraham, M., & Crawford, J. (1994). Training and staff development: Integrated or isolated? *Asia Pacific Journal of Human Resources, 32*(2), 112–132.

Kohli, A. K., Jaworski, B. J., & Kumar, A. (1993). MARKOR: A measure of market orientation. *Journal of Marketing Research, 30*, 467–477.

Kumar, N., & Puranam, P. (2012). *Inside India: The emerging innovation challenge to the West*. Boston, MA: Harvard Business Review Press.

Laleman, F., Pereira, V., & Malik, A. (2015). Understanding cultural singularities of "Indianness" in an inter-cultural business setting. *Culture and Organization, 21*(5), 427–447.

Long, M., Ryan, R., Bourke, G., & Hopkins, S. (1999). *Enterprise focussed education and training: A literature review*. ACER and Monash University. Melbourne: Centre for the Economics of Education and Training.

Lynham, S. A. (2002). The general method of theory building research in applied disciplines. *Advances in Developing Human Resources, 4*(3), 221–241.

Malik, A. (2009). Training drivers, competitive strategy, and clients' needs: Case studies of three business process outsourcing companies. *Journal of European Industrial Training, 33*(2 and 3), 160–177.

Malik, A., & Nilakant, V. (2011). Extending the 'size matters' debate: Drivers of training in three business process outsourcing SMEs in India. *Management Research Review, 34*(1), 111–132. doi:10.1108/01409171111096504.

Malik, A., & Blumenfeld, S. (2012). Six Sigma, quality management systems and the development of organisational learning capability: Evidence from four business process outsourcing organisations in India. *International Journal of Quality and Reliability Management, 29*(1), 71–91.

Malik, A. (2013a). Connecting work design and business ecosystems: Fostering innovation in information technology firms. *Journal of Economic and Social Policy, 15*(2), 1–23.

Malik, A. (2013b). Post-GFC people management challenges: A study of India's information technology sector. *Asia Pacific Business Review, 19*(2), 230–246. doi:10.1080/13602381.2013.767638.

Malik, A. (2015a). Innovative people management approaches from three software research and product development firms. In A. Malik & C. Rowley (Eds.), *Business models and people management in the Indian IT industry: From people to profits* (1st ed., pp. 118–136). Oxon and New York: Routledge.

Malik, A. (2015b). Innovative HR practices: Evidence from three IT software services organisations. In A. Malik & C. Rowley (Eds.), *Business models and people management in the Indian IT industry: From people to profits* (1st ed., pp. 93–117). Oxon and New York: Routledge.

Malik, A., & Nilakant, V. (2015). Knowledge integration mechanisms in high-technology business-to-business services vendors. *Knowledge Management Research & Practice*, doi:10.1057/kmrp.2015.9.

Malik, A., & Rowley, C. (2015a). *Business models and people management in the Indian IT industry: From people to profits* (1st ed.). A. Malik & C. Rowley (Eds.). Oxon and New York: Routledge.

Malik, A., & Rowley, C. (2015b). Towards an integrated model of human capital development for business model innovation: Synthesis and new knowledge. In A. Malik & C. Rowley (Eds.), *Business models and people management in the Indian IT industry: From people to profits* (1st ed., pp. 219–231). Oxon and New York: Routledge.

Malik, A., Sinha, A., & Blumenfeld, S. (2012). Role of quality management capabilities in developing market-based organisational learning capabilities: Case study evidence from four Indian business process outsourcing firms. *Industrial Marketing Management, 41*(4), 639–648.

Mark, S. K., & Akhtar, S. (2003). Human resources management practices, strategic orientations, and company performance: A correlation study of publicly listed companies. *Journal of American Academy of Business, 2*(2), 510–515.

McLean, G. N. (1998). HRD: A three-legged stool, an octopus or a centipede? *Human Resource Development International, 1*(4), 375–377.

Morris, L. (2013). Three dimensions of innovation. *International Management Review, 9*(2), 5–10. Retrieved from http://search.ebscohost.com/login.aspx?direct=true&db=bth&AN=91879701&site=eds-live

NASSCOM. (2004). *Key statistics: IT sector.* Retrieved January 7, 2005, from www.nasscom.org

NASSCOM. (2005). *Key statistics: ITeS/BPO sector.* Retrieved January 7, 2005, from www.nasscom.org

NASSCOM. (2012). Retrieved from http://www.nasscom.org/quarterly-industry-review-september-2012

NASSCOM. (2014). Retrieved March 31, 2014, from http://www.nasscom.in/positive-outlook-itbpm-industry-fy-2014

NTITSD (1998). *National taskforce on information technology and software development.* New Delhi: Government of India.

OECD (1994). *The OECD jobs study: Evidence and explanations.* Paris: OECD.

OECD. (1999). Training of adult workers. *Employment Outlook*, June, OECD, Paris.

OECD/CERI (1986). *New technology and HRD in automobile industry*. Paris: OECD.

OECD/CERI (1988). *Human resources and corporate strategy: Technology change in banks and insurance companies*. Paris: OECD.

Osterman, P. (1995). Skills, training, and work organisation in American establishments. *Industrial Relations, 34*(2), 125–146.

Pereira, V, & Fontinha, R. (2014). Global talent management in knowledge intensive firms in and between Western Europe and India: Future research directions. In A. Al Ariss (Ed.), *Global talent management: Challenges, strategies, and opportunities*. Management for professionals. Springer, Berlin. ISBN: 9783319051253.

Pereira, V., & Budhwar, P. (2015). HRM and firm performance: The case of Indian IT/BPO industry. In A. Malik & C. Rowley (Eds.), *The changing face of business models and people management in the Indian IT industry: From people to profits*. Working in Asia. Routledge, London. ISBN: 9781138783188.

Pereira, V., & Malik, A. (2015). *Human capital in the Indian IT/BPO industry* (1st ed.). London: Palgrave Macmillan.

Pereira, V., & Scott, P. (2014). Neither Western not Indian: HRM policy in an Indian multinational. In P. Konara, J. H. Yoo, F. McDonald, & Y. Wei (Eds.), *The rise of multinationals from emerging economies: Achieving a new balance*. Academy of International Business (UKI) series. Basingstoke: Palgrave Macmillan. ISBN: 9781137473103.

Pereira, V., Sharma, K., & Malik, A. (2015, in press). Colliding employer-employee perspectives of employee turnover: Evidence from a born-global industry. *Thunderbird International Business Review*.

Porter, M. E., Schwab, K., Sala-I-Martin, X., & Lopez-Claros, A. (2004). *The global competitiveness report*. Geneva, Switzerland: World Economic Forum.

Prajogo, D., & Ahmed, P. (2006). Relationships between innovation stimulus, innovation capacity, and innovation performance. *R&D Management, 36*(5), 499–515.

Rao, T. V., & Abhraham, E. (1986). HRD practices in Indian industries: A trend report. *Management and Labour Studies, 2*, 73–85.

Ridoutt, L., Dutneall, R., Hummel, K., & Smith, A. (2002). *Factors influencing training and learning in the workplace*. Leabrook, SA: NCVER.

Rogers, M. (1999). Innovation in Australian enterprises: An empirical analysis. *Australian Bulletin of Labour, 25*(4), 334–350.

Senge, P. (1990). *The fifth discipline: The art and practice of learning organisation.* New York: Doubleday.

Sinkula, J. M., Baker, W. E., & Noordeweir, T. (1997). A framework for market-based organisational learning: Linking values, knowledge, and behaviour. *Journal of the Academy of Marketing Science, 25*, 305–318.

Slater, S. F., & Narver, J. C. (1995, July). Market orientation and the learning organization. *Journal of Marketing, 59*, 63–74.

Smith, A., & Hayton, G. (1999). What drives enterprise training? Evidence from Australia. *The International Journal of Human Resource Management, 10*(2), 251–272.

Smith, A., Courvisanos, J., Tuck, J., & McEachern, S. (2012). *Building the capacity to innovate: The role of human capital.* Research Report, Adelaide: NCVER.

Smith, A., Oczkowksi, E., Noble, C. & Macklin, R. (2002). *New management practices and enterprise training.* National Centre for Vocational Educational Research, Leabrook, SA: NCVER.

Sparrow, J., & Pettigrew, A. (1985). Britain's training problems: The search for a strategic HRM approach. *Human Resource Management, 26*(1), 109–127.

Stevens, J., & Walsh, T. (1991). Training and competitiveness. In J. Stevens & R. Mackay (Eds.), *Training and competitiveness.* London: Kogan Page.

Swanson, R. A. (1999). HRD theory, real or imagined? *Human Resource Development International, 2*(1), 2–5.

Swanson, R. A. (2001). Human resource development and its underlying theory. *Human Resource Development International, 4*(3), 299–312.

Taylor, P., & Bain, P. (2001). Trade unions, workers rights and the frontier of control in UK call centres. *Economic and Industrial Democracy, 22*(1), 39–66.

Taylor, P., & Bain, P. (2004, April). Call centre offshoring to India: The revenge of history? *Labour & Industry, 14*(3), 15–24.

Teicher, J., & Grauze, A. (1996). Enterprise bargaining, industrial relations and training reforms in Australia. In C. Selby Smith & F. Ferrier (Eds.), *The economic impact of vocational education and training* (pp. 254–272). Canberra: AGPS.

UNI-APRO. (2004, October). *IT/ICT-driven outsourcing in globalizing Asia: Capital mobility, labour flexibility.* Discussion paper prepared for UNI-APRO Four, Sector Conference.

van den Broek, D. (2002). Monitoring and surveillance in call centres: Some responses from Australian workers. *Labour & Industry, 12*(3), 43–58.

Verma, P. (2004, July 29). Forum to tackle unfair HR practices in BPO industry. *The Financial Express*, India. Retrieved January 7, 2005, from www.financialexpress.com

Wright, P. M., & McMahan, G. C. (1992). Theoretical perspectives for strategic human resource management. *Journal of Management, 18*(2), 295–320.

Yadapadithaya, P. S. (1999). *HRD policies and practices in Indian industries.* Unpublished research monograph, Mangalore University.

Zeytinoglu, I. U. C., & Gordon, B. (2009). On-the-job training in Canada: Associations with information technology, innovation and competition. *Journal of Industrial Relations, 51*(1), 95–112.

Index

Note: Page numbers with "n" denote endnotes.

© The Author(s) 2017
S. Kundu, S. Munjal (eds.), *Human Capital and Innovation*,
DOI 10.1057/978-1-137-56561-7